THE BEST UTAH Children's HIKES

Adams Canyon Falls in summer.

COLORADO
MOUNTAIN CLUB
GUIDEBOOK

THE BEST UTAH Children's HIKES

COURTNEY JOHNSON

The Colorado Mountain Club Press
Golden, Colorado

WARNING: Although there has been an effort to make the trail descriptions in this book as accurate as possible, some discrepancies may exist between the text and the trails in the field. Hiking in the desert and mountains involves some risks. This guidebook is not a substitute for your experience and common sense. The users of this guidebook assume full responsibility for their own safety. Weather, terrain conditions and individual technical abilities must be considered before undertaking any of the routes in this guide.

The Best Utah Children's Hikes

PUBLISHED BY
The Colorado Mountain Club Press
710 10th Street, Suite 200, Golden, Colorado 80401
303-996-2743 | cmcpress@cmc.org | http://www.cmc.org

CORRECTIONS: We greatly appreciate when readers alert us to errors or outdated information by contacting us at cmcpress@cmc.org.

Courtney Johnson: photographer, unless noted otherwise
Erika Arroyo: designer
Jodi Jennings: copyeditor
CMC Publication: publisher

Cover photo: Lower Calf Creek Falls in Escalante. Courtney Johnson

DISTRIBUTED TO THE BOOK TRADE BY
Mountaineers Books
1001 SW Klickitat Way, Suite 201, Seattle, WA 98134, 800-553-4453
www.mountaineersbooks.org

We gratefully acknowledge the financial support of the people of Colorado through the Scientific and Cultural Facilities District of greater metropolitan Denver for our publishing activities.

TOPOGRAPHIC MAPS are created with CalTopo.com software

Printed in Korea

First Printing

ISBN 978-1-937052-69-0

ACKNOWLEDGMENTS

Special thanks to my husband, AJ, for supporting me through this project. He was there to lift me up when I needed encouragement and helped keep my daughter happy on the many hikes we did together. He gave up holidays and breaks to travel with me and never complained while I accomplished this lifelong goal of mine.

Thanks to my daughter, Emma, who joined me on most of the hikes. By the end, she was reminding me to start my GPS and never forgot to tell me she was proud of me. She positively shared the enthusiasm of her mom's dream of writing a book, and never missed an opportunity to tell strangers about it.

Thanks to my sister-in-law Kathy and her family for opening their home to me, so I could have a free place to stay while exploring the vast hiking areas in the Salt Lake City area. The family camped with us, hiked with us, and took care of Emma when I needed to complete multiple hikes.

Thanks to strangers and friends who gave me photos for the book, especially Heather and Nic Sims, Jamie Recio, Kristin Mason and the Wild Outsider Club. These photos helped me fill in the spaces for those hikes where a kiddo was not to be found except for maybe my own. Additional thanks to Stephanie Barkmeyer Vrablik for her photo help as well. Gratitude goes to Megan Humbrecht for her help with creating the overview maps.

Thank you to my family and friends that supported and encouraged me along the way. You helped me stay positive from my pitch to the finished product!

Lastly, thanks to CMC Press for trusting me to create a great guide book for hiking with kids in Utah.

There are so many amazing hikes for kids in Utah including many in the Uinta Mountains.
Photo: Heather Sims

NORTH CENTRAL UTAH

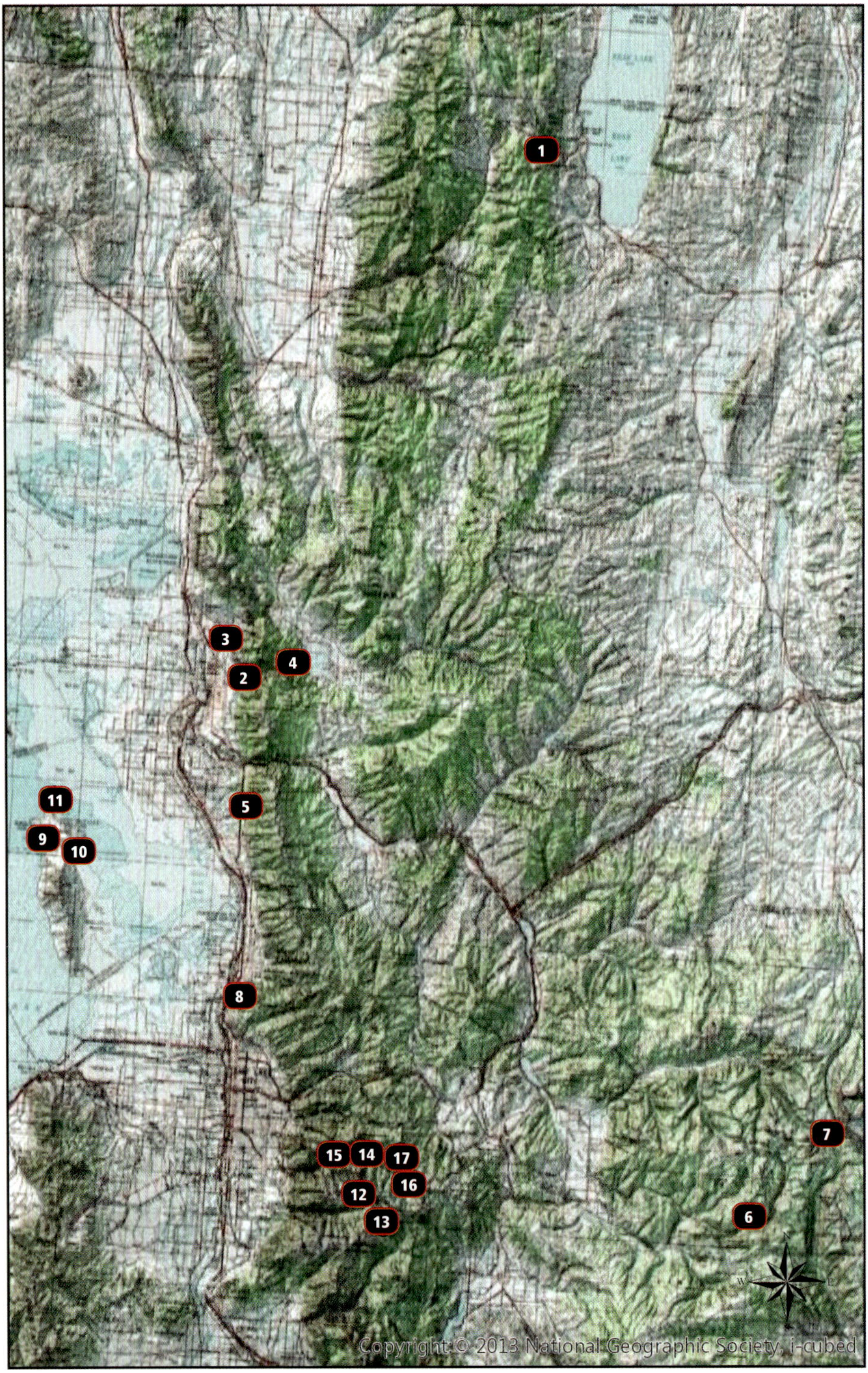

NORTH AND NORTHEAST UTAH

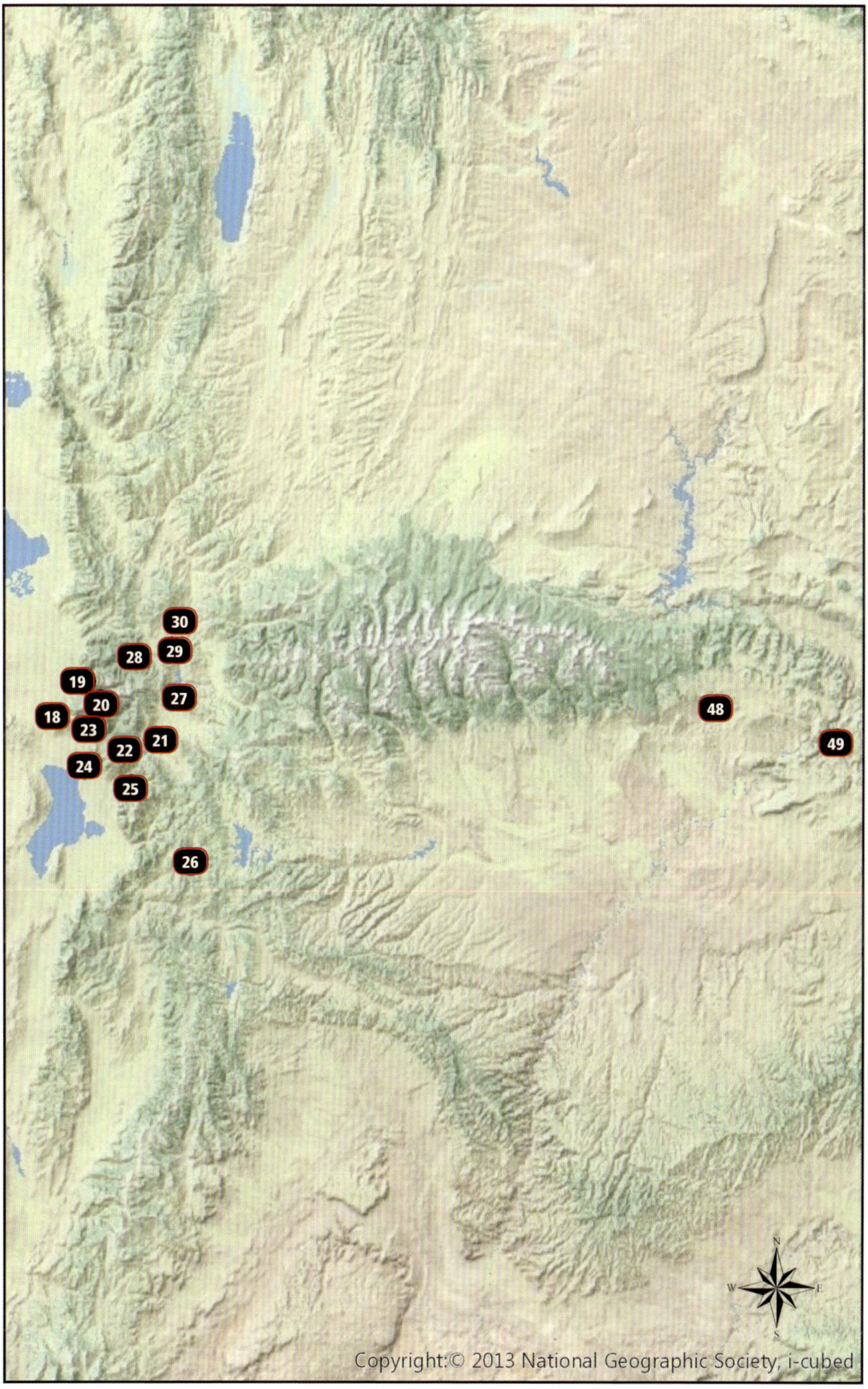

SOUTHEAST UTAH

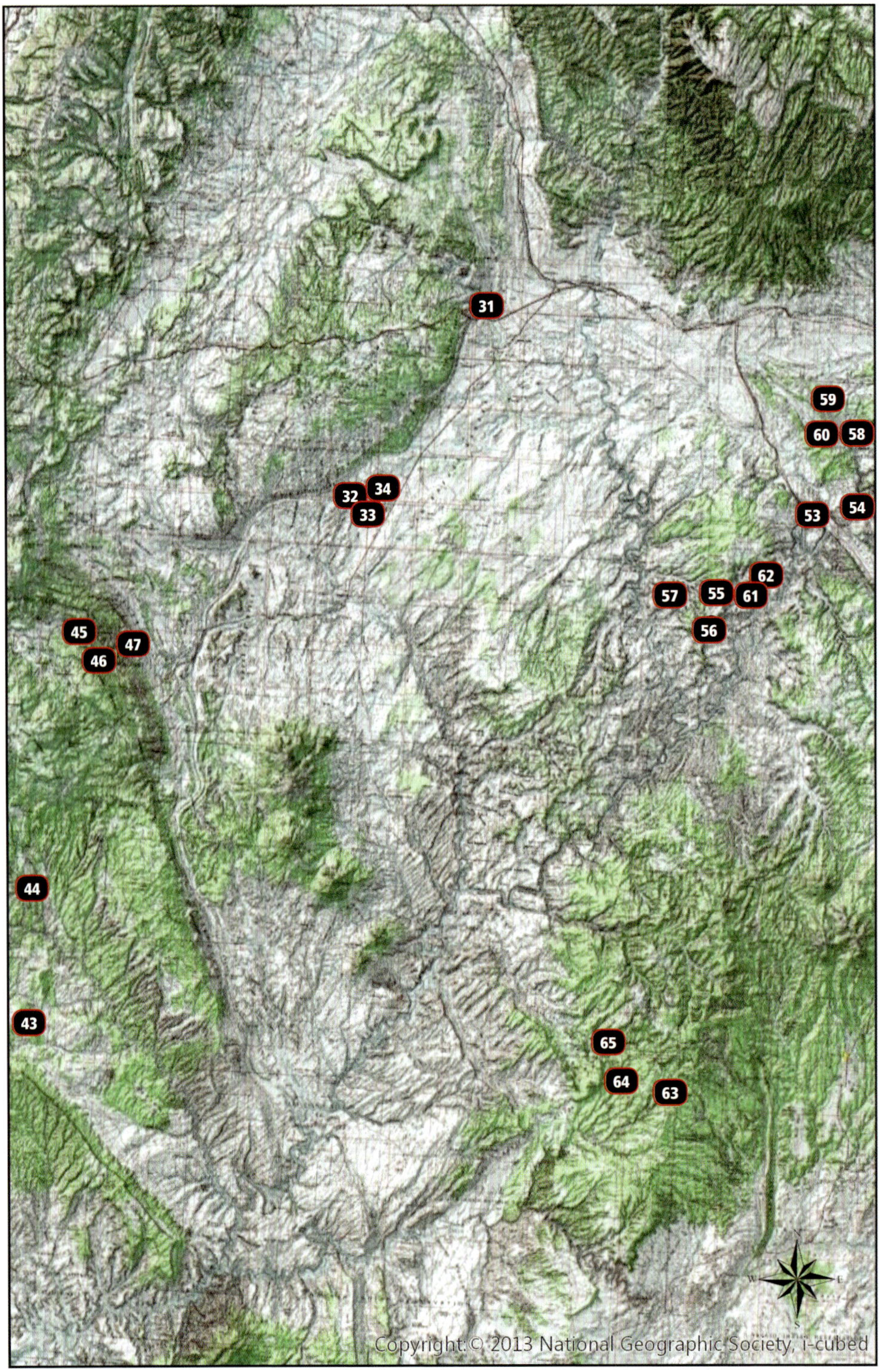

SOUTHWEST MAP 1

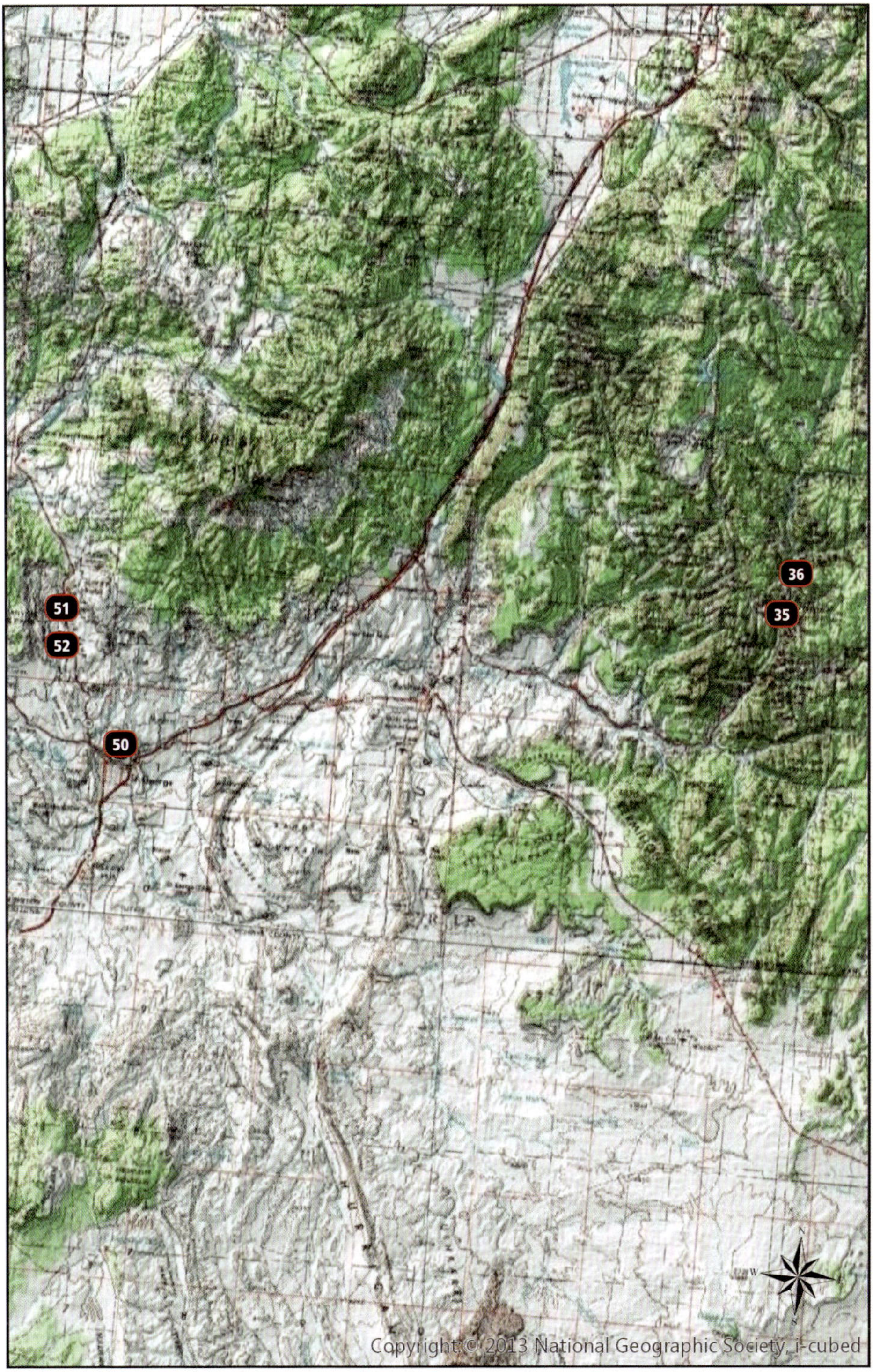

SOUTHWEST MAP 2

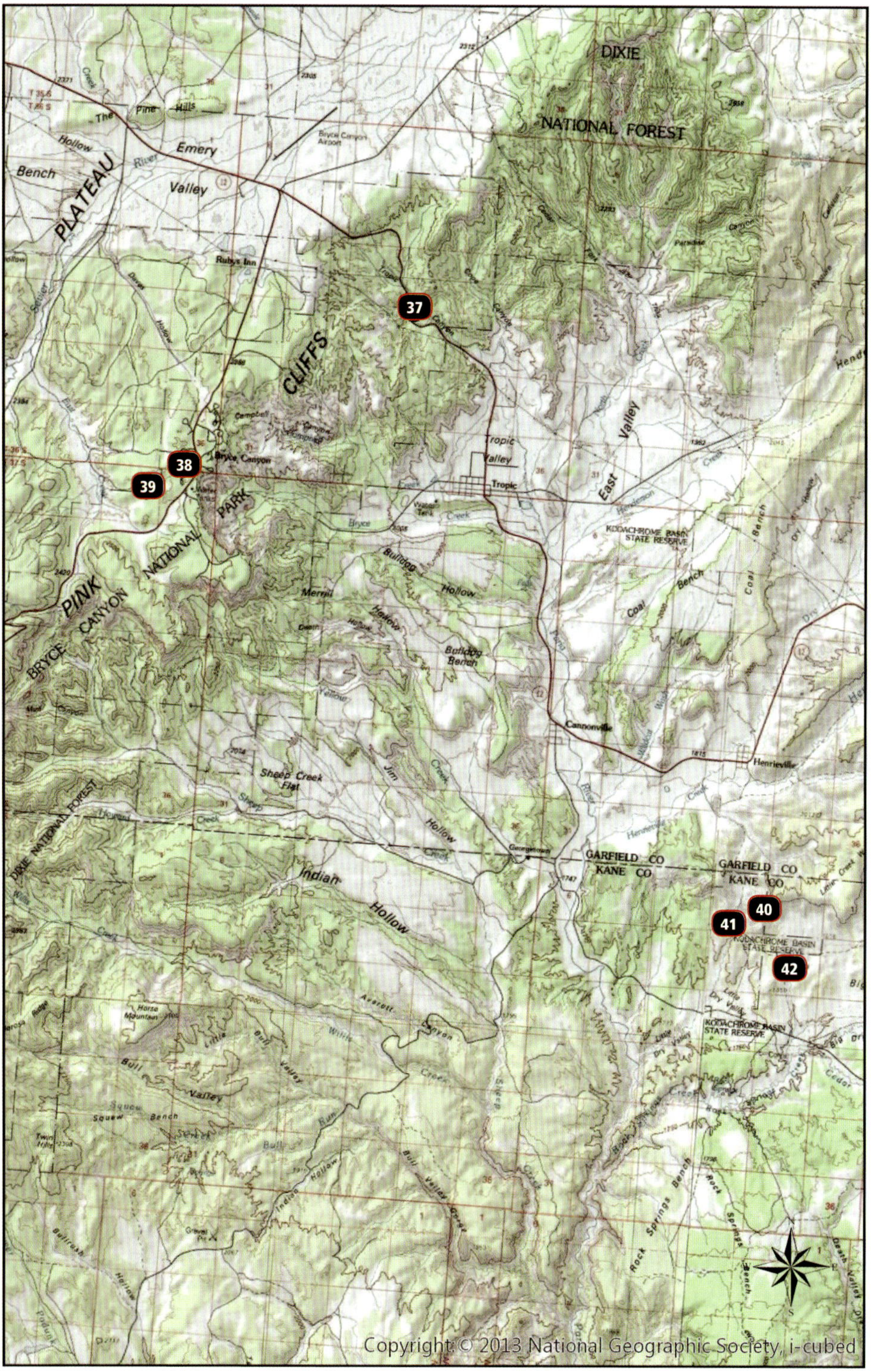

Contents

CAPITOL REEF NATIONAL PARK

VERNAL AREA

DINOSAUR NATIONAL MONUMENT

ST. GEORGE AREA

SNOW CANYON STATE PARK

MOAB AREA

CANYONLANDS NATIONAL PARK

ARCHES NATIONAL PARK

DEAD HORSE POINT STATE PARK

CEDAR MESA AREA

NATURAL BRIDGES NATIONAL MONUMENT

FOREWORD

There is no shortage of wonderful hikes around Utah. With only one year to complete the book, we couldn't hike all of them. I'm not sure we could have gotten to all of them if we had 10 years. This book features hikes we felt were the best for kids in terms of location to major cities, overall beauty, and sometimes just simplicity. In fact, they were all kid tested and approved!

Don't let some of the trail distances shy you away from a hike. There is always the option to turnaround at any place along the trail. Taking breaks is essential and encouraged. Our family and kid suggested tips will help you get on the trail.

This year has been an incredible time for my family. We got to travel around the Beehive State to see some of the best natural wonders: waterfalls, dinosaur bones, and battle sites, and mountains red, yellow, and green in the heart of fall. Every hike brought a new opportunity to stimulate our senses and a new chance to connect with each other through nature. I hope the hikes in this book encourage you to get out with your own family to experience the beauty of the state.

Happy Hiking,
Courtney Johnson

Courtney, her daughter Emma and husband AJ on the Landscape Arch and Double O Arch Trail in Arches National Park.

INTRODUCTION

WHY TRY HIKING?

The impact even minimal time in nature has on one's well-being can't be denied. The mental and physical benefits hiking generates far outweigh the risks. Hiking helps reduce stress and anxiety and improves memory and other cognitive functions.

Hiking is merely an extension of something we do naturally everyday from around age 1. It's inexpensive and can be done with minimal effort. There is no real learning curve. The more you hike, the longer and harder hikes you can complete.

From an early age, children's lives are scheduled from day care and school to church and swim lessons. Hiking offers a break from the regimen. It allows children to be in touch with their surroundings, gives them a chance to get dirty, and creates an opportunity for imagination to run wild and adventure to be had. Most families can use more quality time together free from distractions. Hiking gives people the opportunity to talk and listen.

Children learn to overcome obstacles, meet goals, and build confidence all along the trail. Hiking gives parents a chance to teach life skills including weather and animal safety, map and compass reading, and leadership.

Hiking will be different than it was when you hit the trails without children. But that's all for the better. The phrase "seeing the world through a child's eyes" will have a whole new meaning as you leave no stone unturned looking for dinosaur tracks, while cooling off in a waterfall, or standing on top of a mountain smiling. It takes patience, advanced preparation, and an open attitude.

We are not born with a genetic appreciation for the outdoors. Early experiences in nature set children up for a lifetime of curiosity, exploration, and appreciation for the natural wonders of the world. From the first animal they spy on the side of the trail to the first mountain they summit, the memories of hiking will last a lifetime. The lasting bond you create with your children through hiking will translate to your child's lasting bond with nature.

WHY THIS GUIDE?

There is no scarceness of hikes to choose from in the Beehive State. *The Best Utah Children's Hikes* lists 65 child-friendly hikes that were chosen to pique a variety of interests and engage different levels of challenge. Many were picked because of their proximity to major towns and cities, while some were chosen for their natural beauty and wonder. For safety reasons, slot canyon hikes weren't included in the book.

A good hike is one that can be navigated from start to finish safely. It makes children ask questions. It stimulates the senses and makes them wonder. It has you looking forward to the next time you can hit the trail with your little one.

If you have new walkers (hikers), the book includes simple trails to introduce them to the wonderful opportunities hiking brings. Throughout the book, you will also find trails to engage dinosaur lovers, hikes that will lead to natural wonders, and others that travel past historical sites, including old mines. Longer hikes will challenge young hikers but will bring a sense of accomplishment when they complete them.

The book also includes ADA accessible trails. According to the U.S Forest Service, to be considered ADA accessible the trail must have a stable surface, be 36 inches wide, and have no more than an 8.33 percent incline.

HOW FAR TO GO

The trail descriptions in this book contain the trail name, trail length, time to complete (this will vary by age), elevation changes, location, nearest landmarks, fees, dog friendliness, restroom availability, and the operating hours. Note that all times are approximate and depend on how much time your party spends during the hike exploring its various attractions.

The Comment section features an overall explanation of each trail. It also includes special historical information, suggestions about when it's best to hike the trail, and other practical tips.

In the Getting There section, readers will find information about accessing trailheads. Mile markers, parking lot descriptions, mileage, and turns are included.

The Route section describes what to expect, from distance to specific mileage markers. It includes landmarks, trail surfaces, and point-to-point instructions.

Some hike descriptions have information on possible route extensions. The book includes alternative routes as well. Maps may include text showing the date and time hikes were completed to show more precise trail data. On the Way Home makes suggestions for museums and other interesting places not to miss before heading home. History in Hiking offers more in-depth historical information on certain areas.

MILEAGE RECOMMENDATIONS

1–2 years old: 1.0 mile or less
2–4 years old: 1.0 to 2.0 miles
4–6 years old: 2.0 to 4.0 miles
6–9 years old: 5.0 to 6.0 miles
9 years and older: up to 10 miles

Remember these are just general suggestions. Your child(ren) may be able to hike farther, or may not want to venture out that far. At 4.5 years, our daughter was able to complete hikes over five miles with over 1,000 feet of elevation gain. This included hiking the 6.5 mile Lower Calf Creek Falls Trail, and safely navigating about 12 water crossings on the five-mile-plus Morning Glory Bridge Trail. Base your hikes on past experience and your personal know how.

TRAIL RATINGS

Experimenter: Simple nature trails up to 1.0 mile

These trails are a good introduction to hiking for parents and kids alike. This distance is suitable for children from 1 to 3 years old, or novices up to age 5. Use games such as I-Spy and scavenger hunts to help keep your little trail experimenters happy. Parents may want to bring a child carrier along in case their young hiker gets tired. These hikes build a young hiker's confidence and wonder for longer hikes in the future.

Searcher: Trails no more than 2.0 miles in length with minimal elevation change

These trails are a step up from introductory trails and are suitable for the 2- to 4- year-old range. Children should be able to complete these hikes on their own without being carried. Take breaks for snacks and water along the way. Games continue to be helpful on these types of trails.

Seeker: Trails range from 1.75 miles to 3.0 miles round-trip with more elevation changes and may feature uneven surfaces and rocks

More experienced hikers ranging in age from 4 to 6 will enjoy the slight challenges of seeker rated trails. This is also about the age when children should be able to start carrying their own water and snacks in a correctly fitting backpack. Children this age should average approximately 1.0 mile per half hour. Considering that pace, these hikes should take no more than two hours, not including time for breaks and additional exploring.

Wanderer: Trail distances for this category vary from 2.5 miles to 4.0 miles and may include elevation changes upwards of about 500 feet

Move on to this distance when children are able to carry their own gear and complete seeker-length trails with a steady pace of about 1.0 mile per half hour without struggle. With the elevation changes in this trail distance, teach them about the importance of taking breaks and hydration. By the time they master wanderer trails, they should be able to complete this distance at a pace of about 2.0 miles per hour.

Pathfinder: Distances from 3.5 to 5.0 miles round trip, uneven trail surfaces, and descents and ascents may lose or gain over 500 feet

With these changes, the pace of your hiker may slow down to 1.0 mile per hour. This is understandable with the elevation and the challenge of rocky and steeper terrain. Additional nutrition and hydration are necessary for these hikes. Stepping up to a daypack for your child is advisable once you reach these distances.

Adventurer: Distances of 4.5 miles to 6.0 miles round-trip featuring uneven terrain and altitude changes of over 500 feet
When young hikers can handle hiking 2.0 to 4.0 miles per hour at a moderate pace, they are ready for Adventurer-rated trails. I suggest beginning longer hikes with little elevation change and gradually increasing elevation changes. Hydration, nutrition, and rest breaks are an important part of meeting the challenge of these longer trails.

Leader: Trails over 6.0 miles with higher elevations and terrain that varies
These trails are recommended for children or an experienced hiker with the stamina to tackle higher altitudes and steep inclines and declines. The terrain will vary and may include water crossings. These hikes require endurance and a few years of hiking experience. Once children can tackle a Leader-rated trail, they are ready for more serious day hikes throughout Utah.

TRAIL GAMES AND OTHER FUN

One easy way to make the miles tick away is to play games on the trail or do other activities while hiking. The art of distraction can be very beneficial when trying to get your hiker to the trailhead and back.

GAMES TO TRY

- Fistful of Fingers Full of Sounds: Take a break along the trail along some water, near some rocks, or on a tree stump (but make sure to move over to let other people pass you safely). While silent, close your eyes and listen to the sounds you hear. If your child is older, have them keep track of all the sounds they hear on their fingers. If they are younger, they can try and "capture" the sounds in their hands clenching a fist. After a minute, talk about what sounds you heard.
- I-Spy: As you head down the trail, play a game of I-Spy, taking advantage of all your senses. For example: I spy something yellow. I spy something that makes a caw-caw sound.
- Treasure/Scavenger Hunt: You can find many great pre-made scavenger hunts online, or create your own. Be on the lookout for animal tracks, something soft, a feather, something that is your favorite color, a certain color leaf, something round, etc. Don't forget to collect some treasures on the way where allowed!
- ABC's in Nature: Write down (or keep track) of the things you see on the trail. Try to find one object per letter in the alphabet.

- Silly Story: Make a story up as you hike using objects you see along the trail. An adaptation of this is to pick an object you see on the trail as you hike and try to come up with as many words as you can that rhyme with the name of the object.
- Add a Story: One person starts telling a story. Each person takes turns adding two to three sentences to the story to keep it going. From personal experience, this game helped us tremendously through some of the longer hikes in this book.
- Follow the Leader: Someone gets to lead the group on the trail while choosing how the group will walk, such as having everyone walk like a crab or a monster, rub their bellies while walking, or make silly faces while you head down the trail.

ADDITIONAL SUGGESTIONS

- Keep a journal: Stop and draw pictures (best for little ones) or write down what you see on your hike. Add photos you have taken from the trail to complete the journal.
- Become a Junior Ranger: At national parks and monuments and many state parks, you can pick up an age appropriate ranger activity book to complete while you explore the trails. Be sure to bring your completed book back to the ranger station or visitor center to receive your Junior Ranger pin or patch.
- Go on a kid friendly ranger hike: Ranger led hikes are a great way to experience trails. The rangers have a wealth of knowledge to share about the trails while you head down the path.

KID SUGGESTED HIKING TIPS

- Bring snacks, lots and lots of snacks. Our hiking friends recommend a variety covering salty, sour, and sweet tastes.
- Pick hikes with a fun destination. Hikes that lead to waterfalls or feature fossils or rocks for scrambling are big hits.
- Leave no trace on the trail.
- Stay on the trail. It is the safest choice and you won't disturb the soil around it.
- Wear good hiking shoes, bring a hat, and don't forget to carry water.
- Don't forget water shoes or a towel for hikes with water. Quick dry clothes are also a good idea.
- Socialize with other hikers along the trail. They can often provide useful safety information about trail conditions.

BIOMES

Utah has four biome areas: forests, wetlands, desert, and alpine.

- Wetlands: Less than 1 percent of Utah land is considered wetlands, and 75 percent of the wetlands are near the Great Salt Lake. Trees are very unlikely in wetland areas.
- Desert: This is the most typical biome found in Utah, and many of the hikes suggested in this book in the western and southern areas of the state are in a desert biome. Sandy terrain, hot days and cooler nights, nocturnal animals, and a lack of precipitation are all common in the desert biome.
- Forest: The forest biome comprises about 25 percent of the Utah landscape and is common in the Uinta, Wasatch, and other mountain ranges. All four seasons occur in this biome. Trees, plants, wildflowers, and abundant animal life are in the forest biome. There are some hikes within this biome in this guide.
- Alpine: This biome is found at altitudes of 10,000 feet or higher in Utah. These areas support vegetation that does not grow quickly or very tall. This biome area is rocky and typically windy.

HIKING SAFETY AND PRECAUTIONS

10 ESSENTIALS DAY HIKE GEAR LIST

- Backpack
- Water (hydration system or BPA free bottles and filter)
- Basic first aid kit
- Bug and tick spray
- Sunscreen, sunglasses, hat
- Map, compass, and GPS (do not depend on cell service)
- Extra food
- Extra clothing, including rain gear
- Safety items (flashlight/headlamp, waterproof matches, whistle, extra batteries)
- Knife or multi-tool
- Appropriate footwear

Additionally, consider bringing

- Duct tape
- Hand sanitizer
- Bag for food waste, dirty/wet clothes, and anything else to be packed out
- Benadryl, if hiking with anyone with allergies
- Emergency shelter (tarp, large bag, or space blanket)
- Cord or rope for securing shelter
- Lip balm with SPF

ITINERARY

It is always smart to let someone outside your group know your hiking itinerary, including who is in your group, the trail you plan to hike, and the time you should be gone. In the unfortunate event of an emergency, this will make it easier to locate your party.

STAY TOGETHER

One of the number one rules of staying safe on the trail is to stay together. Don't let anyone in the party get too far ahead or lag too far behind. If anyone in the group is tired, turn around and head back to the trailhead together.

When possible, be sure to sign in at the trailhead for safety reasons.

HELP, WE ARE LOST

Knowing your route beforehand, observing markers while on the trail, and carrying navigation tools can help minimize the chance of getting lost. If you do get off route, follow these tips.

- Stay calm, especially around little children.
- Stop and view your surroundings.
- Listen in the distance for familiar sounds, voices, etc.
- Backtrack or stay put on the trail. Do not continue forward.
- Blow your whistle. The universal distress signal is a pattern of three: three whistle blows (a whistle carries farther than yelling), or three piles of rocks, or three mirror signals. Stop and see if anyone responds to your signals.
- If you have cell service, contact authorities if none of the above tips help you get back on the right track.

NO RESTROOM IN SIGHT?

Not all trailheads have restrooms, and mother nature can call at anytime when you are with young kids. The general rule is to keep human waste at least 200 feet from a trail, water supply, or camping area. If there is the need to go in the wild, dig a small hole at least eight inches deep and cover with leaves and dirt. Do not bury wipes or diapers; dispose of them properly.

POISONOUS FLORA

You will encounter poisonous flora on some trails, including in Zion and Escalante, and exposure to it can cause major discomfort. Poison ivy, poison hemlock, and snow-on-the-mountain are some of the poisonous flora found on Utah trails. Donkey's tail can be found in the foothills of northeastern Utah while baneberry is found at elevations of 8,000 feet or higher. The best way to avoid poisonous flora is by staying on the trail. Be mindful of what hands, arms, legs, and feet touch.

If someone comes into contact with poisonous flora, keep the exposed area isolated. Avoid spreading the poison compounds by not touching the exposed area. Wash the area with water (preferably warm) and soap. Apply calamine lotion or baking soda, if available. Call the poison control center at 800 222-1222 if you have any questions or concerns.

ANIMAL ENCOUNTERS

If you spend enough time in nature, an animal encounter is inevitable. The experience can be positive and memorable if you remember some basic safety tips:

- Watch wildlife from a distance. Wildlife is more active during dusk and dawn, pre- and post- hibernation, mating season, and when babies are born.
- Do not try to approach, feed, or follow wildlife.
- Pay attention to the trail ahead of you. If you notice tracks or scat, are they fresh?

- Stay on the trail.
- Although the scenery may be peaceful and quiet, make some noise on the trail to eliminate the element of surprise.
- Wear closed-toed shoes when hiking.
- Be careful when sitting on a rock or log or if you need to leave the trail for any reason.

BEARS

Utah is home to black bears (sometimes brown in color). Be especially vigilant during dusk and dawn when they tend to be most active, and in and around campsites.

If you encounter a bear close on the trail, stop and give it space for an escape route. Your instinct may be to turn your back and run, but this is the opposite of what you should do with a black bear. If the bear doesn't retreat after seeing you, pick up small children or position children in between adults. Try to look as large as possible and avoid eye contact. Begin to back up slowly.

If you are attacked, fight back and aim for the bear's nose. Use any objects around you to hit the bear. Do not give up! Seek medical attention immediately.

Bear spray is also a smart deterrent to carry if you frequently hike in active bear country. Spray if a bear approaches within 30 feet and back away from the area as quickly as possible without running.

MOUNTAIN LIONS

Mountain lions are the second largest predator in Utah. Deer are its main source of food, so be more cautious if you encounter deer on the trail. Mountain lions attack from behind and are most active at dusk and at night. Keeping children in the front of the group on the trail is recommended.

If you encounter a mountain lion close on the trail, stop and give it space for an escape route. Your instinct may be to turn your back and run, but this is the opposite of what you want to do. If the mountain lion doesn't retreat after seeing you, pick up small children or position children in between adults. Try to look as large as possible and avoid eye contact. Begin to back up slowly.

Just like with bears, fight back if you are attacked. Use any objects around you to hit the cougar. Try and protect your head and neck, the spots that the lion will most likely aim for. Do not give up! Seek medical attention immediately.

COYOTES

If you encounter a coyote on the trail, do not run. It will think you are prey trying to escape. Instead, make yourself look bigger, yell, and throw rocks and other items at it to scare it off.

ELK, MOOSE, AND DEER

Although an attack from these animals is unlikely because they are more apt to run away than charge, it is possible especially during rutting season, between late

August through October. Moose are strong and large while deer and elk have strong hooves and sharp antlers. If you see one, back away and change the direction you are headed, but do not turn your back. If one of these animals charges or attacks, try and get away by placing something large between you and the animal, such as a tree or a car. You may also run, as these types of animals are not likely to chase you. Climbing a tree, rock, or other object is also recommended. If you are attacked, curl up, and cover your head. Hold still and wait for the animal to move on. Seek medical attention immediately.

BISON

While bison encounters on a trail are not common, one of the largest herd of wild bison in the United States roams the trails of Antelope Island. If you happen upon a bison, do not approach it. Give the bison space; at least 100 yards or more is recommended. Bison can run three times faster than a human, but running or climbing is your best safety mechanism. Taking cover behind something large can also be helpful. If a bison butts you, try to protect your head and organs until the animal retreats. Seek medical attention immediately.

SNAKES

There are seven types of venomous snakes in Utah, six of which are the rattlesnake variety. They hibernate in winter and are most active at dusk and dawn. In the heat of the summer, rattlesnakes tend to seek shade, so be especially mindful when taking breaks along the trail. When the temperature is cooler, snakes will seek warmth from rocks and parts of the trail that receive sun exposure. If it is possible to do safely, walk in the middle of trail to avoid snakes.

Do not touch or poke at a snake. If you see one, give it space to escape and warn others around you of the snake's presence. The sound of a rattle means the snake feels threatened and wants you to move away. Back away slowly. If one does come toward you, stomp your foot once and back away quickly (do not run) and safely.

If a snakebite occurs, keep the victim calm. Move away from the area, as snakes often strike more than once. Keep the area of the bite below the heart, and remove all restrictive clothing and jewelry. Keep the victim calm, still, and help them control their breathing to keep the venom from spreading. Seek medical attention quickly. Snakebite kits are totally ineffective.

GILA MONSTERS

Present in southern Utah, the bite from a Gila monster is poisonous but not likely to kill you. They live and sleep underground for approximately 95 percent of their lives and are very slow. In the off chance that someone you are with is bit by one, treat the victim similar to a snake bite and seek medical attention.

BITING INSECTS

Insects are the most likely type of wildlife you will encounter on the trails. Biting gnats and mosquitoes are the most common biting insects during the warmer and

A bison heads towards the Great Salt Lake in Antelope Island State Park.

wetter months. Insect repellent (DEET is recommended) is effective for mosquitoes, but biting gnats (also known as no-see-ums) are not repelled by repellant in most cases. Antelope Island is known for its bug population, especially from April through July. Long-sleeved clothing and mesh nets are recommended for no-see-ums.

BEES AND STINGING INSECTS

To avoid bees and stinging insects, wear light colored clothing. Never disturb or get too close to a nest. If a bee or other stinging insect circles you, it is putting out a warning to leave the area. When stopping for a break, listen for the buzzing sound; avoid stopping in the area if you hear one. If bees or other stinging insects attack, running is the best mechanism to deter them.

In the event that someone is stung, have them try to protect the face, head, and eyes while continuing to run. Swatting at the insects will only attract them to continue stinging.

If someone in your party is bit or stung, the first thing to do is to leave the area and seek shelter. Insects send out distress signals, and this can provoke additional stings and bites. Remove any tight clothing, including jewelry, in case swelling occurs. If anyone in your party is allergic to insect bites and stings, having Benadryl in your first aid kit is recommended, and consider carrying an Epi-pen. If possible, remove any stingers by scraping. Do not squeeze the area, as additional venom will be released under the skin. Treat the wound by washing the area with soap and water. Ice can also help. If the person is stung more than 10 times, has a known allergy to stings, begins to feel sick, shows signs of distress, or has swelling outside of the wound area, seek immediate medical attention.

ARACHNID BITES

The desert recluse, black widow, and the hobo spider (often mistaken for a brown recluse) are the most venomous spiders common to the Utah desert and mountains. Most spider bites can be treated with the RICE method: rest, ice, compression, and elevation. Be on the lookout for symptoms that mean medical attention is necessary. The following symptoms can all be signs of an allergic reaction, necrosis, or systemic poisoning, which are the three major dangers from spider bites:

- hives,
- elevated heart rate,
- rapid breathing or shortness of breath,
- sweating,
- head and body aches,
- cramps, and
- boils or ulcers.

TICKS

The two most prevalent ticks found in Utah's mountain ranges are the light brown American dog tick and the dark brown or black wood tick. Although they are most common in spring and summer, ticks can be found year round. Grassy and bushy areas are the most common places ticks are found. Wear tick repellant if you are headed to an area known for ticks. Wearing long shirts and pants can also deter ticks. After a hike in a tick area, removing clothing, inspecting for ticks, and showering are recommended preventive measures.

If a tick has bitten you or someone in your group, remain calm. Take tweezers and remove the tick by going under the head of the tick to pull out the tick's mouth. If you try and remove it by the body, it is likely that the contents of the tick's stomach will empty under the skin. This makes it more likely for an infection to spread. If you were in an area with a high level of Lyme disease risk, try and save the tick. Monitor symptoms. A red rash is the most common symptom to look for. If one appears, seek medical attention.

SCORPIONS

While present in Utah, scorpions are not very common. Be especially careful on desert hikes in and around rocks, tree limbs, or anything on the ground. At night, you can easily spot scorpions with a flashlight equipped with a UV bulb; they are fluorescent. Wearing long clothing can help prevent stings. Scorpions are more active during the evening than the day.

Symptoms from a scorpion sting range from a burning or stinging sensation where stung to cramping, drooling, and convulsions. If someone is stung, apply ice to the area. Have them remain calm and seek medical attention.

INJURIES

From blisters to twisted ankles, injuries are inevitable when you hit the trail. Have a basic first aid kit with you containing pain medication, band-aids, medical tape, petroleum jelly, and antibacterial cream. Carrying an extra pair of dry socks and wearing boots or shoes that fit correctly can also help reduce the risk of injury.

MINOR CUTS OR ABRASIONS

Cuts and abrasions are almost a right of passage of being a hiker. It's best to wear latex gloves when treating a wound. At a minimum, wash your hands before treating yourself or someone else. Apply pressure to wounds that are bleeding. Wash cuts and abrasions with water. Remove debris with tweezers. Dry the wound. Apply an antibacterial gel and bandage if needed. Watch abrasions and cuts over the next few days to make sure proper healing is happening and no infection is occurring. If bleeding continues, seek medical attention.

BLISTERS

The best way to keep a blister from forming is to wear proper fitting boots or shoes and socks when hiking. If you or any other hikers in your party feel discomfort in the foot or heel area (also known as a hotspot), don't ignore it until it becomes a bigger problem.

Adjust socks, or change them if wet. Adjust boots or shoes if they are too tight or too loose. Apply moleskin, duct tape, or athletic tape to any hotspots before a blister forms.

If someone in your group has already developed a blister, clean the area with water. There are two ways to treat the blister: you can pop it with a clean needle and drain it, apply antibiotic cream, and cover it with a bandage or athletic tape. If the blister isn't large or may pop on its own, you can cover it with duct tape and let it pop naturally. Cover it with duct tape to reduce any painful friction until you finish the hike.

THORNS, CACTUS NEEDLES, AND SPLINTERS

In your first aid kit, you should carry a pair of tweezers for removing things like thorns and splinters. Use duct tape to remove a large amount of small needles, like those from a cactus.

TWISTED ANKLE

Because many of the trails in this book have uneven terrain that is sometimes covered in rocks and roots, rolled or twisted ankles are a hiking hazard that might occur. If an ankle twist or roll occurs, sometimes it can be fixed by walking it off. If the injury is beyond that, elevation, rest, and bracing is the best treatment plan.

SUNBURN

Sunburn is one of the most common ailments when hiking. The higher the altitude, the more intense the sun will be. Apply sunscreen before a hike and carry additional sunscreen to apply while on the trail. Many companies make clothing with SPF built in. Wearing long sleeves, pants, and a hat also help aid in sun protection. Choosing hikes that have plenty of shade, especially in the summer months, will cut down the risk of burns. Starting early before the sun becomes intense is a good practice.

DEHYDRATION

Our bodies are made mostly of water. It is important to remember to take breaks before you become thirsty to make sure you are adequately hydrated. Most of the hikes in this book are in dry areas and often in direct sunlight.

The minimum daily water need per person for a day hike is one gallon (four 32-ounce/one-liter water bottles). Most of the hikes in this book are shorter than a day hike, but it is never a bad idea to have extra water with you.

Early indicators of dehydration include lack of urination and fatigue. Take a break every 10 to 15 minutes and encourage frequent sips of water. It is a good rule of thumb to not trust natural water sources that you may find on the trail, no matter how clear the water appears. Therefore, carrying hydration packs and a water filter

Smaller waterfalls offer the perfect place for cooling off like this one on the Adams Canyon Trail.

(they are lightweight and inexpensive) is recommended. Older children should be capable of carrying their own water, while younger children will likely need some help. Keep additional water in your car for post-hike hydration.

REGULATING BODY TEMPERATURE

Children (especially those under age 4) are more at risk for having trouble self-regulating body temperature in both cold and heat. Age, medications, and health conditions including diabetes, obesity, and heart and lung conditions can all affect a body's ability to adjust to heat.

Body temperature issues, including heat exhaustion and heat stroke, are often directly related to the heat index. As the index climbs, the risk of heat-related illness increases. Additionally, humidity only has to be at 60 percent to affect a body's ability to cool itself.

To decrease dehydration risk, avoid long exposure to heat by hiking earlier in the day or choosing routes that contain shade. Beginning a hike hydrated is also a good way to regulate body temperature.

HEAT ILLNESSES

Heat Exposure, heat exhaustion, and heat cramping are caused by a lack of fluids and electrolytes (mainly salt) in the body. Symptoms include dizziness, fatigue, heavy sweating, cold skin, and cramping. To treat these conditions:

- Place the person in shade.
- Remove any tight clothing.
- Give liquids every 15 minutes or so (avoid caffeine or alcohol).
- Apply something cold.
- Massage areas of cramping.

If you do not see improvement after 15 minutes, seek medical attention.

When the body temperature exceeds 104°F, heat stroke occurs. Symptoms are more severe and include dry skin, confusion, loss of consciousness, erratic behavior, a rapid weak pulse, and shallow rapid breathing. Seizures are one of the most severe symptoms. If someone shows symptoms of heat stroke:

- Seek immediate medical attention.
- Move the victim to a shady area.
- Remove any tight or sweat-soaked clothing.
- Give liquids every minute or so (avoid caffeine or alcohol).
- Apply something cold to the face, neck, and other areas, and ice to the groin, under arms, and wrists.

HYPOTHERMIA

Hypothermia occurs when the body drops in temperature. Common symptoms include shivering, slow and shallow breathing, confusion, skin that is cold to the touch, and a slow and weak pulse. Children that are not dressed properly or don't consume enough food are especially susceptible. Take extra precautions if you plan to hike in the evening. The sun sets earlier in the mountains. The sand, rocks, and dirt of mountain or desert trails do not hold heat. Dry air doesn't keep heat either. Cloudless nights are especially cold. To treat hypothermia:

- Remove any wet clothing.
- Change the person into dry, warm clothes and/or wrap them in blankets.
- Move to a warm, dry place.
- Provide warm liquids.
- Seek medical attention. If person is unconscious or unresponsive, call 911 right away.

ALTITUDE SICKNESS

Altitude sickness (also known as acute mountain sickness (AMS)) can strike anyone despite age or physical fitness. Although the effects of higher altitudes can be felt starting around 5,000 feet, AMS most often occurs when above 8,000 feet. AMS symptoms are nonspecific and often mimic common symptoms of other conditions. The first and earliest indicator of AMS is often a headache. Lack of urination and appetite, shortness of breath or rapid breathing, vomiting and/or nausea, and fatigue are also common symptoms. Altitude sickness strikes approximately 12 to 24 hours after being at higher altitudes.

To prevent AMS, get proper rest before a high altitude hike. Go slowly and take breaks. Drink plenty of fluids, but avoid caffeine and alcohol. Eat adequately before, during, and after your hike. If symptoms occur, move to a lower elevation. Rest, fluids, and over the counter medication should help with any pain. If symptoms persist or worsen, seek medical attention.

WEATHER

It is important to always observe weather conditions before and during a hike, no matter how short it is. Before leaving, check the forecast and visit with a ranger at a visitor center to check specific trail and weather conditions. Always be ready to turn around when the weather takes a turn for the worse.

LIGHTNING

Utah is one of the top states for lightning injuries and deaths (number two to avalanches). The highest potential for lightning strikes is between May and August. Before you head out for your hike, check the forecast. Listen for thunder and watch for increasing clouds as you hike. Getting out earlier in the day, especially in the summer months, decreases the potential for getting caught in a lightning storm. This means being below treeline before early afternoon.

If you get caught in a storm, find shelter, if available, or the lowest spot safe from potential flooding that is away from poles, fences, trees, or anything metal. If you are in a tree-dense area, take shelter under short trees. Split apart and keep distance between the people in your party. If you feel your hair standing up or tingling, squat low on the balls of your feet and put your head between your legs to make yourself a small target.

If someone is struck by lightning, move to safety as quickly as possible. Call 911 but do not remain on the line with dispatch because phone lines can cause electrical build up. Administer first aid until help arrives: treat burns, administer CPR, or perform any other life saving measures that can be administered until a medical team arrives.

FLASH FLOODS

The most likely places you will see a flash flood are slot canyons, steep slopes, and narrow valleys. The hikes in this book were selected because of their minimal flash flood risk, but it is still important to know what to do if one occurs while you are on the trail.

Six inches of water is enough to knock someone off their feet. Floods can occur from storms that took place miles away and that drop even minimal amounts of water quickly. Beyond checking the weather forecast before heading out, it is a good idea to check in at visitor centers about the potential for flooding.

There is a difference between a flash flood "watch" and "warning." A flash flood watch means a flood is possible; a flash flood warning means a flash flood is currently occurring or will occur soon.

The National Weather Service gives the advice "Turn Around, Don't Drown" for flash floods. This means it is safer to leave the area of a flash flood than to try to cross it. If one occurs, seek higher ground immediately, keeping in mind that flash flood levels can reach over 30 feet high.

AVALANCHE

Some of these hikes can also be enjoyed in late fall, winter, and early spring. This means that there is potential for an avalanche to occur near the trail. Just as you check the weather before a hike, it is important to check the avalanche danger before heading out in the snowy months. Look around for potential avalanche chutes and have an escape plan. Warning signs of avalanches include evidence of recent avalanches, rapidly warming temperatures, heavy snowfall or rain in the past 24 hours, high winds, and unstable snow.

ROCKSLIDES

Although heavy rain, earthquakes, and rapid snowmelt are big causes of rockslides, slides can happen at any time and are unpredictable. Some of the hikes featured in this book travel past scree fields and are on trails susceptible to rock fall. One of the warning signs of a potential rockslide or fall is the sound of clapping. If you hear a clapping sound, curl into a ball and protect your head.

MINIMIZING YOUR IMPACT

Most of Utah is a fragile desert environment. To make sure these natural wonders are around for future generations to enjoy, it is important to minimize our impact as we enjoy them. Make sure to observe these guidelines:

- Stay on the designated trails.
- Do not feed wildlife.
- Pack in and pack out what you bring with you.
- If you must go while on the trail, dig a four to six-inch deep hole at least 200 feet away from campgrounds and water sources.
- Avoid using soap in a freshwater source.
- Be considerate of others and keep your noise levels to a minimum.
- Leave gates as you found them (opened or closed).

Fall makes its presence on the Limber Pine Trail near Logan, Utah.

Logan Area

Logan City is often referred to as Logan. The main campus of Utah State University is found within the city. The town is named for fur trapper Ephraim Logan and was founded by settlers in 1859 surveying the land near the Logan River for Brigham Young.

Bear Lake as seen from the Limber Pine Trail.

Rank 2

1. Limber Pine Trail

RATING	Searcher, due to length and some elevation change
ROUND TRIP DISTANCE	1.4-mile loop
ROUND-TRIP TIME	45 minutes to 1.5 hours
ELEVATION CHANGE	101 feet (from 7,800 to 7,901 feet)
MAP	Trails Illustrated Logan, Bear River Range
NEAREST LANDMARK	Bear Lake Summit
FEES	None
RESTROOMS	Pit Toilets
DOGS	Must be leashed
OPERATING HOURS	One hour before sunrise to one hour after sunset

COMMENT: This trail is a part of the U.S. Forest Service Yellowstone to Unitas Connection, a 350-mile wildlife corridor. Make sure to bring plenty of water for this hike as there is no access to any on the trail. The 500 to 1,000 year old limber pines and other trees provide excellent shade on this hike, but there are open areas of sun. This hike is best from June through October with the chance for patches of snow in June. Can you say summer snowball fight? The higher altitude means packing a jacket is a good idea. Afternoons bring thunderstorms in the summer. This hike is a part of the forest biome. Head to this trail in the winter to snowshoe.

GETTING THERE: From Salt Lake City, take US Highway 89/ Logan Canyon Scenic Byway for 30.0 miles. Watch for the sign for Rich County. The parking lot is shortly after this sign around mile marker 492. Park in the large parking lot that holds about 14 cars. Typically parking is not an issue in the large lot, but sometimes summer weekends mean a full trailhead.

THE ROUTE: Although this route climbs a bit, switchbacks help hikers young and old reach the jewel of this hike: the large limber pine, which is several trees estimated to be about 600 years old that have grown together. The trail is fairly smooth, but there are sections that are rocky.

From the parking lot, walk approximately 60 yards to a junction. This is a loop hike, so head left or right. Be sure to grab a pamphlet in the wooden box before the start of the hike. Please note that the text for this book details what you will see if you head to the right. Benches along the way provide opportunities to take a break and take in the view. The first bench is about 578 feet from the trailhead.

Limber pines line the trail offering a great place to take a break.

Aspens and gamble oak bring color almost from the start. Be sure to look for the signs on the sides of the trail discussing the area and asking insightful questions. These 13 interpretive signs on both sides of the trail help slow down the pace and teach hikers about the ecosystem of the area, including the story of the "Nutcracker's Forest," about how the limber pines came to be. Questions on the signs suitable for adults and children make for a fun hike activity.

Shortly into the climb, look east for the first views of Bear Lake. The trail opens up now before returning into the pines. There are additional views of Bear Lake along the hike, especially near the top. Mountain mahogany lines the trail. Wildflowers bloom in mid-summer.

At 0.3 mile look down on the left to see where the trail loops around. At 0.4 mile on the right you will see interpretive sign 5. This is a great place to stop to do a little downed tree climbing while you hydrate. When you reach 0.5 mile, the trail returns to the pines and aspens. Interpretive sign 8 on the left at 0.6 describes the tree hotel, an old Douglas fir tree to the side of the trail that fell in 1993.

The famous limber pine lives about half way through the hike at 0.7 mile at interpretive sign 10. There is a bench to enjoy the tree from a distance. Once thought to be the biggest limber pine in the world, it was discovered to be multiple trees that have grown together with a circumference of about 25 feet. There is a tree that looks like an elbow on the right at 0.75 mile. The trail now begins to descend slightly.

There are lots of downed old growth trees and lots of hiking sticks to be had in this area. You may encounter a downed tree to climb over at 0.9 mile, and may see animal dens on the left shortly after the downed tree. The trail meanders in and out of shade depending on the time of day. As it continues, it begins to climb slightly and gets rockier. Look to the right at 1.1 miles through the pines for a possible view

At about 0.7 miles on the right, you will see the famous limber pine.

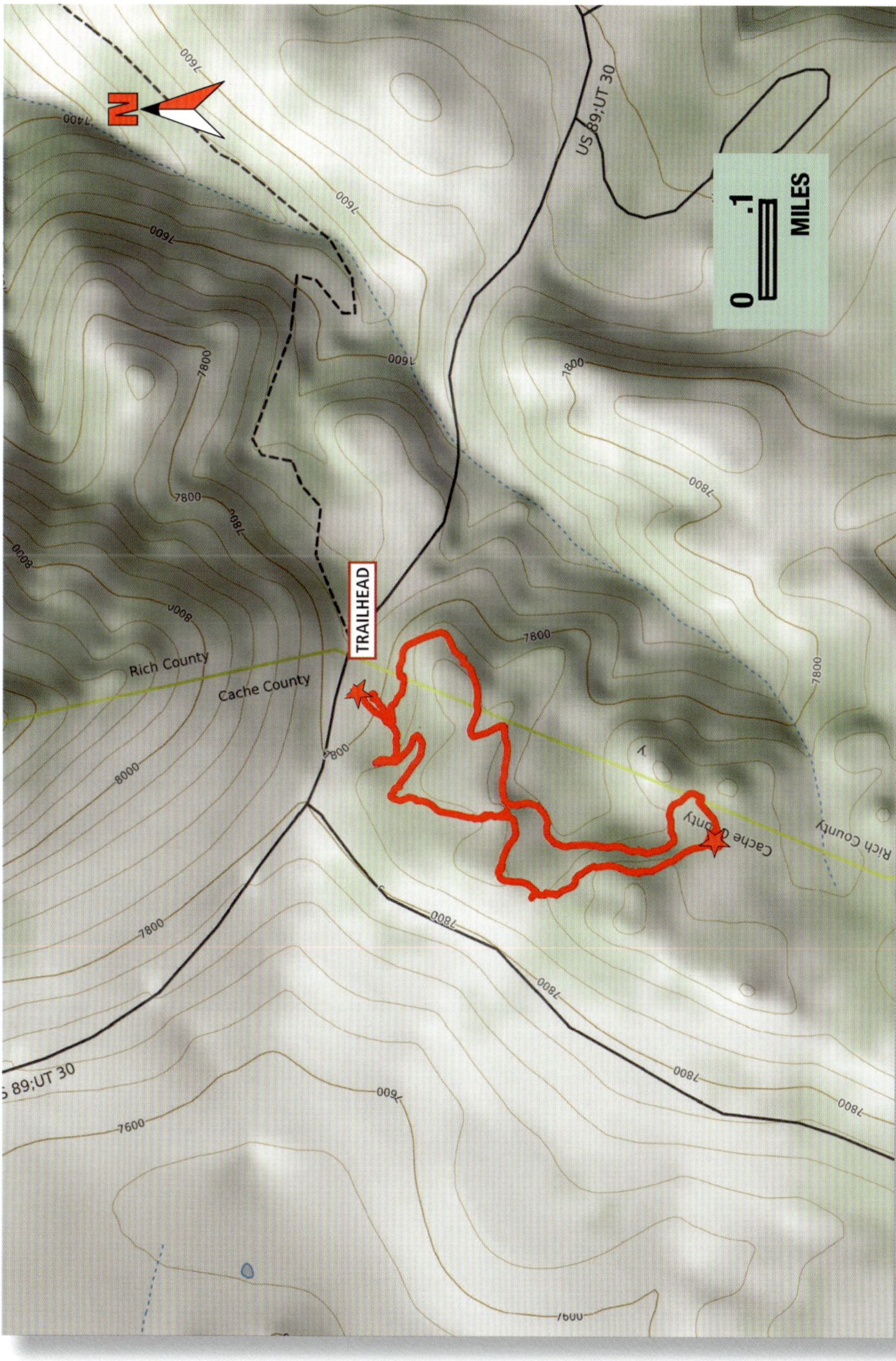

LIMBER PINE TRAIL

Take some time to enjoy the limber pines that have grown in this area for 500 to 1,000 years.

of Bear Lake. If you didn't catch it, don't fret because at 1.2 miles you will get a pretty clear view. Another bench and view can be found at 1.25 miles near sign 12.

As you get close to the trailhead, the trail descends. You will hear the road before you see it at 1.3 miles. The last sign, "Trails end," is a fitting close to the hike. Turn right slightly after the last information sign to head back to your car.

On the Way Home

THE ALLEN & ALICE STOKES NATURE CENTER

The Allen & Alice Stokes Nature Center is a nationally recognized children's forest. There is a preschool section for younger learners and a hands-on activities section for children and adults. Live animals are also a part of the visit. The beautiful but short hike of 0.3 mile from the parking lot to the nature center is not the only outdoor experience to be found. There is a swing and water for water play, and camps, nature preschool, and workshops are all held at the center. Be sure to check their calendar for special programs, free weekly program, music jams, and more.

Allen & Alice Stokes Nature Center
2696 E. US Highway 89
Logan, UT 84321
(435) 755-3239
http://logannature.org
Hours: Summer only on Friday and Saturday 10 a.m. to 7 p.m., except holidays
Cost: Free, unless it is a special program

Ogden Area

Utah's 7th largest city, trappers first named the town Fort Buenaventura in the 1840s. Its name was then changed to Brownsville in honor of Captain James Brown who purchased the land. Eventually the name was changed to Ogden in memory of fur trapper Peter Skene Ogden, a leader of the Hudson's Bay Company. Ogden butts up to the foothills of the Wasatch Mountains making it a popular destination for hikers, skiers, and rock climbers.

Overlooking the mountains of Ogden from the Birdsong Trail.

Rank 3

2. Birdsong Trail

RATING	Seeker, due to length and elevation gain
ROUND TRIP DISTANCE	1.7 miles out and back
ROUND-TRIP TIME	1–2 hours
ELEVATION CHANGE	180 feet (from 4,400 to 4,580 feet)
MAP	Trails Illustrated Ogden, Monte Cristo Range
NEAREST LANDMARK	Rainbow Gardens
FEES	None
RESTROOMS	At Rainbow Gardens
DOGS	Must be leashed
OPERATING HOURS	One hour before sunrise to one hour after sunset

COMMENT: This is a popular urban trail for bird lovers. This trail is multi-use, so expect to share it with runners, hikers, horses, and bikers. Keep small hikers close because the trail is eroded in places. Although the hike is about two-thirds shaded, grab water at Rainbow Gardens if necessary. This trail is a part of the forest biome. Have those binoculars ready from the start of this loop trail! And be on the lookout for rattlesnakes, which frequent the trail.

GETTING THERE: From Salt Lake City, take Interstate 15 north. Keep right at the fork onto US 89 and follow signs for I-84/South Ogden. Make a slight right onto S 1200 E/Harrison Blvd. and continue for 12.0 miles to 20th St. Turn right onto 20th St. and drive 5.0 miles to Valley Dr. Turn left onto Valley Dr. and continue for 1.0 mile to Rainbow Gardens on the right. If you park at Rainbow Gardens, make sure to pick a spot with a snowflake on the sign to avoid a ticket or getting towed4 miles northwest to Deer Ridge Junction. There is parking on both sides of the road.

THE ROUTE: As the name states, the habitat around the trail is a haven for birds. It begins in the southwest corner of the parking lot for Rainbow Gardens. Look for a large wooden Rainbow Trail sign. Shortly down the trail, at the Bonneville Shoreline sign, head left for the Birdsong Trail. At the trail fork, keep right and travel up the hill. The trail narrows, but it is still wide enough to walk side by side with a hiking pack. This spot can be tricky when multi-users are present at the same time.

Look right for views of the surrounding mountains at 0.2 mile. Then you will pass a beautiful bunch of Gamble oaks that turn red in the fall. The trail now opens up and is exposed. You can see Rainbow Gardens down to the right. The trail bends and switchbacks just shy of 0.3 mile. You can tell which way the winds blow most often here from the way the trees bend. At 0.30 mile an overlook trail goes off to the right. It is a short 0.1-mile trail that is not shaded but offers the chance to see a variety of wildflowers and prickly pear cactus. The trail overlooks the east bench area of Ogden and the golf course. Head right to take the short overlook, or left to remain on the main trail.

The main trail continues through trees and leads to a bench that is perfect for a water break at 0.6 mile. A small stream provides soothing background noise. If you have children that enjoy skipping rocks, they will enjoy this part of the trail. Wildflowers still hanging onto to summer can be seen in early fall. At 0.7 mile, the trail opens up again in grasses. You can see where animals cut through the grasses that are smashed down. The trail winds past an elementary school on the right and to the trailhead end, where there is a picnic table and water bowl for dogs. After taking in the views and some water, head back the way you came. You will pass the overlook loop at 1.3 miles on the left. Complete the loop again or for the first time. If your hiker(s) are tired, skip it and head to the trailhead.

A rainbow along the Birdsong Trail. *Photo: Wild Outsider Club*

Signs help hikers stay on the trail along the Birdsong Trail.

On the Way Home

GEORGE S. ECCLES DINOSAUR PARK

Don't miss the chance to visit the George S. Eccles Dinosaur Park while in Ogden. Open year round, there are 100 dinosaur sculptures based on fossil skeletons within the park. Enjoy outdoor paths lined with dinosaurs and minerals and fossils inside the museum. Hands on activities include a dino dig in sand. You may even see some fossil extractions. An outdoor playground and picnic tables are available.

George S. Eccles Dinosaur Park
1544 East Park Blvd.
Ogden, UT 84401
(801) 393-3466 ext. 56
www.dinosaurpark.org
Hours: Vary by season, so check the website for details
Cost: Adults 18 and up, $7; students 13–17, $6; children 2–12, $5; children under 2 free

BIRDSONG TRAIL

Rank 1

3. Quail Loop Trail

RATING	Experimenter, due to easy terrain
ROUND TRIP DISTANCE	0.82-mile loop
ROUND-TRIP TIME	45 minutes to 1 hour
ELEVATION CHANGE	187 feet (from 4,390 to 4,557 feet)
MAP	Trails Illustrated Ogden, Monte Cristo Range Map
NEAREST LANDMARK	Ogden Nature Center North
FEES	None
RESTROOMS	None
DOGS	Must be leashed
OPERATING HOURS	One hour before sunrise to one hour after sunset

COMMENT: Be on the lookout for mountain bikers and runners along this trail. Geocaching is also popular in the area. There is no access to water, so bring plenty as parts of the trail are fully exposed. The trail has small streams that flow from Pine Tree Reservoir, and it is known for spotting wildlife, particularly quail (hence the name) and rabbits. It is also known for mosquitoes when water is present, so put on some bug spray. A spattering of wildflowers may yet be visible through mid-September. Downed trees and rocks create many places to take breaks. This trail is a part of the forest biome.

GETTING THERE: From Salt Lake City, take Interstate 15 north. Keep right at the fork to continue on US 89 north, following signs for I-84 E/South Ogden. Take a slight right onto Harrison Blvd/S 1200 E and continue to Mountain Rd. Turn right on Mountain Rd. Look for a rock on the right that says "Ogden Nature Center North." The parking lot will be after that on the right. The 16 parking spots fill up on the weekends, as there are access two other trailheads here.

THE ROUTE: Begin this hike by going under the pergola-type structure. You will come to a trail junction for the Power Line Trail, Bonneville Shoreline Trail, and the Quail Trail Loop. Head left on the wide dirt Quail Trail Loop. This is a fairly easy hike with enough variation and challenges for a wide age and experience range of little hikers.

Under the canopy of trees at the beginning of the hike there is a sign reminding visitors to stay on the trail to help prevent erosion. This is a reminder to stay off

QUAIL LOOP TRAIL

Not even a little snow kept these young adventurers from enjoying the Quail Loop Trail.
Photo: Wild Outsider Club

the social trails along this hike. After this sign, there is a trail that heads off right; continue straight. The trail meanders through thick vegetation, but there are only a few rocks to maneuver around or over on this hike. Listen for the croaking of frogs and toads, and birds singing. If you have a nature collector in your family, this is a good trail for them. Nuts, pinecones, and leaves of a large variety, including maple and oak, are plentiful. You may even get hit in the head with a nut!

At 0.15 mile, the trail reconnects with the offshoot that went to the right earlier. The first of many footbridges appears just shy of 0.2 mile. At 0.25 mile, head left to continue on the Quail Trail Loop, then cross some planks of wood put in place for water runoff. Older kids will enjoy the challenge of balancing across them, and they are wide and stable, so even little ones can manage. The planks continue at 0.3 mile. You may find some water here, depending on recent weather. The trail comes close to the road now and is exposed to the sun. You can feel quite a temperature difference between the shade and the exposed areas. There is another trail junction past 0.3 mile; head right here for a short climb and another footbridge. Turn left at the sign at 0.4 mile as the trail turns direction back toward the trailhead.

Another footbridge at 0.45 mile is followed by a series of bridges crossing over the slowly trickling stream. Climb up and over the rock at 0.5 mile. You may have to duck under a hanging tree branch at 0.52 mile, and there will be a few more rocks to navigate and another bridge or two as you head back on this loop trail back to your car.

Rank 5

4. Wheeler Creek Trail

RATING	Pathfinder, due to distance and elevation gain
ROUND TRIP DISTANCE	3.8 miles out and back
ROUND-TRIP TIME	2–3 hours
ELEVATION CHANGE	660 feet (from 4,853 to 5513 feet)
MAP	Trails Illustrated Ogden, Monte Cristo Range
NEAREST LANDMARK	Ogden Canyon
FEES	None
RESTROOMS	At turnaround point at Art Norda Road Trailhead
DOGS	Must be leashed
OPERATING HOURS	One hour before sunrise to one hour after sunset

COMMENT: Mountain bikers heavily use this trail, and horses may also be seen, so use caution. The trail is also popular in winter for snowshoeing, winter hiking, Nordic skiing, and fat biking. The trail suffers from erosion and can be quite muddy during the spring runoff and after rain. This trail is a great place for collecting leaves including oak, maple, and cottonwood. This trail is a part of the forest biome.

GETTING THERE: From Salt Lake City, take Interstate 15 north. Take Exit 344 for 12th St and follow 12th St. up Ogden Canyon toward Pineview Reservoir. There is a parking lot on the right as the canyon begins to open up that has 20 spots. It fills up quickly, especially on summer weekends. You can also park at the top at the turn off at the lot off Ogden Canyon Road. You will be able to see the dam on the left. If you see the water for the Pineview Reservoir, you have gone too far. Follow the dirt road at the end of the parking lot down to the trailhead.

THE ROUTE: The wide trail begins under the shade. From the start, you will notice the trail is rocky, making footing difficult for young hikers, so be ready for a few falls.

At 0.1 mile there is a large rock in the middle of the trail. Kids enjoy climbing this rock, which is a good place to stop and get ready for hiking in the sunshine by taking in some water. The trail opens up shortly after you pass by the rock. Look left and you will begin to see Wheeler Creek. This begins the areas of erosion and drop offs on the left. It's better to keep everyone over to the right. The trail leaves the canopy of the shade and becomes exposed.

There is beauty to capture all along the Wheeler Creek Trail.

The water noise begins to drown out the road noise, and at 0.3 mile, there are man-made cement falls on the left. As you continue on the trail, look left for natural falls. You will continue to climb slightly as the wide and rocky route continues. There are big rocks on the sides to sit on and take a break all along the trail.

A scree field at 0.50 mile on the right is the first of many. There is a big area of erosion on the left, and the rocky walls of the canyon begin to close in on the right. A fun rock on the right at 0.6 mile almost looks like a throne to sit on.

The water of Wheeler Creek is on the right at 0.8 mile. There is a perfect place to take a break on the right close to 0.9 mile, known as "Nature's Cul De Sac." Hike leader Susan from Wild Outsiders Club named this shady spot perfectly. It sort of goes around in a loop and is a prime place to explore the water, skip rocks, have lunch or a snack on top of a log, and just explore. It is also a backcountry campsite area. This is a good place to turn around if you have small hikers.

If you continue, scree fields become more prevalent on the right. You will now encounter blind corners on the trail, but you can hear mountain bikes before you see them and be prepared. At 1.08 miles there is a bridge on the right, and a trail sign points slightly right for Ice Box Canyon, which is a more shaded trail.

Head straight to continue on the Wheeler Creek/Art Nord Trail. Be on the lookout for elk and moose, which go through a rut during the fall making them

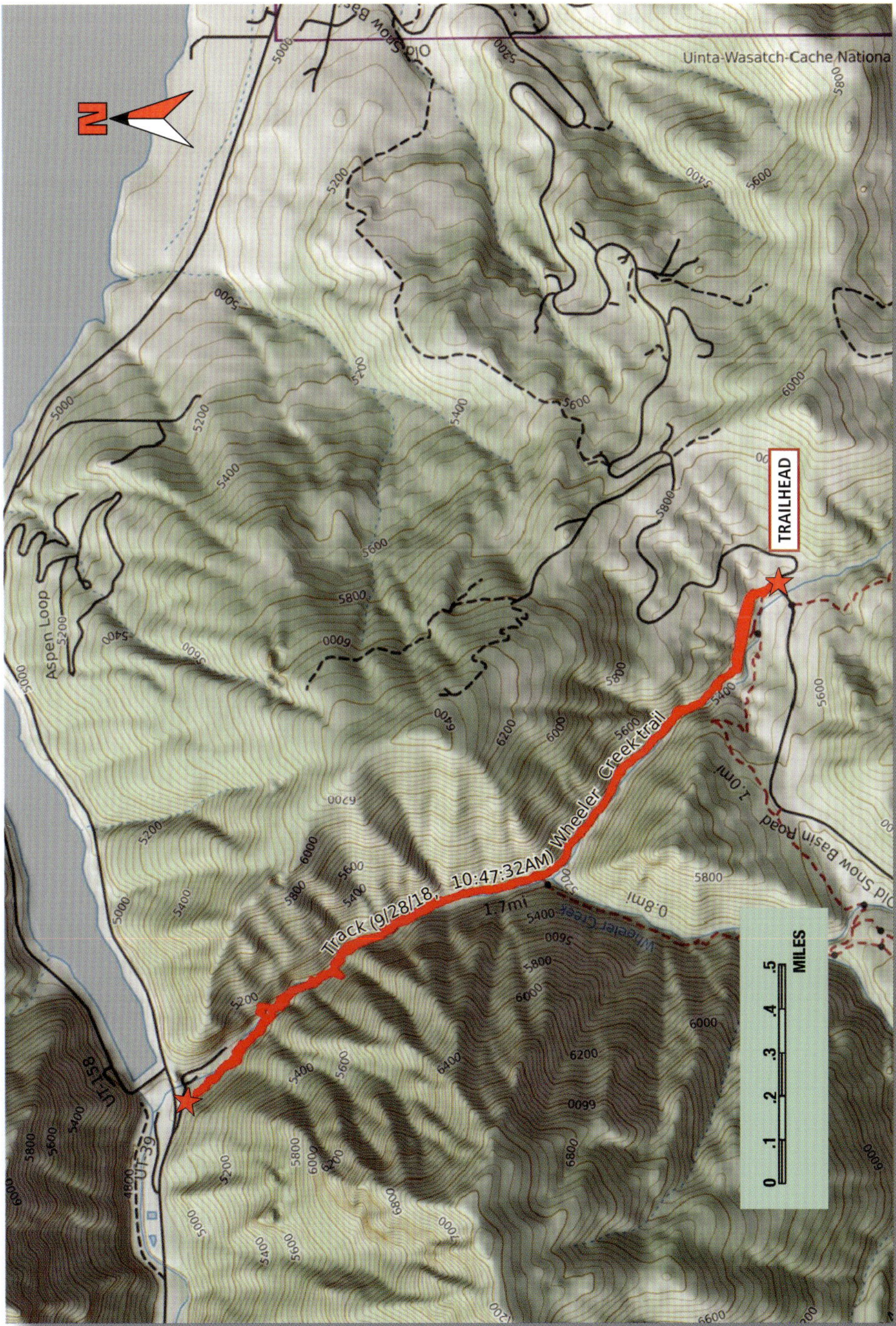

WHEELER CREEK TRAIL

more aggressive during this time. Art Nord was a leader in the restoration of watersheds and development of recreation areas in the area including Snow Basin and the Pineview Dam before he passed away in 1957. He was a member of the U.S Forest Service from 1915 until 1956. As you hike along, be thankful to him and the many others who value preserving outdoor lands and building opportunities for people to enjoy them.

The trail continues to be exposed as it climbs. The sound of water disappears as you continue up the gentle incline. Steep drop offs continue on the right. At 1.3 miles there may be possible water access. Be wary of wasps here, as they tend to be prevalent. Don't forget to turn around to see the views of the canyon behind you. Some cairns can be found on the left near 1.6 miles. The trail opens up again passed the cairns but continues to be in the direct sun.

Look for a rock with a plaque on the right at 1.8 miles for information about Art Nord.

At 1.9 miles, you will come to the parking lot off of Art Nord Drive. There are pit toilets here. Follow the trail back to the trailhead, enjoying the views from the other direction.

HIKE EXTENSION: If you complete all the loops of Wheeler Creek, including Icebox Canyon and the Upper Wheeler Creek Trail, it is about a 9.2-mile day hike that climbs over 1,500 feet.

The scenery along Wheeler Creek is beautiful.

Layton Area

Named after Mormon Leader Christopher Layton, the town was first settled in the 1850s. It lies within the Wasatch Front. Hill Air Force Base is located in Layton. It stands at an elevation of approximately 4,350 feet.

American flags align the Adams Canyon Trail in Layton, Utah.

Rank 5

5. Adams Canyon Trail

RATING	Pathfinder, due to elevation gain, rock scrambling, and steep terrain
ROUND TRIP DISTANCE	4.65 miles out and back
ROUND-TRIP TIME	3–4 hours
ELEVATION CHANGE	1,575 feet (from 4,800 to 6,375 feet)
MAP	Trails Illustrated Ogden, Monte Cristo Range
NEAREST LANDMARK	Layton
FEES	None
RESTROOMS	None
DOGS	Must be leashed
OPERATING HOURS	One hour before sunrise to one hour after sunset

COMMENT: This popular hike features three waterfalls, two small ones and the larger Adams Canyon Falls. The best time to visit the falls is from spring through fall. Butterflies and dragonflies abound on the trail. Rattlesnakes and deer are common to this area as well. Rocks and tree stumps offer plenty of places to stop and take a break. Campsites can be found all along the trail.

The beginning portion of the hike has full sun exposure. The trail, located in a forest biome, becomes more difficult as you get closer to the falls, with water crossings and rocky terrain. Scrambling may be needed in places. While difficult, it is possible to get to the falls wearing a kiddo in a pack. The trail is hikeable year round. Spikes are recommended in the winter..

GETTING THERE: From Salt Lake City, take Interstate 15 north to Highway 89. Take Hwy 89 north to Layton. Turn right onto East 1200 North, and then make a quick right on Eastside Rd. Find a dirt parking lot on the left that can fit 25 to 30 cars, close to the end of Eastside Road. Parking is allowed on the street as well.

THE ROUTE: From the start, the trail climbs a series of exposed switchbacks in thick sand. A chain link fence surrounds the initial steps on the trail. At 0.15 mile there is a rock that explains how Adams Canyon got its name. You may pass eight American flags flying in the wind as you make your way to the top of the switchbacks. The flags are a good visual as the trail climbs 500 feet up to the top. Sections of the trail may be washed out in this area based on recent weather.

The first part of the hike into Adams Canyon offers little shade, so be sure to hydrate.

The largest of falls in Adams Canyon is 40 feet tall.

At 0.35 mile, you will notice some social trails. Continue to head straight as you approach a bench that offers a sunny place to take a break. At a little over 0.5 mile, the trail hits a junction with the Bonneville Shoreline Trail, which heads left and right. Head right (east). You will begin to hear the waters of Holmes Creek as you

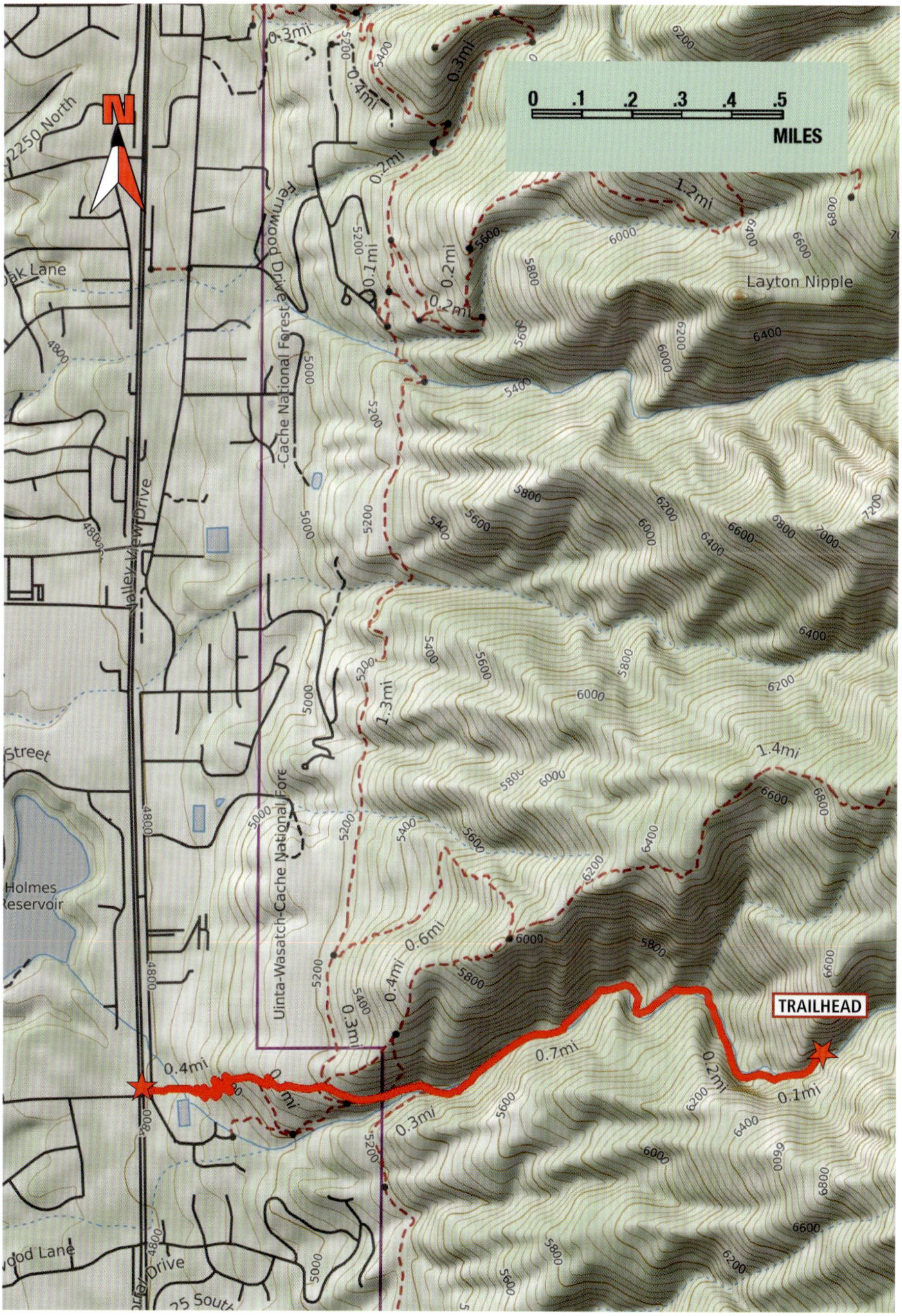

ADAMS CANYON TRAIL

The falls at Adams Canyon offer a great place to cool down.

approach the shade of the pines and Gambel oak. Fall brings a blaze of red as you travel through the oak.

The trail levels off at this point and meanders up and down in and out of shade. At 0.75 mile, turn left at the fork where the wooden Adams Canyon Trail sign is located. Water access at 0.8 mile offers a good place to dunk your hat for relief from the heat. The wasps are big fans of the water here. Close to 0.9 mile, there is a series of downed trees to navigate. Shortly after the trees, the trail hugs the wall of dirt and rock. Depending on recent weather, the water from Holmes Creek may be high enough to cover the trail. There is a massive pine on the right near the one mile mark. The trail continues to get rockier as you get closer to the first set of falls. The trail follows Holmes Creek, and the water level comes close to the trail on the right just shy of the 1.0-mile mark. The trail climbs again just past this point. At 1.2 miles, the trail opens up on the right for an Adams Canyon view.

Make sure to continue right/straight on the trail around 1.3 miles. Shortly after, the trail opens up to a canyon view on the left. The 1.5 mark offers another good spot to dunk your hat to cool off in the summer months. Head between rocks as you hug the water. The trail crosses a bridge on the left. After the bridge, the trail becomes more difficult. The creek will now be on the left as you scramble up a steep hill. At 1.7 miles, the trail hugs a wall of dirt and requires you to navigate the creek by moving from rock to rock. You will see the first of the three waterfalls on the left shortly after.

The trail continues to become rockier as it climbs. At 2 miles, the second waterfall appears on the left. You can dunk your heads here directly in the stream.

The trail steepens and the terrain becomes more difficult as you get closer to Adams Falls. You may need to use your hands to get up and over the rocks. Taking a few breaks along the way is advised. As you approach the falls, which you will be able to hear before you see, use rocks to cross Holmes Creek. Once across the creek, around the corner you will see the approximately 40-foot Adams Canyon Falls. There is a pool under the falls to cool off in, and you may find a brown trout at your feet! Several large rocks near the falls offer the perfect spot for removing socks and shoes. Although you can climb up to the top of the falls, it is not recommended. After cooling off in the spray (or under the falls if you can brave the cold), retrace your steps back to the trailhead.

Kamas Area

With the nickname of "Gateway to the Uintas," Kamas is appealing to those seeking isolation amongst natural wonder. Hiking, climbing and fishing are popular in the area. Ranching and lumber are the most popular industries in the area. Look west to see the Wasatch Mountains while the Uinta Mountains surround the area to the east. The Weber River runs north while the Provo River runs south. The town was settled in 1859 by Mormon Pioneers after Native Americans moved on. The name comes from Camassia quamash- a food for Native Americans.

The mountains reflect in Mirror Lake. *Photo: Heather Sims*

Rank 1

6. Fairy Forest Trail

RATING	Experimenter, due to easy terrain and short distance
ROUND TRIP DISTANCE	1 mile out and back
ROUND-TRIP TIME	1 hour plus
ELEVATION CHANGE	39 feet (from 8,032 to 8,071 feet)
MAP	Trails Illustrated High Uinta Wilderness
NEAREST LANDMARK	Mirror Lake/Shady Dell Campground
FEES	$6 to drive the Mirror Lake Scenic Byway
RESTROOMS	Pit toilets at campground
DOGS	Must be leashed
OPERATING HOURS	Sunrise to sunset

COMMENT: One of the most unique trails in Utah, the Fairy Forest Trail brings a sense of wonder and delight to hikers young and old. In 1997, local Scott Hayes and friends created a rock garden, complete with fairy houses, wind chimes, and ribbons that today is known as the Fairy Garden. Due to issues with garbage and the use of materials that are not natural to the environment, no additions to the garden are allowed.

This trail requires a stream crossing over rocks or logs. The water can be moving fast, especially during spring runoff or recent rains. This hike is in the forest biome. It is best hiked from May through October, before the first snow.

GETTING THERE: From Salt Lake City, take Interstate 80 east to Exit 146/

Some of the many fairy houses along the Fairy Forest Trail.
Photo: Heather Sims

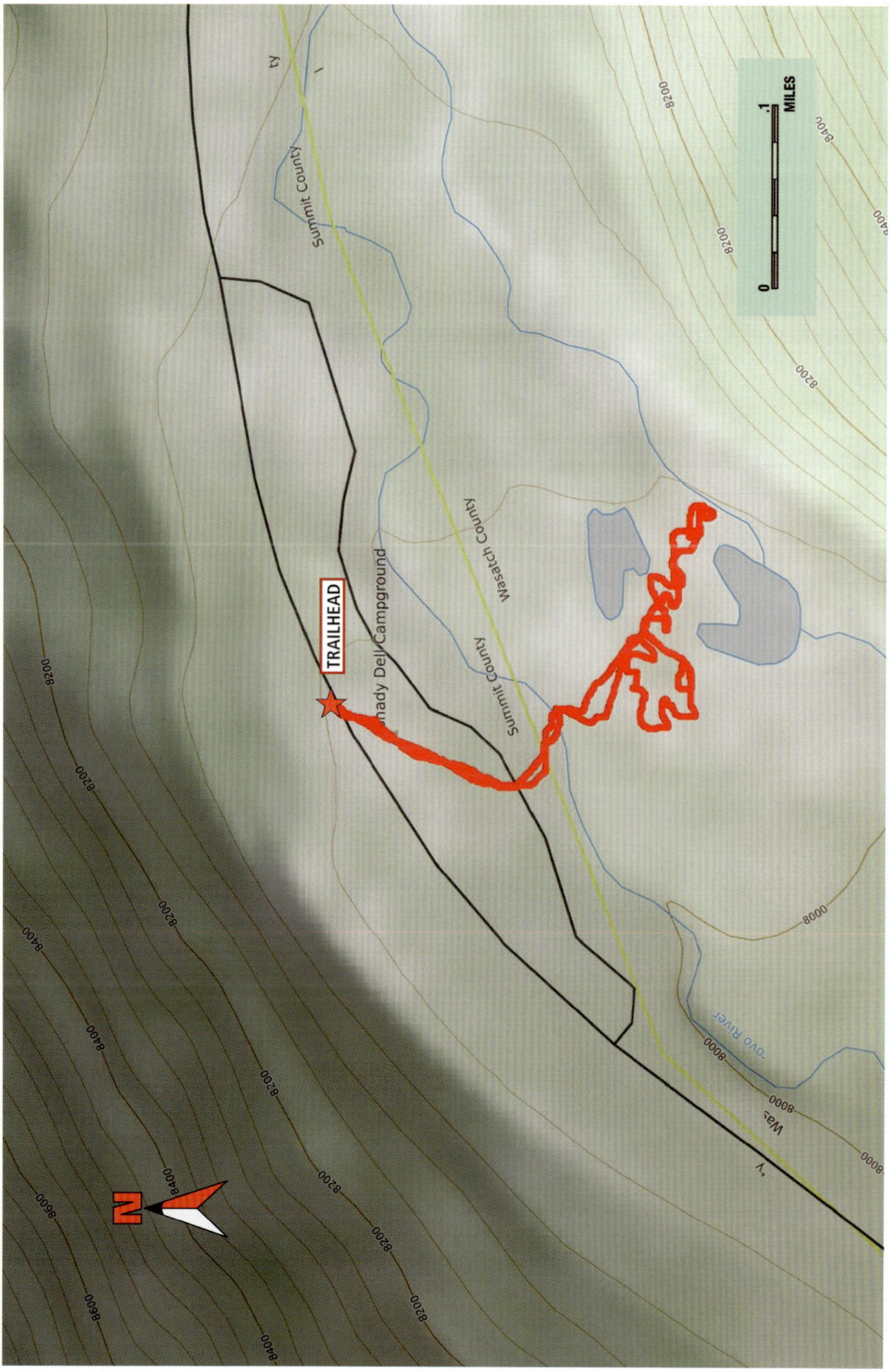

FAIRY FOREST TRAIL

Logs and rocks are perfect for playing on the Fairy Forest Trail. *Photo: Heather Sims*

UT 40. Continue on UT 40 for 3.0 miles and take Exit 4, Park City/Kamas. Head east on SR-248 toward Kamas for less than a mile. Turn left on Main St. (the first light). Make a right shortly after onto Center St. Center St. will turn into the Mirror Lake Scenic Byway. Follow the Mirror Lake Scenic Byway for 17.0 miles. Look for the pullout at mile marker 17. Park in the pullout lot.

THE ROUTE: Begin your hike on the trail on the right as you look into the forest. This trail leads to the Shady Dell Campground. Continue through the campground following the trail. Watch for arrows painted on the rocks pointing you in the correct direction.

The fairly flat path leads to a creek bed, which may be wet or dry, depending on the time of year. Use rocks or logs to cross the creek bed when necessary. Once across the creek, conquer the hill (the only place with elevation gain). A log may or may not be at the top designating that you are close to the Fairy Forest. Use hushed voices as you take a few more steps. Head to the right, and just ahead enter the forest. Skip among the rocks. Listen to the peaceful sounds of the wind chimes as you navigate through the whimsical fairy houses and gardens. Be sure to stay on the designated paths lined by the rocks. Some spots are in memory of lost loved ones, while others bring the fairy world to life. You can look, but do not disturb the collection or add to it. The Fairy Forest is the perfect place to put down a blanket and have a picnic while keeping a keen eye out for fairies. Or, enjoy a snack while visiting a replica Stonehenge.

The fall brings vibrant colors. Leaves floating in the autumn breeze add to the magic of this place. Retrace your fairy steps across the water, through the campground, and to your car. After viewing the gardens and homes, retrace your fairy steps across the water, through the campground, and to your car.

Rank 3

7. Mirror Lake Shoreline Trail

RATING	Seeker, due to length and starting elevation
ROUND TRIP DISTANCE	2.9 mile loop
ROUND-TRIP TIME	1.5–2 hours
ELEVATION CHANGE	70 feet (from 10,400 to 10,470 feet)
MAP	Trails Illustrated High Uinta Wilderness
NEAREST LANDMARK	Mirror Lake
FEES	$6 to drive the Mirror Lake Scenic Byway
RESTROOMS	Pit Toilets
DOGS	Must be leashed
OPERATING HOURS	One hour before sunrise to one hour after sunset

COMMENT: You may see people kayaking, stand-up paddleboarding, and fishing while on this alpine biome hike. The occasional horseback rider may also be seen. This hike is best between late June and October, as the snow lasts through June. The trail is quite shaded but is especially busy on summer weekends. Pack extra clothing

Moose are popular visitors on the Mirror Lake Trail. *Photo: Heather Sims*

Clear skies bring mountain reflections along the Mirror Lake Trail. *Photo: Heather Sims*

for the higher altitude. The weather can change quickly and lightning is common on summer afternoons.

Wildflowers bloom in the summer bringing a splash of color to the lakefront and trail around it. Fall brings vibrant yellows from the aspens mixed in with the greens of the pines. Look up on the hillsides for unmatched scenery, especially come September.

GETTING THERE: From Salt Lake City, take Interstate 80 east for 30.0 miles. Go south on Highway 40 Park City/Heber City/Vernal exit 146 for one mile to the Kamas exit. Follow HWY 189 southeast for 12 miles. Turn right onto Hwy 150/Mirror Lake Scenic Byway. Drive for 32 miles to reach the campground.

MIRROR LAKE TRAIL

THE ROUTE: The Mirror Lake Shoreline Trail begins near the Mirror Lake Campground area off the Mirror Lake Scenic Byway. From the boat launch, look for the bathrooms. Just past the bathrooms there is a sign designating the trailhead.

The trail is wide in most spots. Occasionally rocks and roots pop up along the path around the lake, but none that are too difficult, even for new hikers. The trail is often muddy because of the weather at this high altitude. This makes the use of a stroller or wheelchair on the trail not recommended. The trail passes through some marshy areas, but boardwalks help visitors stay dry and navigate across. It is almost impossible to get lost as long as you keep on the main trail. The Uinta Mountain Range runs east to west.

Enjoy the reflection of the mountains in the lake, especially Bald Mountain, as you make your way around the loop. You can see how the lake got its name! It is one of several Mirror Lakes around the United States all named for the glass-like water that reflects the beauty around it.

Don't miss the opportunity to read the plaques around the trail with information on local animals, including mule deer. Moose frequent the lake area. Less frequently, bear have been spotted in the area. Birds enjoy the water and chipmunks enjoy trying to steal a snack or two. Various benches around the lake offer the perfect opportunity to slow down and enjoy the scenery while refueling. Since this hike is more like a stroll, there is no reason to rush. Take in the sights, take in the smells, and take in the beauty of this place. Follow the loop around and back to the trailhead.

On the Way Home

HI-MOUNTAIN DRUG

A local secret (until now), don't miss the chance to fuel up on the way home by stopping at Hi-Mountain Drug. The name is confusing, because at one time the building had a pharmacy. But now it serves old-fashioned milkshakes, home style fries, and delicious burgers. It's perfect post hike grub!

Hi-Mountain Drug
40 N. Main St.
Kamas, UT 84036
(435) 783-4466
www.facebook.com/himountainburgers
Hours: Monday through Saturday, 8 a.m. to 9 p.m.

Salt Lake City Area

Serving as the capital city for Utah, Salt Lake City is named after the Great Salt Lake. Sometimes called Salt Lake, or SLC, the city was founded in 1847 by Brigham Young. The city serves as the world headquarters for the Church of Jesus Christ of Latter Day Saints. The city hosted the 2002 Winter Olympics and is surrounded by the Oquirrh Mountains to the west and Wasatch Mountains east.

A view of the Salt Lake area from the Wild Rose Trail.

Rank 3

8. Wild Rose Trail

RATING	Seeker, due to elevation change
ROUND TRIP DISTANCE	2-mile loop
ROUND-TRIP TIME	1.5–2 hours
ELEVATION CHANGE	307 feet (from 5200 to 5507 feet)
MAP	Trails Illustrated Ogden, Monte Cristo Range
NEAREST LANDMARK	Wild Rose Trailhead Park
FEES	None
RESTROOMS	Seasonal bathrooms with water mid-April through mid-October
DOGS	Must be leashed
OPERATING HOURS	One hour before sunrise to one hour after sunset

COMMENT: This is a multi-use trail that shares access with mountain bikers, so it is important to keep your head up at all times. Wildflowers line the trails in late May until July, depending on the weather. Most of this trail is exposed, but pockets of trees provide shade and perfect places to stop and grab a drink or snack. This hike can be snowshoed in the winter. Sunsets are a popular hike time because of the views looking over Salt Lake. This hike is an example of the forest biome.

GETTING THERE: From Salt Lake City, take Interstate 15 north for 4.0 miles. Take Exit 313 for US 89N/Beck Street. After 1.5 miles, turn right onto E. Eagle Ridge Dr.. Go through the roundabout and continue on E. Eagle Ridge Dr. Make a right onto Eaglepointe Dr. Take that to Sky Crest Ln. and make a left. The park and trailhead are on the left. The parking lot fits about 15 cars.

THE ROUTE: Begin on the cement path from the parking lot that is just to the left of the large map and sign. When the cement ends, turn right. The beginning of the hike is shaded and there are many butterflies. There is a good sign about respecting the trails and nature. Take the time to stop and read it with your little hikers.

At almost 0.2 miles, continue straight. If you head right, you will be on a downhill mountain bike trail; a trail sign marks the correct direction. At this point, the trail begins to climb. Just shy of 0.3 mile, you will see the shortcut for the Wild Rose Loop, which is designated with a sign. A map also shows your location within the area. Stop to take a look back at the valley and grab a drink of water. There is more shade less climbing coming up.

WILD ROSE TRAIL

The Wild Rose Trail offers the opportunity to overlook many cities including Bountiful.

The trail continues to switchback up the hillside. Look right around the 0.4-mile mark for valley views and continue left to stay on the loop trail. Heading right leads to a lookout. The trail begins to level off a bit now and there are pockets of shade. The trail narrows and becomes a bit rocky here. It might be difficult to hike side by side, but there is room for a hiking pack without getting scratched by the trees and scrub.

At 0.58 mile, the downhill mountain bike trails are on the right. At the T at 0.6 mile, continue to the left for the Wild Rose Loop. Heading right goes to the Chukar Loop (see hike extension) and the downhill mountain bike trails.

You will come to a sign for the Eagle Ridge, Woodbriar Game, and Jeep Trails at 0.65 mile. Here you can begin to see the B on the hillside for the town of Bountiful, and mountains are on both sides now. At 0.75 mile, go either right or left; you will end up at the same place: Sunset Point, at 0.8 mile. There is no advantage to taking one over the other.

A bench at 0.9 mile is a good place to take a break. Social trails appear at 1.1 miles. Follow the main trail right into pockets of shade. The Gambel oaks here offer beautiful pockets of red in the fall. Another bench in the shade is at 1.26 miles. More social trails begin to pop up with most leading to the neighborhoods below.

Before the 1.5 miles mark, the trail leaves the eastern view behind for a western view. Shade will continue to keep you cooler as you get closer to the trailhead and park. You will hit the fork where the trail began at around 1.7 miles. Go right at the map sign to finish your hike.

HIKE EXTENSION: To hike a longer route, choose the Chukar Loop. At the Wild Rose shortcut, head straight (right) instead of left. The loop is 0.7 mile long and loops back to the Wild Rose Trail Loop. The extension trail changes to a Seeker rating due to distance.

Antelope Island State Park

The topography and location of Antelope Island attracts a variety of animals and insects. No-see-ums, usually present from April through June, are the peskiest because spray doesn't keep them away, so visit outside those months or on a breezy day. Other bugs are harmless or respond to insect repellant. Antelope Island is a wetland biome, so it lacks trees.

Antelope Island on a rainy day creates a dramatic backdrop.

9. Buffalo Point Trail

RATING	Seeker, due to elevation change
ROUND TRIP DISTANCE	0.8 mile out and back
ROUND-TRIP TIME	45 minutes to 1 hour
ELEVATION CHANGE	300 feet (from 4,520 to 4,820 feet)
MAP	Trails Illustrated Ogden, Monte Cristo Range
NEAREST LANDMARK	Antelope Island State Park Visitor Center
FEES	$10 per car, or free if staying at a park campsite; Utah State Parks pass
RESTROOMS	Pit toilets
DOGS	Must be leashed
OPERATING HOURS	6 a.m. to 10 p.m. daily, except Thanksgiving and Christmas

COMMENT: Buffalo Point is a popular hike, especially during sunsets. Star gazers also enjoy this hike for open star viewing. The hike offers viewpoints of the park throughout including the herds of bison.

An interpretive center and an observation deck are located next to the parking lot. This hike is part of the wetland biome and can be hiked year round needing spikes or snowshoes in the winter months. Because this hike is treeless, there is no shade, and it tends to be more crowded in the morning and evening.

Hiking back down to the trailhead on the Buffalo Point Trail.

GETTING THERE: From Salt Lake City, take Interstate 15 north to Exit 332 UT 108 N/W 2000 N/Antelope Dr. in Layton. Take Exit 332 onto UT 108/Antelope Dr. and continue for 15.0 miles. Follow the main entrance road for Antelope Island State Park to the right. Turn left at the sign for Bridger Bay Campground. Follow the sign for Buffalo Point. There is a large parking lot that holds about 40 cars.

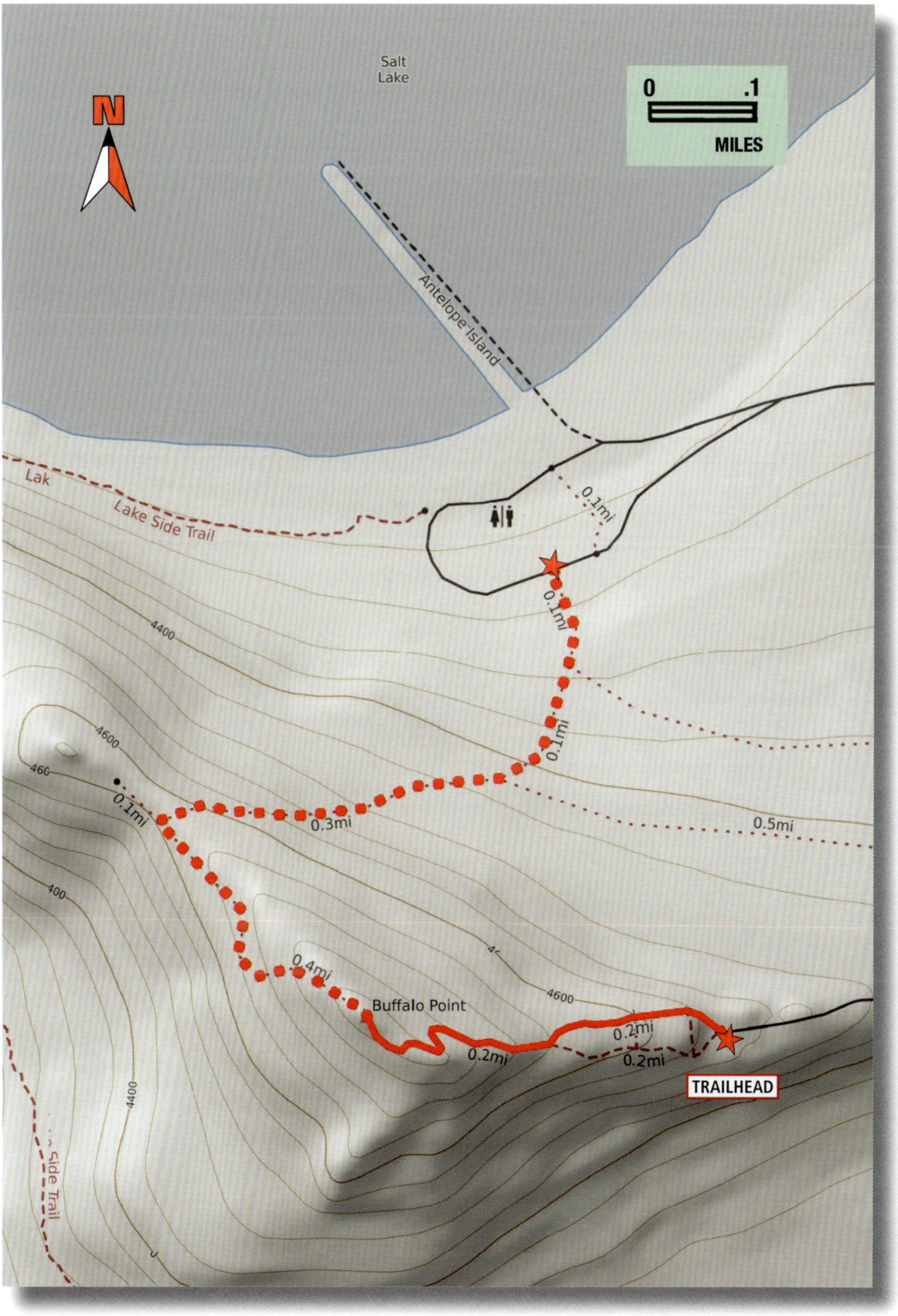

BUFFALO POINT TRAIL

The rocks provide a natural signal for the turnaround point of the trail.

THE ROUTE: The Buffalo Point Trail begins to the right of the observation deck and interpretive center. The trail gradually climbs from the start. At about 0.3 mile, the trail heads to the right. Avoid the social and other trails and stick to the main trail while you hike out to Buffalo Point. This helps with erosion and restoration.

Take a break on one of three benches if you need a breath during the climb. You can see Bridger Bay on the right and White Rock Bay on the left. Because the island is home to many animals, be on the lookout for herds of buffalo (and buffalo patties), bighorn sheep, and pronghorn antelopes. Chukar can also be found around the trail. Follow the trail back to the parking lot after viewing the rocks, wildlife, and flora of 28,000-acre Antelope Island.

There is no clear end to the trail; carefully venture out on the rocks no farther than you feel comfortable. Panoramic views open at the top of what is said to be the 4,240th highest mountain peak in Utah. You can also scan for wildlife and look for tufa deposits, the youngest rocks on the island that resemble concrete. Believed to be 550 million years old, tintic quartzite can also be found around Buffalo Point and is typically brown and tan.

ALTERNATIVE HIKE: You can also start this hike from the Bridger Bay Campground. There is a trail that begins from the left hand side of the campground. This trail heads up and up and includes some rock scrambling. The hikes is approximately 2 miles round trip and is a Seeker (but close to Wanderer) rated hike due to elevation change.

Rank 4

10. Dooley Knob Spur Trail

RATING	Wanderer, due to elevation gain and length
ROUND TRIP DISTANCE	3 miles out and back
ROUND-TRIP TIME	1.5–2 hours
ELEVATION CHANGE	645 feet (from 4,545 to 5,190 feet)
MAP	Trails Illustrated Ogden, Monte Cristo Range
NEAREST LANDMARK	Antelope Island Visitor Center
FEES	$10 per car, or free if staying at a park campsite; Utah State Parks pass
RESTROOMS	None
DOGS	Must be leashed
OPERATING HOURS	6 a.m. through 10 p.m. daily, except Thanksgiving and Christmas

COMMENT: This trail is named after John Dooley, Sr. who is credited with saving the American Bison. He bought Antelope Island in 1884 and brought over 12 bison to the island. The bison graze often in and around the trail, so use caution. It is safest to give them plenty of space. You might spot a herd in the distance near the Fielding Garr Ranch.

Coyote, mule deer, and pronghorn are a few animals you can see from this trail. The scenery makes this trail a must-do; it evokes Lord of the Rings and the rolling hills of Ireland and its coastline. Rocky knolls provide places to grab a snack and explore. Yarrow and other wildflowers line the trail along with other scrub. This hike is treeless, so there is no shade. This means it tends to be more crowded in the morning and evening. Insects are also plentiful.

Sunrise and sunset are popular times for this hike. Fairly mild fall and spring temperatures make this a year-round destination. Animals are more active during these months too. There is a full moon hike here in November that is open to children 8 and older. Antelope Island is a wetland biome, which explains the lack of trees.

GETTING THERE: From Salt Lake City, take Interstate 15 north to Exit 332 UT 108 N/W 2000 N/Antelope Dr. in Layton. Take Exit 332 for UT 108/Antelope Dr. and continue for 15 miles. Once on the park causeway, follow signs for the Frary Peak Trailhead. The causeway is a little less than 8.0 miles long; take a left when the

The green hillsides of Antelope Island provide a beautiful backdrop.

causeway ends. The trailhead is approximately 6.0 miles up the road on the right. There is parking for about 20 cars and a few horse trailers.

THE ROUTE: From the trailhead, take the trail on the right of the main trailhead sign, Frary Peak Trail, to Dooley Knob Spur. The trail begins to climb immediately up the peak's west side. Switchbacks make the climb easier, but you may want to take water breaks along the way.

There is an overlook on the right around 0.2 mile. Many hikers choose to stop here and climb up a series of rocks to take in the view. At 0.3 mile, the trail flattens out for a bit but continues to climb. The trail is wide enough to hike side by side until the rocky section near the top of the knob. Hiking packs are not an issue on this terrain. As you hike up, look left to see if you can see a herd of buffalo below the trailhead parking lot. Bison pies are often found along the trail as buffalo use the area to cross from the east to the west and vice versa within the park.

At 0.75 mile, the trail comes to a T. A wooden sign denotes Dooley Knob Spur to the right and Frary Peak to the left. Follow the trail to the right (north). The trail switchbacks in the final push to the summit, and close to the top, the obvious path stops. Cairns at the top of the knob guide hikers to the safest paths. Kids will feel quite a sense of achievement in getting to the top! The trail ends at the top of the knob at 1.5 miles.

Once you catch your breath, take in the views from all sides, including the Wasatch Mountains and the Great Salt Lake, which is the largest natural lake west of the Mississippi. Follow your path back to the trailhead while enjoying the views from another direction.

DOOLEY KNOB TRAIL

Rank 3

11. Ladyfinger Trail

RATING	Seeker, due to rocky surface
ROUND TRIP DISTANCE	0.5 mile out and back
ROUND-TRIP TIME	30 minutes
ELEVATION CHANGE	About 10 feet (from 4,250 to 4,260 feet)
MAP	Trails Illustrated Ogden, Monte Cristo Range
NEAREST LANDMARK	Antelope Island State Park Visitor Center
FEES	$10 per car, or free if staying at a park campsite; Utah State Parks pass
RESTROOMS	Pit toilets
DOGS	Must be leashed
OPERATING HOURS	6 a.m. through 10 p.m. daily, except Thanksgiving and Christmas

COMMENT: The Ladyfinger Trail is popular for visitors wishing to catch a view of Egg Island, which is a bird-nesting site. Sunsets are a spectacular time to visit the point. This hike is treeless, so there is no shade, and it tends to be more crowded in the morning and evening.

GETTING THERE: From Salt Lake City, take Interstate 15 north to Exit 332 UT 108 N/W 2000 N/Antelope Dr. in Layton. Take Exit 332 for UT 108/Antelope Dr. and continue for 15 miles. Follow the main entrance road for Antelope Island State Park to the right. From the visitor center, drive southeast on Antelope Island Rd. Make two lefts to continue on Antelope Island Rd. Turn right onto Egg

The Ladyfinger Trail is short but provides unobstructed 360 degree views.

Looking out towards Egg Island and the Great Salt Lake.

Island Overlook Rd. for the Ladyfinger Trailhead. The large parking lot can hold over 30 cars. The picnic shelter is a popular place to have lunch or dinner.

THE ROUTE: What the Ladyfinger Trail lacks in length and elevation change, it makes up for in views. The trail begins as a wide gravel path. Interpretive signs describe the Great Salt Lake and Antelope Island. Benches provide spots to stop and

The scenery from the Ladyfinger Trail.

take in the views. At 0.1 mile the trail turns from wide gravel to rocky. Once you reach the rocks, there is no set route to navigate over them to the trail's end. Use the path that works best for you and your little hikers. Rocks provide good hand holds at points, but some are jagged. Some of these rocks are tintic quartzite. Believed to be 550 million years old, these rocks are typically tan and brown.

There are panoramic views if you can find some level ground to look around. Look northwest at Egg Island and the countless birds that nest there—an estimated 4 million during the year, including California gulls, one of 250 bird species known to reside on the island. You might also see ibises and pelicans. To the west, you can see Bridger Bay, the campground area, and beach access. East faces toward Salt Lake City. Beside birds, you'll probably see butterflies and lizards, and spiders enjoy building webs among the rocks, so look out for eight legs. Blaze your own rocky (but safe) path back to the parking lot after checking out the views and birds.

On the Way Home

ANTELOPE ISLAND STATE PARK

Antelope Island State Park is a hidden gem, making it a unique day or multi-day trip if you choose to camp overnight. After a hike or two, check out the herds of bison (from a distance) and Fielding Garr Ranch, or attend an educational program. Take time to visit the shoreline of the Great Salt Lake. Its oolitic sand, formed similarly to pearls, is unique, with circular grains.

The Bridger Bay area has a sandy beach along with restrooms and coin showers. It's named after American explorer Jim Bridger, who may have been the first non-Native American to see the lake in 1824. Covered picnic tables offer a great place to have a meal and watch the sunset. Or eat at Island Buffalo Grill, which serves buffalo burgers and other food and drinks. Its hours vary depending on the season. Take a salty swim, build a sand castle, or skip rocks. Kayaking, canoeing, and stand-up paddleboarding are allowed on the lake. Hit the coin showers to wash off the salt before heading home, and give equipment a rinse as well.

Bridger Bay Beach at Antelope Island State Park

4528 West 1700 Street
Syracuse, UT 84075
(801) 773-2941
https://stateparks.utah.gov/parks/antelope-island
Admission: Free with $10 park entrance fee
Hours: 6 a.m. through 10 p.m.; closed on Thanksgiving and Christmas

LADYFINGER TRAIL

Wildflowers are abundant during the summer in the Wasatch Mountains.

Little Cottonwood Canyon

A U-shaped canyon carved during the last ice age, Little Cottonwood Canyon is in the Wasatch Mountain Range. Two ski resorts, Alta and Snowbird, are based in the canyon. Fishing, hiking and rock climbing are also popular, and it's common to see road cyclists powering up the canyon road in the summer months.

Little Cottonwood Canyon provides year round recreation including hiking in the spring, summer, and fall.

Rank 4

12. Albion Meadows Trail

RATING	Wanderer, due to starting altitude and elevation gain
ROUND TRIP DISTANCE	2.14 miles
ROUND-TRIP TIME	1.5–2 hours
ELEVATION CHANGE	571 feet (from 8,600 to 9,171 feet)
MAP	Trails Illustrated Wasatch Front North
NEAREST LANDMARK	Alta Ski Resort
FEES	None if you start at Alta Ski Resort; past the ski resort $7 per car
RESTROOMS	Vault toilets at the campground and restrooms at the resort
DOGS	Not allowed
OPERATING HOURS	One hour before sunrise to one hour after sunset

COMMENT: This trail takes you through the forest biome. Almost from the start of the hike, wildflowers come into view and are generally in full display from mid-June through August, followed by the changing of the leaves in late September and early October. This hike is mostly exposed, making it hot in summer. There is virtually no shade on this hike, so get an early start and carry plenty of water. Brown signs mark the way, but note that summer construction may alter the route.

GETTING THERE: From Salt Lake City, take Interstate 80 east to I-215. Head south on I-215 and take the 6200 south exit. This becomes Wasatch Blvd. Bear left at UT 210 and head up Little Cottonwood Canyon Rd. for a little over 10.0 miles. You will pass Alta Ski Resort, where the road turns to gravel. Two-wheel drive cars can navigate the gravel portion safely. After you pass the resort, there is a parking lot 2.5 miles up the road on the left before you reach the Albion Basin Campground. Park here and follow the signs for the Cecret Lake Trail.

From the suburbs of Salt Lake City, including Sandy and Draper, it is faster to head east on UT 209 to UT 210, Little Cottonwood Canyon Rd. Go right on Little Cottonwood Canyon Rd. and continue for 8.0 miles to Alta Ski Resort. Park at the large Alta Ski Resort parking lot.

Parking along the road is forbidden and may result in a ticket or towing. Summer construction occurs every year on this road and may cause delays.

Wildflowers can be found on both sides of the Albion Meadows Trail.

THE ROUTE: The route begins at the Albion base east of the Snowpine Lodge. At 0.28 mile you will cross under the first set of ski lifts (Albion). The trail continues to wind around and under the lifts, following the Sunnyside lift.

Make sure to stop and read the Ske-cology books placed on the trees on the left and right sides of the route. They contain interesting facts about the animals that call the basin home, including the snowshoe hare and the ermine. These books are typically located in the shade of the pines, so taking time to read them offers a break from the sun and the opportunity for a water and snack break.

At 0.6 mile, the trail opens up more, and wildflowers surround you on both sides. Literally, take the time to stop and smell the flowers! Look left, right, in front, and behind as you climb up. The smells of the flowers are as vibrant as the colors. Lupine, coneflowers, yarrow, Indian paintbrush, and Wasatch penstemon are just some of the flowers you can see while strolling through the meadow. Butterflies are abundant along this hike.

At 0.88 mile notice multiple brown wooden signs on the right for the Albion Basin Campground, town of Alta, Cecret Lake, the Wildcat Trailhead, and Germania Pass. Stay straight toward Cecret Lake and the Albion Basin Campground. A mile up the canyon, you will see the overlook on the left for the meadow where cars can park for hiking or to view the flowers. The trail comes to a T with a dirt path at the 1.07 miles mark. You can retrace your steps from here back to the Alta Ski Resort.

HIKE EXTENSION: Continue to the Cecret Lake Trail by heading left. (You can also combine the two hikes.) If you continue, the connector trail that takes you past Al's Restaurant and the Supreme Lift to the campground offers a bit of shade

Ski lift signs along the Albion Meadows Trail.

as it meanders through the alpine. Water running on the left makes the area quite serene. A bench offers a great place to stop and take it all in. From the T near Al's Restaurant and the Supreme Ski Lift, it is just shy of 0.5 mile to the Albion Basin Campground via a connector trail. From the campground, it is 1.6 miles round-trip to the lake and back. Hiking Lower Albion Meadows and Cecret Lake is a total of 4.7 miles, bringing the hike rating to Pathfinder with the mileage, altitude, and elevation change. Refer to the next hike map for Cecret Lake for extension route details.

HISTORY IN HIKING

Running its first lift on January 15 1939, Alta Ski Resort is one of only three ski resorts in the country that is skier-only. The Collins Lift, named after 1800s prospector Charles H. Collins, carried paying skiers up Collins Gulch. It was a wooden single-chair lift, the first in the Wasatch and the fifth in the United States. Officials say it may have also been the fifth operating lift in the world, but that has not been verified.

The lift was built from the metal from an old aerial tram that was used to bring ore down the canyon. According to the Alta Historical Society, it cost a mere $.25 for a one-time ride and $1.50 to use it all day. Three hundred and fifty people rode the lift that first day.

Celebrating its 80th anniversary in 2018, the ski resort has come a long way since those early mining days of the 1800s. Not only is Alta a winter destination, it also boasts a number of summer activities. Dine at one of the restaurants. You can camp for a night or two at the Albion Basin Campground, or stay at one of the lodges open for summer. Special summer events include cooking classes, outdoor yoga, the ever-popular Wildflower Resort, and kid specific events. And don't forget about the amazing mountain bike trails at the Albion Base as well as other hiking trails.

ALBION MEADOWS TRAIL

Rank 2

13. Cecret Lake Trail

RATING	Searcher, due to because distance and the rocky push to the lake
ROUND TRIP DISTANCE	1.6 miles out and back
ROUND-TRIP TIME	1–2 hours
ELEVATION CHANGE	350 feet (from 9,550 to 9,900 feet)
MAP	Trails Illustrated Wasatch Front North
NEAREST LANDMARK	Albion Base Campground, Alta Ski Resort
FEES	None if you start at Alta Ski Resort; past the ski resort $7 per car
RESTROOMS	Vault toilets at the campground
DOGS	Not allowed
OPERATING HOURS	One hour before sunrise to one hour after sunset

COMMENT: Pronounced like secret (and sometimes spelled that way too), the Cecret Lake Trail is a popular hiking destination in the Central Wasatch in the ski off-season. It can get exceptionally crowded, especially when the wildflowers are peaking. Dogs, horses, and bikes are not allowed, so you will only have to navigate among hikers, and maybe a trail runner or two.

This trail takes you through the forest biome. Beyond the wildlife, this trail is known as a gem for wildflower seekers, which typically peaking in early to mid-August in an array of colors. Expect to see flowers on the first part of the hike and around the lake. Indian paintbrush, sunflowers, and lupine are just some of the varieties you can expect to see. The abundance of flowers serves as a reminder to teach about being good trail stewards and to look but not touch or pick the flowers. The fall brings yellows, reds, and oranges in late September and early October. Several other trails intersect the route, but Cecret Lake Trail is well marked. This trail is used by climbers headed to Sugarloaf Mountain, Mount Baldy, or Devil's Castle, all of which can be seen from this trail. This hike is best done from mid-June to early October, based on snow conditions. The trail is a bit dusty and loose, so good-traction shoes are recommended, especially for the final steep switchback section.

GETTING THERE: From Salt Lake City, take Interstate 80 east to I-215. Head south on I-215 and take the 6200 south exit. This becomes Wasatch Blvd. Bear left at UT 210 (Little Cottonwood Canyon Rd.) and continue for a little more than 10 miles.

The reflection of Cecret Lake on a bluebird day.

You will pass Alta Ski Resort, where the road turns to gravel (two wheel drive cars can navigate it safely). In 2.5 miles, there is a parking lot to the left before the Albion Basin Campground. Park here and follow the signs for the Cecret Lake Trail.

If the Albion Campground parking lot (about 50 spots) is full, you may have to park at the main Alta Ski Resort parking lot and walk up a dirt road 2.5 miles to the trailhead. On holidays and weekends, there is a free shuttle operating from 9 a.m. to 4:30 p.m. that begins in mid-July and runs through September from the Alta Albion Base parking lot to the trailhead. The shuttle runs about every 20 minutes. Parking along Little Cottonwood Canyon Rd. is forbidden and may result in a ticket or towing. Be sure to check if the summer road where the road turns to gravel is open (usually around the beginning of July). If it is not, it is an extra 2.5 miles each way to the trailhead and back to your car. Summer construction occurs every year on this road and may cause delays.

From the Salt Lake City suburbs, including Sandy and Draper, it is faster to head east on UT 209 to UT 210 (Little Cottonwood Canyon Rd.). Go right on UT-210 and follow the road for 8.0 miles to Alta Ski Resort. It is another 2.5 miles on gravel to the Albion Basin Campground.

THE ROUTE: Beginning at the south side of the Albion Campground parking lot, follow the narrow singletrack trail for 200 yards or so on the west side of the Albion

Basin Campground, where the trail starts. Don't forget to look up to see the ski lifts overhead; you will cross under the Supreme Ski Lift at the beginning of this hike. Be prepared for some easy to cross post spring runoff at around 0.35 mile and at a few more spots on the trail.

Continue to follow a service road for less than 0.5 mile. When the service road forks, head left for the Cecret Lake Trail. If you head right, it will lead you to a cabin. The trail widens as you continue toward the lake. Be sure to also take some time to read the interpretive signs that teach about the geology and other facts about the basin. Keep those eyes on the lookout for moose, which frequent the area, especially around the shores of the lake. Marmots, deer, and squirrels are residents of the basin as well and can be seen often, in spite of the large amount of people on the trail.

You will pass numerous spur trails as you head toward the lake. Continue to follow the trail signs for the lake. Plenty of rocks offer opportunities for climbing or taking a snack or water break. As you get closer to the lake, the peak of Devil's Castle, Sugarloaf Peak, and Mount Baldy come into view.

The last and steepest part of the hike, with the most elevation change, begins as you begin the push up to Cecret Lake at about the 0.6 mile mark. Switchbacks make it a bit easier, but this part is also rocky and lacks shade. Younger kids can manage the switchbacks (but there is no shame in taking a few breaks), and they will feel a sense of accomplishment when they see that beautiful lake. A small tunnel, possibly

Hikers on the trail up to Cecret Lake.

CECRET LAKE TRAIL

The trail to the lake is fairly wide most of the way.

for the Emma Mines or other mines in the area, on the right is a fun place to explore. There will most likely be a bit of water inside it. Test your Yodel-ay-hee-hoo as you climb through the valley.

Now at the top, catch your breath, take a break, and enjoy the rewarding views of the craggy peaks and the lake. Tiger salamanders and their larvae can be seen in the lake waters. Mosquitoes often appear, especially in mornings and evenings. After that final steep pitch, it might be tempting to cool off at the lake, but wading and swimming in Cecret Lake is off limits because the lake is the main source of drinking water for the Salt Lake City area. But you might be lucky enough to find some snow patches up around the lake for some quick sledding or a snowball fight!

Sunset is often picturesque, but note that it gets dark earlier at this elevation and the temperature changes dramatically as the sun sets. If you are still hungry after a snack break at the lake, bring firewood and coolers and enjoy post-hike S'mores or hot dogs over a fire pit at the campground.

HIKE EXTENSION: After returning to the trailhead, some hikers choose to continue to hike a few hundred yards on the Albion Meadows Trail to a meadow where the moose like to feed. Or extend the hike by beginning at the Albion Meadows Trailhead, which begins at the base of the Alta ski lifts near the shuttle drop off and the Albion Lodge and Grill, for an extra 1.5 miles each way. This changes the hike to a rating of Wanderer because of the distance covered and the elevation change. Refer to the map for the hike to Albion Meadows for extension route details

Big Cottonwood Canyon

This 15-mile long canyon is a part of the Wasatch Range. Two ski resorts Brighton and Solitude are within the canyon boundaries. Fishing, hiking and rock climbing are also popular, and it's common to see road cyclists powering up the canyon road in the summer months.

Downed trees and rocks are abundant near Donut Falls. *Photo: Kristin Mason*

Rank 2

14. Donut Falls Trail

RATING	Searcher, due to distance and the short scramble down to the falls
ROUND TRIP DISTANCE	1.5 miles out and back
ROUND-TRIP TIME	30 minutes to 1.5 hours
ELEVATION CHANGE	341 feet (from 7,493 to 7,834 feet)
MAP	Trails Illustrated Wasatch Front North
NEAREST LANDMARK	Jordan Pines Picnic Area
FEES	None
RESTROOMS	One pit toilet at trailhead closed during winter
DOGS	Not allowed
OPERATING HOURS	One hour before sunrise to one hour after sunset

COMMENT: This hike is a good example of the forest biome in Utah. Look for various holes and other habitats along the trail. Various tree stumps and large rocks along the trail provide spots to stop and rehydrate.

There is no access to drinking water, so bring your own. The majority of the hike is shaded but temperatures can reach in the 90s in the summer. Wildflowers line the trail from July through August. Fall leaves are vibrant. If you choose to scramble up the rocks for a dip, note that a recent rockslide has made the entrance to the falls fairly narrow. The trail is open year round, but the best time to visit is March through October. This trail can be hiked in winter with the use of snowshoes or spikes. The turn off for Cardiff Rd. and the bathroom are closed during winter.

GETTING THERE: From the Interstate 215 belt route, take Exit 6/6200 South. Head east on Wasatch Blvd. and follow the signs to Solitude and Brighton ski areas. Turn onto Big Cottonwood Canyon Rd. and follow the road for approximately 9.0 miles. Take a right onto Cardiff Road, which is the turn off for the trailhead. You will drive past the Jordan Pines Picnic Area before you reach the trailhead. The main parking lot only has approximately 20 parking spaces and fills up early on the weekends. Additional spaces are available a mile up the road at the Cardiff Road turn off.

THE ROUTE: Taking its name from a unique waterfall feature where the water falls through a round hole, this is a popular hike due to its relatively flat terrain. Starting from the parking lot just right of the bathroom, head straight up the rocky hill following the wooden trail signs. The wide trail meanders through aspens and pines as

The hike up the falls to the "donut" of Donut Falls is recommended for older children.

Large rocks and downed tree limbs are all obstacles climbing up to the "donut."
Photo: Kristen Mason

you climb to the top of the hill. Turn right at the top and continue to follow the trail sign. At 0.5 mile, cross a stream via a footbridge. Just after the footbridge, the trail opens up a bit. Kids can put their feet in the water here, and it's a good alternative for little kids who are not able to ascend the rocky terrain where the waterfall comes into view. Many people choose this shaded area to enjoy a picnic or quick snack.

The trail continues through the forest until it intersects a four-by-four road. At this point, turn left (south) and follow the road for 100 yards until the trail begins again on the left. Continue to follow the trail with the stream on your left. A few minutes later, you will reach a rock outcropping/drop off. More than likely, children will need a hand descending and climbing back up the outcropping at the rocky bottom of the falls runoff. Cross the log bridge to access the east side, where a better view of the falls can be had.

Spend some time listening to the peaceful sound of the falls and watching adventurous people climb to the "donut." The shadiness of the area makes it a perfect spot to grab some water and enjoy a snack before heading back. Moose are known to frequent the area as well as skunks, birds, and chipmunks. Retrace your steps back to the trailhead.

HIKE EXTENSION: Recommended for older children with climbing experience, the hike up to the falls is a scramble of approximately 100 feet. The rocks can be quite slippery, depending on the strength of the falls and recent storms. The water is cold, but most people brave it to experience standing under a waterfall.

DONUT FALLS TRAIL

Rank 1

15. Hidden Falls Trail

RATING	Experimenter, due to short distance
ROUND TRIP DISTANCE	0.25 mile
ROUND-TRIP TIME	15–30 minutes
ELEVATION CHANGE	53 feet (from 6,220 to 6,273 feet)
MAP	Trails Illustrated Wasatch Front North
NEAREST LANDMARK	Mill B South Interpretive Trail
FEES	None
RESTROOMS	None
DOGS	Not allowed
OPERATING HOURS	One hour before sunrise to one hour after sunset

COMMENT: You will be able to hear Hidden Falls for most of your hike. This forest biome hike is mostly shaded, and the best time to visit Hidden Falls is late spring through October. The trail is rarely crowded, especially on weekdays.

This is said to be the easiest waterfall hike in the state. The peak waterfall flow occurs with the snowmelt in April and early May when it is advised to not try and cross the river to the falls. Although the water will not run as high or as quickly as at other points in the canyon, use extra caution, especially during the spring runoff. Later in the summer the flow slows down allowing for children to walk into the base of the falls. Fall brings bursts of reds and yellows. Late fall and winter bring ice and snowy conditions, making it more difficult to navigate the trail.

GETTING THERE: From the Interstate 215 belt route, take Exit 6/6200 South. Head east on Wasatch Blvd. and follow the signs to Solitude and Brighton ski areas. Turn onto Big Cottonwood Canyon Rd. and follow it for 4.4 miles. Look for a small parking lot inside the "S" curve on the right just past the larger lot for the Mill B South Interpretive Trail. There are approximately 12 parking spots in the lot. Additional parking is available roadside.

THE ROUTE: To get to the trailhead, cross the road from the parking lot to the other side. As you cross the road, you can either go straight or climb the stairs on the right. Continue straight and follow the trail to the right of the creek.

There are two ways to access the falls. If your explorers don't mind getting wet, you can head left, cross the stream, and walk to the falls. Downed logs are useful for crossing the stream. If the water levels are low enough, you may cross by hopping from large rock to large rock. There is also a trail on the right that heads straight and ends at the falls after a short climb.

You can spy the falls at various points when crossing over rocks, making the falls not so hidden despite the name. Toddlers may need help, but older children should be able to navigate the varied terrain on their own whatever path you choose. You will also pass the gated entrance to an abandoned mine on the right just before the falls. Make sure to test out your echo in the mine entrance from behind the fence. There may be an opening into the mine, but abandoned mines are dangerous and should not be explored.

The falls provide a perfect place for skipping rocks, and there are plenty of rocks to scramble upon on the left side of the falls. Keep in mind that Big Cottonwood Canyon is a watershed, so playing in the water is not advised. Rock climbers can sometimes be seen on the rocks near the falls. In the winter, the frozen falls become a destination for ice climbers. Return to your car the way you came.

TRAIL EXTENSION: Because the Hidden Falls Trail is so short, you may want to add a few waterfalls to your trip, and you don't even have to move your car or hike

You can hear Hidden Falls before you can see it.

The author and her daughter cross a log on the Hidden Falls Trail. *Photo: AJ Johnson*

much farther to do so. Two waterfalls are located along the Mill B South paved trail. To start the trail, head down to the lower (south) lot of the S-curve and start on the paved trail at the far east side of the lot. Along the paved trail, you will pass one waterfall near the beginning of the Lake Blanche Trail. When you reach the end of the pavement, continue on the dirt for a few minutes to get to the second waterfall. This adds 0.7 mile round-trip and makes a good addition to the Hidden Falls hike. Many people actually choose to start with this hike and end with Hidden Falls.

Farther on, the trail reaches the impressive Tourmaline Gorge after you round a bend to the left at just over 4 miles. There are the majestic, windswept winter visages of Notchtop (12,129 feet), Knobtop (12,331 feet), and the Little Matterhorn (11,586 feet). Their snow-covered slopes make what seems like a rather casual jaunt in the summer much more of an achievement and wilderness experience in winter. It is a long 0.5 mile of hazardous travel to reach the northern shore of Odessa Lake. It is safer and much easier to approach Odessa from the Fern Lake Trail. If you do get off track, it is fairly easy to keep Mill Creek Basin on your left and go south until you reach the Bear Lake Basin and the cliff band.

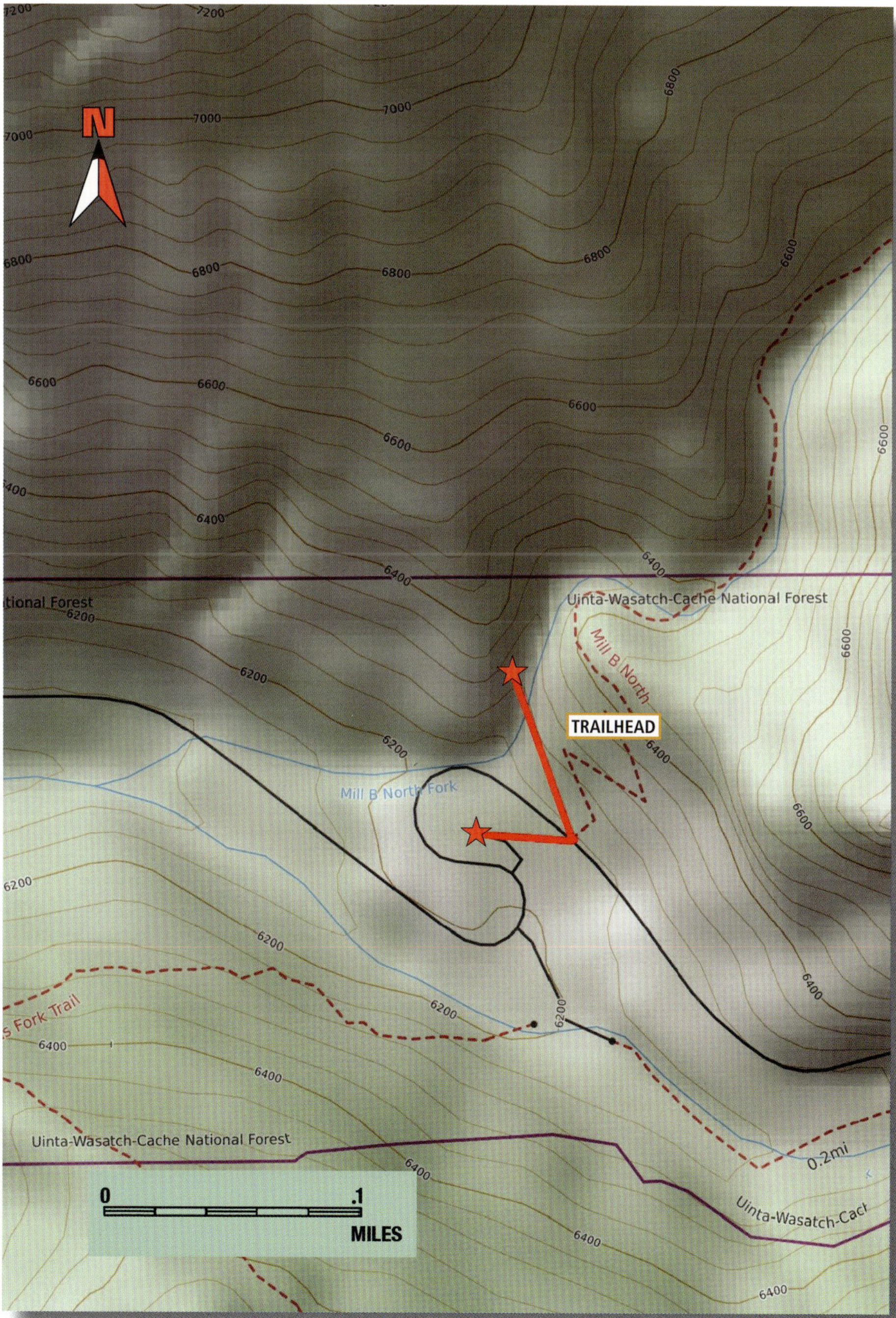

HIDDEN FALLS TRAIL

16. Lake Solitude Trail

RATING	Wanderer, due to length and altitude
ROUND TRIP DISTANCE	3.5 miles out and back
ROUND-TRIP TIME	2–3 hours
ELEVATION CHANGE	320 feet (from 8,730 to 9,050 feet)
MAP	Trails Illustrated Wasatch Front North
NEAREST LANDMARK	Brighton Ski Resort
FEES	None
RESTROOMS	Bathrooms at the Information Center/Solitude Nordic Center, when open
DOGS	Not allowed
OPERATING HOURS	One hour before sunrise to one hour after sunset

COMMENT: The hike to Lake Solitude begins at Silver Lake and heads toward Brighton Ski Resort. This trail is part of the forest biome. Wildflowers bloom from the end of June through the end of August, including columbines and geraniums. Be advised that you might have to trek through some snow in several locations if visiting before mid-June. The information center, run by the Forest Service in the summer, is a great resource for maps and other information. While visiting there you can see insect specimens and animal skulls and find a pamphlet describing the flowers native to the area. It's typically open from 9:30 a.m. to 5:30 p.m., Monday through Sunday.

You may encounter trail, ski run, and maintenance road construction, especially during early summer. Be on the lookout for trucks and workers, and the trail may divert a bit because of this, so keep following the signs, which could include forest service signs and an arrow carved into a downed tree stump.

GETTING THERE: Head east up Big Cottonwood Canyon. Just past the 14-mile mark the canyon road becomes one-way at a fork. Be advised that the road may be under construction or closed, so access to Silver Lake may not be available at times. Head west on the one-way loop for a short distance until you see the parking lot on the right for the Silver Lake Trailhead. It is large but fills quickly, especially on the weekends, as it is the start to many hikes in the area. The paved parking lot holds over 30 cars. There is a small cafe that may be open adjacent to the parking lot if you need snacks, a quick small meal, or the restroom.

THE ROUTE: Follow the Silver Lake Trailhead counterclockwise for 0.3 mile where you will see a trail junction on the right. Follow the dirt junction and the signs for the Lake Solitude Trail. This is also the junction for the Twin Lakes Trail. Watch for signs that lead to Lake Solitude at the 0.4 mile mark. The trail is dirt with rocks and roots. Most of the hike is under the canopy of pines and aspens. If the course is set up, you will pass a disc golf hole along the way. Be on the lookout for rogue Frisbees as you hike along.

Don't miss the chance to stop for a moment and breathe in the fresh mountain air. Moose frequent the area as well as deer, pika, chipmunks, and birds such as woodpeckers to stellar jays. The noise of the woodpeckers can be heard on this serene and quiet trail.

Moss covered rocks and trees and animal dens line the trail. Just before the 1.0-mile mark, you will cross under the ski lifts for the first time. At 1.2 miles, there are ski run signs and the Zip a Dee blue ski run. The trail continues to meander up and down. Just shy of 1.5 miles, you will begin to pass some scree fields. Use caution here in case rocks come loose and fall. There are a few more scree fields as you make

Solitude and peace can be found at Lake Solitude.

Snow can last through June and July on the Lake Solitude Trail.

your way toward the lake. Thankfully, there are plenty of larger rocks, tree stumps, and downed trees along the way for taking a rest, so stopping in the scree areas isn't necessary.

Closer to the lake there may be sections of snow that add some adventure, but also make for slippery terrain and wet shoes. Before the lake, you will see trails leading left and right marked by blocks of wood. Continue on the trail that heads straight to Lake Solitude. The most quick elevation gain happens right before the lake; it's a climb of 250 to 300 yards that is rocky and rutted. There is no clear path that goes all the way around the lake. If you are up for some bushwhacking, by all means go for it. But the vegetation is thick and thorny. Skip some rocks and search the lake for tiger salamanders before returning the way you came.

HIKE EXTENSION: Follow the boardwalk/dirt trail to the right/counterclockwise around Silver Lake for an additional 0.4 mile. The loop around the lake will return you to the information center/parking lot.

LAKE SOLITUDE TRAIL

Rank 1

17. Silver Lake Trail

RATING	Experimenter, due to flat terrain and short distance
ROUND TRIP DISTANCE	0.75-mile loop
ROUND-TRIP TIME	45 minutes to 1 hour
ELEVATION CHANGE	8,730 at trailhead, minimal gain
MAP	Trails Illustrated Wasatch Front North
NEAREST LANDMARK	Brighton Ski Resort
FEES	None
RESTROOMS	Bathrooms at the information center/Solitude Nordic Center, when open
DOGS	Not allowed
OPERATING HOURS	One hour before sunrise to one hour after sunset

COMMENT: What this trail lacks in length, it makes up for in scenery. This is an ADA-accessible trail, although there are sections of dirt that may be hard to navigate, depending on weather. Strollers and wagons can navigate the trail. The trail is closed to hikers but open to cross-country skiers during winter. The hike is best from June through October, to avoid snow. The aspens blaze yellow in the fall. There is a small cafe adjacent to the parking lot that may be open if you need snacks, a quick small meal, or the restroom.

The information center, run by the U.S. Forest Service in the summer, is a great resource for maps and other information, such as a pamphlet explaining the flowers native to the area. It also houses insect specimens and animal skulls. It's typically open 9:30 a.m. to 5:30 p.m., Monday through Sunday. Night sky photographers and night viewers may enjoy visiting for views of the Milky Way. This trail is a part of the forest biome.

GETTING THERE: Head east up Big Cottonwood Canyon. Just past the 14-mile mark, the canyon road becomes one-way at a fork. Head west on the one-way loop for a short distance until you see the parking lot on the right for the Silver Lake Trailhead. It can hold over 30 cars but fills quickly, especially on weekends, as it is the start to many hikes in the area. Check for road closure or construction before your visit.

THE ROUTE: From the parking lot, head in either a clockwise or counterclockwise direction. Ducks and geese float on the lake. Lily pads and grasses may hold a frog or

SILVER LAKE TRAIL

Boardwalks cover the marshy areas along the Silver Lake Trail.

toad. You may be lucky to see a boreal toad, which is an endangered species. Fishing is allowed at the lake with a valid Utah fishing license.

Be sure to stop along the route to read the interpretive signs that detail local fauna and the area's geology. There are picnic tables at multiple spots around the lake. Wildflowers add splashes of color to the green of the Wasatch Mountains. Moose and deer are often about, so keep a keen eye out. Squirrels and chipmunks scurry around the trail.

At the 0.3-mile mark (if headed counterclockwise), there is a junction for the Twin Lakes and Lake Solitude Trails on the right. Continue straight along the lake path.

Large pines extend into the sky shading most of the hike, but there are some spots with full sun exposure. Follow the lake around and return to the information center and parking lot.

HIKE EXTENSION: The Twin Lakes Loop and Lake Solitude Trail can both be accessed from Silver Lake. The Granite Lakes Loop is 3.0 miles. Lake Solitude is a 4.0-mile out and back, changing the rating to Wanderer.

Sandy and Draper Area

Sandy and Draper Utah are suburbs of Salt Lake City. Both were likely areas of early settlement for Indians with permanent Mormon settlers moving into the area in the 1870s. Butting up to the Wasatch Mountains, both cities are popular for families looking to be close to outdoor recreation.

The Wadsworth Suspension Bridge can be seen on the Bonneville Shoreline Trail.

Rank 2

18. Bonneville Shoreline Trail to the Wadsworth Suspension Bridge

RATING	Searcher, due to minimal elevation change
ROUND TRIP DISTANCE	1.5 miles out and back
ROUND-TRIP TIME	1–1.5 hours
ELEVATION CHANGE	69 feet (from 5,160 to 5,229 feet)
MAP	Trails Illustrated Wasatch Front North
NEAREST LANDMARK	Wasatch Blvd.
FEES	None
RESTROOMS	Seasonal bathrooms and water mid-March through mid-October
DOGS	Not allowed
OPERATING HOURS	One hour before sunrise to one hour after sunset

COMMENT: The Bonneville Shoreline Trail will one day connect from the town of Nephi, Utah, to the Idaho Border. Over 100 miles is already established. The Wadsworth Suspension Bridge was built in 2015 to keep hikers out of the watershed. The bridge is 185 feet long and is dedicated to Clark Naylor, who began building trails in Draper over 50 years ago. There is plenty of parking at Hidden Valley Park. Note that water and bathroom access are seasonal. This trail is a part of the forest biome. This trail can be snowshoed in the winter.

GETTING THERE: From Salt Lake City, take Interstate 15 south/I-80 east for 14 miles to Exit 292. Take W 11400 S/Wasatch Blvd. for a little over 4.0 miles to Hidden Valley Park, which is located at 11570 Wasatch Blvd. in Sandy.

THE ROUTE: From the parking lot of Hidden Valley Park, head left up the cement path. Take the second trailhead on the left as the cement path bends to the right. The trail climbs gradually as you head up above the rooftops of nearby homes. Wildflowers, butterflies, and bees greet you almost right away. A bench off to the left is a good place to stop and look over the valley area. You may even be able to pick up some fresh cut wildflowers from the maintenance workers to create a bouquet.

BONNEVILLE SHORELINE TRAIL TO THE WADSWORTH SUSPENSION BRIDGE

The Wadsworth Suspension Bridge was built in 2015 to keep hikers out of the watershed.

At 0.4 mile, cross a gravel road. Stay straight on the trail. Just past 0.5 mile, the trail levels off. There is a rock slide area on the left at 0.7 mile; don't stop in this area. You will see several trails on the right that lead down to the neighborhoods, including one at 0.86 mile, but stay on the Bonneville Shoreline Trail.

Just before the 1.0 mile mark there is a fun rock for kids to scale on the left. As you continue down the trail, you will see a water treatment plant above the homes on your right. Look for a cool cavern area with rocks to climb at 1.2 miles.

At 1.25 miles, the trail really opens up on the right for an expansive view of homes and valley. Unlike previous parts of the trail, there are no dense trees here. The wooden sign for the Bear Canyon Loop is on the left at the 1.45 miles mark. Continue straight and see a sign for the Bridge Loop, Aqueduct Trail, Ralph's Trail, and Bonneville Shoreline Trail. Head straight to the bridge and enjoy some time there, around 135 feet above the bottom of the watershed. Trace your steps back on the Bonneville Shoreline Trail to Hidden Valley Park.

Rank 3

19. Lower Bells Reservoir Trail from the Boulders Trailhead

RATING	Seeker, due to rocky and steep terrain
ROUND TRIP DISTANCE	1 mile out and back
ROUND-TRIP TIME	1–2 hours
ELEVATION CHANGE	475 feet (from 5,220 to 5,695 feet)
MAP	Trails Illustrated Wasatch Front North
NEAREST LANDMARK	Wasatch Blvd.
FEES	None
RESTROOMS	None
DOGS	Not allowed
OPERATING HOURS	One hour before sunrise to one hour after sunset

COMMENT: This hike provides access to some of the classic rocks climbs in the Wasatch, so be on the lookout for climbers, as kids may enjoy taking a small break to see a climber complete a rocky pitch. Snakes, birds, and deer call the area home, and mountain goats are often seen bounding about on the rocky outcroppings of the Wasatch Mountains. Wildflowers are abundant in late spring through August. This trail is especially popular in the fall before the first snow because of the contrast between the reds, yellows, and oranges of the changing leaves and the constant green of the pines.

This forest biome trail is very popular, especially on the weekends, because of its proximity to neighboring cities. There is virtually no shade on this hike. Wear shoes with good traction, as the trail is loose gravel or sand in most places. This hike requires bigger steps up and over logs and rocks and back down making it tougher for toddlers and younger walkers. Catch and release fishing is allowed at the reservoir. Cutthroat trout are the most abundant fish in the reservoir. The trail is best for use from March through October, but it can get muddy in spring and fall. Consider snowshoeing this trail in the winter for the beautiful scenery.

GETTING THERE: The Boulders Trailhead to Lower Bell Reservoir (also known as Bell's Reservoir and Bells Reservoir) is located near the mouth of Little Cottonwood Canyon approximately 0.25 mile from the Wasatch Blvd. / 9800 South intersection. The parking lot for the Boulders Trailhead is located at approximately 10245 South

Wasatch Blvd. While the main parking lot off Wasatch Blvd. only offers limited spaces, parking is allowed on the roadside.

You may also start this hike at the Granite Trailhead off Little Cottonwood Road at. This route is less steep than the route from the Boulders Trailhead and is 1.5 miles roundtrip.

THE ROUTE: This hike begins in a residential area with a fenced off area separating the private property of the homes from the trail. It begins to climb almost immediately over logs and rocks under no canopy. Shrub oak surrounds you and water cascades to the right.

The water offers a place to cool off along the trail.

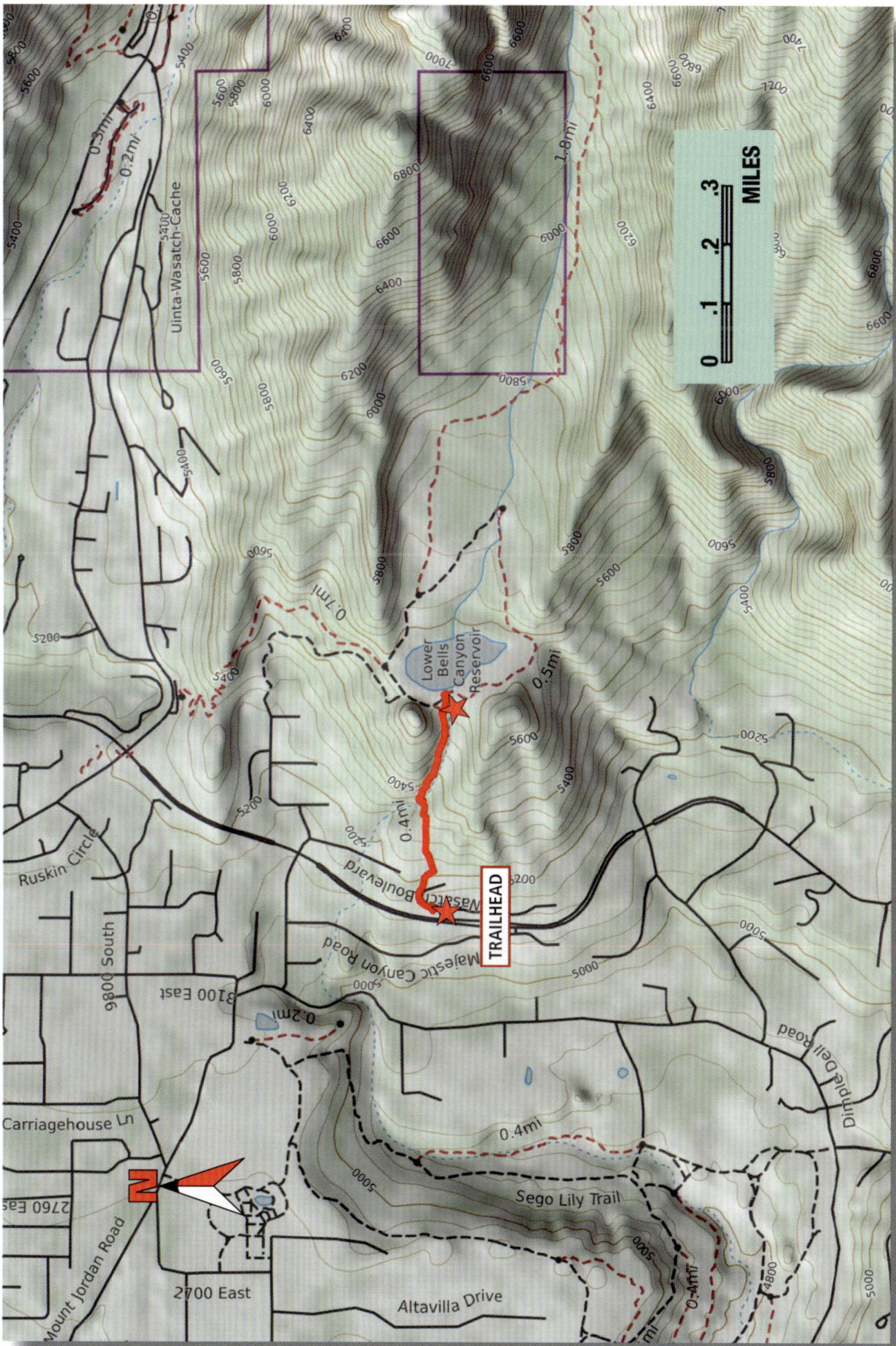

LOWER BELLS RESERVOIR TRAIL

Lower Bells Reservoir is a catch and release reservoir.

The log risers and switchbacks help manage the steepness, but don't be surprised if your little ones' legs tire quickly and they need a break. This offers you a chance to take in the views of the valley below. Close to 0.25 mile into the hike, you will descend and come to a footbridge. Depending on the time of year, the water may be running high, so use caution. The area around the bridge offers a great place to take a break from the climbing and allows kids a chance to put their feet in the water. Enjoy some shade here before crossing the bridge and heading up another steep rocky climb to the reservoir.

Skip stones in the water, check out the mallards and Canadian geese, or catch and release fish between bites of a snack or a picnic. A half-mile trail leads around the reservoir. It can be muddy and hard to follow, and may require some bushwhacking. It isn't maintained and may require water crossing. If your children are more adventurous, you may want to add this to the length of your hike.

After exploring around the reservoir, follow the trail back to the trailhead. On a clear day, the city views are spectacular. Kids may have more trouble with the descent because of the loose terrain, rocks, and steepness. It may take more time to get back to the trailhead for this reason.

HIKE EXTENSION: Some hikers choose to extend the hike and continue to the Lower Falls for a 4.7 miles out-and-back hike. Note that the terrain becomes steep and rocky and includes an elevation gain of over 1,000 feet, which changes the hike rating to Adventurer. This extended hike is recommended for older children due to terrain and exposure.

Rank 3

20. Rocky Mouth Falls Trail

RATING	Searcher, due to elevation gain and rocky terrain
ROUND TRIP DISTANCE	0.9 mile out and back
ROUND-TRIP TIME	30 minutes to 1 hour
ELEVATION CHANGE	300 feet (from 5,125 to 5,425 feet)
MAP	Trails Illustrated Wasatch Front North
NEAREST LANDMARK	Little Cottonwood Canyon
FEES	None
RESTROOMS	None
DOGS	Not allowed
OPERATING HOURS	One hour before sunrise to one hour after sunset (trail sign says 9 p.m.)

COMMENT: The 70-foot Rocky Mouth Waterfall is a natural spring running year-round, with the biggest runoff during spring melt. The trail is one of the easiest waterfall hikes for kids in the state maybe second to Hidden Falls in Big Cottonwood Canyon. Rappelling through the falls and geocaching are popular activities here. The hike is mostly shaded, and the trail is best hiked spring through fall (note that the gate to the hike is often locked during winter). The hike is part of the forest biome.

There are several trails along Wasatch Blvd. This trail is popular because of its proximity to Sandy, Draper, and other towns and because of its shorter length.

GETTING THERE: The Rocky Mouth Trailhead is located at 11248 South Wasatch Blvd. From Salt Lake City, take Interstate 15 south to I-215 east. From I-215 east, take the Wasatch Blvd/6200 exit. As you pass Little Cottonwood Canyon, veer to the right to stay on Wasatch Blvd., and continue for another 3.3 miles. The stone Rocky Mouth Falls Trailhead sign is on the left. About six cars can park in the trailhead lot. Parking is also allowed along Wasatch Blvd., but not along Eagle View Drive or other streets in the neighborhood above the trailhead.

THE ROUTE: The trail to the waterfall begins to climb right away with 82 railroad tie steps. Once you reach the top of the stairs, head to the right (south) along the neighborhood sidewalk along Eagle View Drive and follow the signs to the trail. You will pass approximately four houses before the sidewalk bends to the left. Be respectful of the residents and their property.

The hike to the falls is steep, but the payoff is worth it.

ROCKY MOUTH FALLS TRAIL

Kids love looking for fish, climbing the rocks and cooling off in the falls.

Look for the brown signs indicating the start of the trail on the right at 0.2 mile. The trail follows a fence between two homes and heads up 59 more steps. The climb here is the toughest part of the hike. At 0.3 mile the trail connects with the Bonneville Shoreline Trail. Continue straight to reach the waterfall. You will now be above the homes. If you turn around, you can see the rooftops and the Salt Lake Valley.

Don't miss the little cave and sealed mineshaft among the rocks on the left as you climb to the falls. The trail here is wide but often rocky. Little ones may need some help navigating the safest path. Don't be surprised to see a squirrel or two scampering among the rocks. If you happen upon a cottonwood stick on the ground, break it open at a notch to see if you find a star. If you do, follow the folk tale and make a wish!

The area around the falls is rocky. The moss that grows on the rocks adds color but also makes it slippery. Summer weather brings wasps, so be cautious. Depending on the flow levels, you may be able to climb up to the top to the pool. This climb requires some skill and is not recommended for little hikers.

Alpine Loop

The Alpine Loop is open from late May through late October. It is a twenty-mile scenic drive through the canyons of the Wasatch Mountains. Sundance Resort and Timpanogos Cave National Monument are found along the drive that runs from HWY 92 in American Fork Canyon, through the Uinta National Forest and ends at Provo Canyon on HWY 189.

The first signs of fall on the Cascade Springs Interpretive Trail.

21. Cascade Springs Interpretive Trail

RATING	Experimenter, due to fairly flat terrain and short distance
ROUND TRIP DISTANCE	0.7 mile
ROUND-TRIP TIME	30 minutes to 1 hour
ELEVATION CHANGE	86 feet (from 6,220 to 6,306 feet)
MAP	Trails Illustrated Wasatch Front North
NEAREST LANDMARK	American Fork Canyon
FEES	$6 day use fee; National Parks pass
RESTROOMS	Pit toilets
DOGS	Must be on leash
OPERATING HOURS	One hour before sunrise to one hour after sunset

COMMENT: According to the U.S. Forest Service, 7 million gallons of water flow out of Cascade Springs every day. That is the equivalent of 1,800 glasses of water every second, according to the interpretive signs. Also interesting is that the water temperature stays a consistent 48 degrees year round.

This mostly paved trail is a wonderful sensory experience. It is a mix of blacktop, cement, and boardwalks, and little adventurers will especially enjoy the bridges. If you begin from the lower parking lot, don't skip the posters and photos that tell about the area. As you begin the hike, plaques name the mountain peaks and animals that call the area home. A fire devastated the area in 2003. The progress of regrowth is also detailed on the plaques along the hike.

Rustling in the trees surrounding the trail could be wild turkeys, mule deer, or even moose. Common trees along this hike are oaks, and aspen, bringing a variety of colors in the fall and homes for animals. Summer brings splashes of pinks, yellows, and purples from the wildflowers including columbine, and buttercups. The trail has some spots of shade, but it's mostly exposed. But be sure to stay on the path as stinging nettle lines parts of the trail. Benches along the trail provide good spots to stop and take in Mother Nature or enjoy a water break, but picnicking is not allowed in the area. Snacks along the trail are also discouraged.

For ADA accessibility, park in the lower parking lot and take the trail to the right. Only the first two loops are ADA accessible. The lower lot has about 20 spots with possible access to water to fill up your bottles, but don't count on it. Although water surrounds the trail, fishing and wading are not allowed. The trail is best used

There are peek a boo views through the trees along the Cascade Springs Interpretive Trail.

between June and October, as the road closes in the winter. Be sure to display your day use pass on your window. This hike is a part of the forest biome. Winter offers a completely different experience on this hike.

GETTING THERE: From Salt Lake City, take Interstate 15 south to Exit 284 for UT 92 E. Go east on UT 92 to American Fork Canyon. Pay the day use fee and follow the signs for Alpine Scenic Route. Eleven miles up the canyon, you will reach the summit. Take the turn off for Cascade Springs. It is 6.7 miles to the parking area. This is the recommended route because the route through Midway requires a high clearance car; it is rocky and rutted and a popular area for ATV's and dirt bikes.

THE ROUTE: You can hear the sound of water from the parking lot. Pools greet hikers at the beginning of the hike as the trail follows the spring that feeds the pools. As you hike, you will cross three boardwalks over the pools. Enjoy the soothing sounds of trickling water over rocks and waterfalls.

There are many loop trails to enjoy Cascade Springs that are well marked by signs. At 62 feet on the right, you will see the return to parking trail that is the better route for strollers and wheelchairs. Continue straight and find a bench on the right and the start of interpretive signs about the animals and other parts of the trail. Cross over the bridge into the inviting trees. At 460 feet, the trail curves left and heads across the first boardwalk. The boardwalk ends a little past 0.1 mile.

The trails along the springs wind around amongst the oaks and maples.

The first loop of Cascade begins on the left after the first boardwalk. After another boardwalk, at 0.21 mile, you will see stairs on the left. Instead of taking the stairs, head right to the starting point of the first loop and follow the hill up. There is a bench on the right before 0.3 mile. The trail switchbacks up, lined with Gambel oak and beautiful maples. Water cascades on the left.

There is another bridge on the left at 0.3 mile. Signs continue to teach about the local animal residents wildflowers, and trees, such as river birch and quaking aspen. On the left is an area to get near the water's edge, but remember that wading in the water is prohibited. There are beautiful 360-degree views here.

At 0.4 mile, there is a trail on the right that heads to the upper parking. Continue straight. Shortly after, you can get a peek-a-boo view of part of Wasatch Mountain State Park if you look left. The vegetation becomes so thick that you can't see the water, but you can hear it.

A trail on the left at 0.5 mile leads to the edge of the water. At about 0.2 down the trail, there will be a trail junction. Head right to complete the middle loop. Head left to go back to the upper loop or the lower loop, depending on the direction you turned after the bridge. You still can't see the water, but you can hear it.

There is a bench on the left at 0.55 mile where you can relax and listen to the roaring water under the shade of maples and Gambel oak. A little past the bench, there are rock stairs that lead back down to the footbridge and the path that takes you back to the beginning of the first loop. Head back past the beginning of the first loop (or go around again if you fancy). Back track on the trail, over the boardwalk, and to the car.

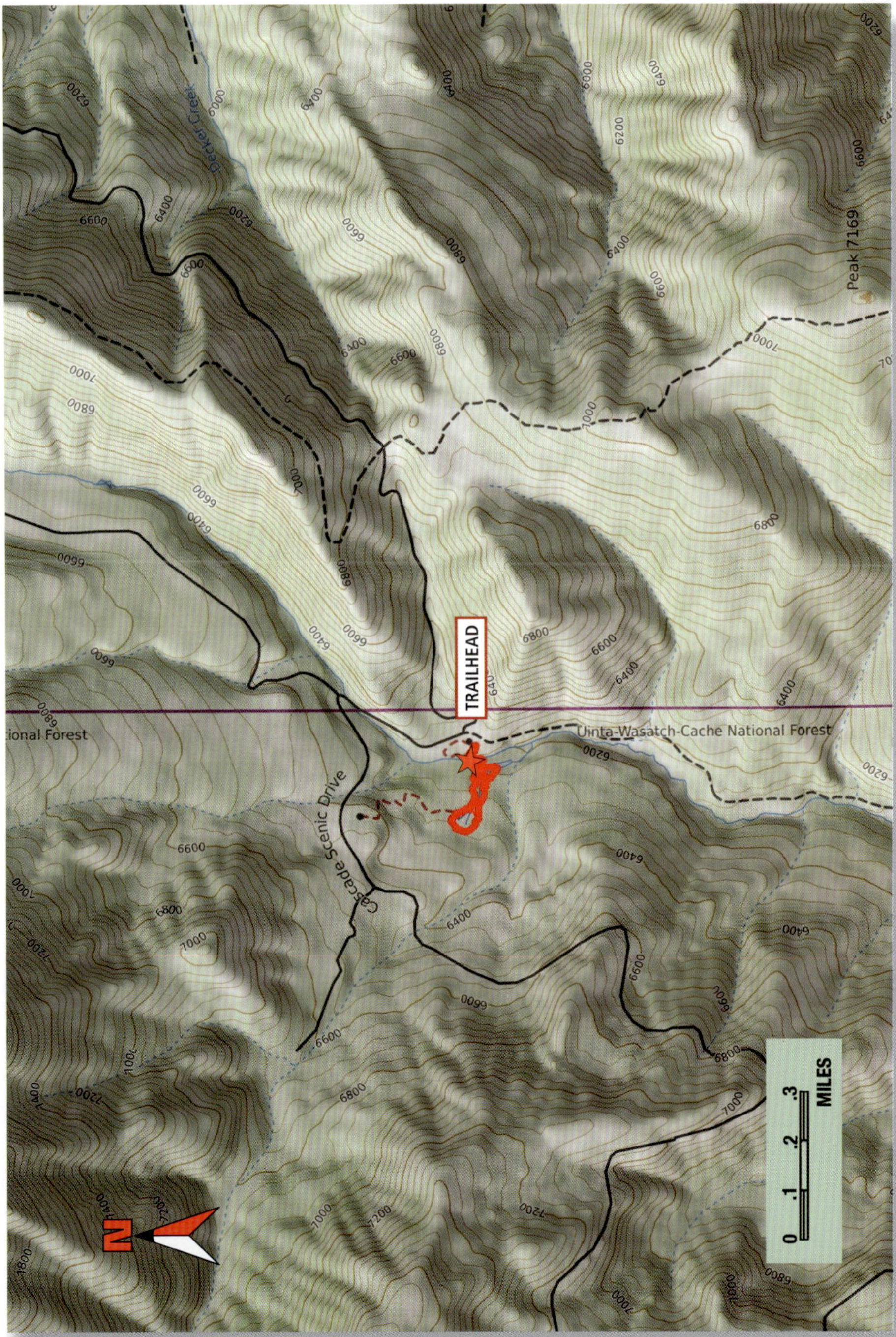

CASCADE SPRINGS INTERPRETIVE TRAIL

Rank 5

22. Stewart Falls/ Stewart Cascade Trail

RATING	Pathfinder, due to elevation changes, distance, and terrain
ROUND TRIP DISTANCE	3.64 miles out and back
ROUND-TRIP TIME	2.5–3.5 hours
ELEVATION CHANGE	618 feet (from 6,900 to 7,518 feet)
MAP	Trails Illustrated Wasatch Front North
NEAREST LANDMARK	Sundance Ski Resort
FEES	$6 American Fork Canyon fee per vehicle; National Parks pass
RESTROOMS	Pit toilets at trailhead at Aspen Grove
DOGS	Not allowed
OPERATING HOURS	One hour before sunrise to one hour after sunset

COMMENT: This two-tiered waterfall is over 200 feet tall. Mid-spring through mid-fall is the ideal time to hike to the falls. Spring and summer bring wildflowers; forget-me-nots, yarrow, columbines, and bluebells line the trail, adding a splash of color to the alpine green of the trees and the ski runs of Sundance Ski Resort. When fall arrives, Gambel oak and aspens show off as the wildflowers dry up and go dormant until spring. While beautiful in winter, this hike is only recommended for older children during that season because of the rocks and terrain. Although the trail has pockets of shade, there are areas of full sun exposure, so carry plenty of water. The trail is popular and is usually crowded, especially on weekends. Horses also use this forest biome trail.

Be on the lookout for moose in the groves of trees and chipmunks and squirrels that dart back and forth across the trail. The familiar squawks of raptors may be heard above. Black bears, mountain lions and mule deer are also residents in the area. If you step off the trail, avoid the stinging nettle and watch out for snakes. Rattlers and bull snakes are frequently found on and just off the trail.

GETTING THERE: From Salt Lake City, take Interstate 15 to Orem 800 north/Exit 272. Take 800 north. Keep left at the curve and follow the road into Provo Canyon, US 189. Continue to follow US 189 for 7.0 miles. Turn left onto UT 92 after a short tunnel. Follow the road past Sundance Ski Resort and Aspen Grove. Pay the fee at

Stewart Falls is a two tiered waterfall.

To enjoy the pool and the falls, you will need to do a bit of rock scrambling.

the ranger station. Past the ranger station, the trailhead will be on your left. The parking lot at Aspen Grove fits over forty cars, but it is also the parking lot for other local trails including the route to Mt. Timpanogos. Parking on the road is permitted during high traffic times.

An alternative route passes Timpanogos National Monument: Take Exit 284 for Alpine-Highland from I-15 north or south. Turn east onto State Highway 92. Take SH 92 to the guard stand. Pay the $6 fee and continue east on UT 92. Turn right onto Alpine Loop Road and continue until you come to the Aspen Grove parking lot on the right.

THE ROUTE: The trail begins on the right near the bathrooms in the Aspen Grove parking lot. There is a brown sign to guide you. The trail follows the east side of Mt. Timpanogos.

Follow the signed trail for about the length of a football field. When it veers left, continue left to Stewart Falls. If you continue straight, you will be on the Aspen Grove Trail that takes you to Mt. Timpanogos.

The trail climbs under a canopy of trees including aspens and pines. Roots, rocks, and loose terrain make the trail a bit more difficult for younger hikers, who may need to take their time or get a little help. At 0.2 mile, look down and left to see the parking lot to take a little break from the climbing. You will encounter some sections of safety fencing for erosion protection.

STEWART FALLS/STEWART CASCADE TRAIL

At 0.3 mile, the private trails for BYU and AG are on the left. The trail continues to climb before it levels off. At 0.4 mile, look for the research camera attached to a tree base on the left as the trail begins to head south. Shortly after, there is a water tank on the left. The area is fun for exploring and taking a quick off-trail break. At 0.5 mile, there is a nice area of shade.

There are interesting bends in the trees around 0.8 mile. Here the trail becomes looser and the dirt becomes thicker as you continue heading south to the falls. At 0.9 mile a beautiful grove of aspens on the left provides some shade. Butterflies may greet you in this section or on other sections of the trail. At the 1.0-mile mark, another grove of aspens provides the perfect place to for a snack and hydration break.

At just over 1.0 mile, you will get your first peak at the ski trails of Sundance Resort on your left. The trail descends a bit as the vegetation opens up for another view of Sundance again on the left. At 1.35 miles, there is a slow slog up as the trail climbs again. There might be a nice log at shortly after the trail begins to climb that is a perfect spot for a break. Keep an ear to the wind; soon you'll hear the falls.

You can catch a glimpse of the falls on the left just shy of the 1.5 mile mark. This begins the rocky descent to the falls. Little hikers may need some extra time, help, and encouragement here. You will pass a large scree field with a smaller few sections of scree ahead on the right. The trail continues to descend and switch back, as you get closer to the falls and the trails end.

The waterfall flows year round but is strongest during the spring runoff. The water temperature remains cold year round. The stream descending from the falls usually moves slowly enough for children to play in it. Large rocks around the falls provide perfect spots to take off your shoes and dry off your feet when done. Rocks and logs from avalanches and rock slides help for crossing the stream. You can also get directly under the falls with some scrambling. Climbing up to the second tier is risky and not recommended, especially for children. After a cool down in the falls, follow the trail back to the trailhead.

ALTERNATIVE ROUTE: You can also hike to Stewart Falls from Sundance Resort. While visiting Sundance Resort is free, there is a fee to take the lift ticket to Ray's Summit. The hike from Sundance is shorter, but still has a Pathfinder rating.

The trail overlooks Sundance Resort.

Rank 5

23. Timpanogos Cave Trail

RATING	Pathfinder, due to elevation changes
ROUND TRIP DISTANCE	3.0 miles
ROUND-TRIP TIME	3.5 hours, including cave tour
ELEVATION CHANGE	1,100 feet (from 5,600 to 6700 feet)
MAP	Trails Illustrated Wasatch Front North
NEAREST LANDMARK	Timpanogos National Monument Visitor Center
FEES	$6 American Fork Canyon fee per vehicle, if you plan to explore beyond the cave; National Parks pass. Basic cave tours range from free to $8.00 based on age. It is free to just hike to the top.
RESTROOMS	Full restrooms at Timpanogos Cave Visitor Center
DOGS	Not allowed
OPERATING HOURS	May 19 through September 3, 7 a.m. to 6 p.m.

COMMENT: The route through this forest biome is paved and includes stairs, but it is exposed. If you plan to also visit the cave, secure tickets ahead of time. Morning is the best time to visit in the summer months because there is little shade. You have 1.5 hours from the starting the time on your ticket to get to the cave entrance, so begin hiking before your start time to allow for extra time. The cave temperature is around 45 degrees, so pack jackets and plenty of water. Strollers are not allowed on the trail. You may carry hiking backpacks, but the packs can't be worn in the cave. Small backpacks have to be worn on the front while exploring the cave with a guide, so make sure your pack size is not too large.

GETTING THERE: From Salt Lake City, take Interstate 15 north or south to Exit 284/Alpine-Highland. Turn east onto State Highway 92 and continue for 10.0 miles to the monument. You will pass a guard stand. Pay the $6 fee if you plan to spend time exploring beyond the cave. There are about 20 parking spots in the main visitor center lot with additional parking across the main road.

THE ROUTE: From the Timpanogos Cave Visitor Center, head left to find the paved trail. A Park Service employee will ask to see your tickets for the cave or a pass if you are just hiking to the top and back. This begins your climb up to the cave.

Follow the paw prints and signs for info along the trail.

The trail winds and switchbacks up the mountainside. On the left, at 0.35 mile there is a good viewpoint with benches. Don't miss the Intermountain Healthcare sign for giving your body a health check during the hike.

Pay attention to the red and yellow lines around the trail. These are areas of known rockslides, so don't stop in these areas for any reason. If you hear a rock slide, which sounds similar to clapping, crouch down and cover your head and neck.

Note the small round discs in the cement on the ground on your left as you climb up. These discs are placed every 100 feet and serve as mileage markers. They range from 79 to 0, from the bottom to the top. At the sign for the 0.25-mile mark there is a cool small tunnel through the rock. There is a bench on the left shortly thereafter.

At 0.55 mile a scree field on the left shows the aftermath of a rock fall. Pass through the area quickly. You will come upon a small tunnel with a gate after the scree field. You may see a ranger there if you your hikers have any questions for their Junior Ranger badges. Gambel oaks, pines, and maples line the trail to the right. Don't get too close to them because the trail drops off steeply on most of the right side as you head up.

Don't forget to look down at the ground as you head to the top. You will see changes in the time periods of the rock formations labeled. There is a 0.5-mark wooden sign on the left. Follow the paw prints on the wall to a hole in the rock, where you can feel cool air coming out.

The trail steepens as you get closer to the 1.0-mile mark, where you'll find another Intermountain Healthcare health check and a bench. At 1.1 miles take a photo of your group to be a part of history. Visitors have been taking family photos in this very spot overlooking the farmland since 1922!

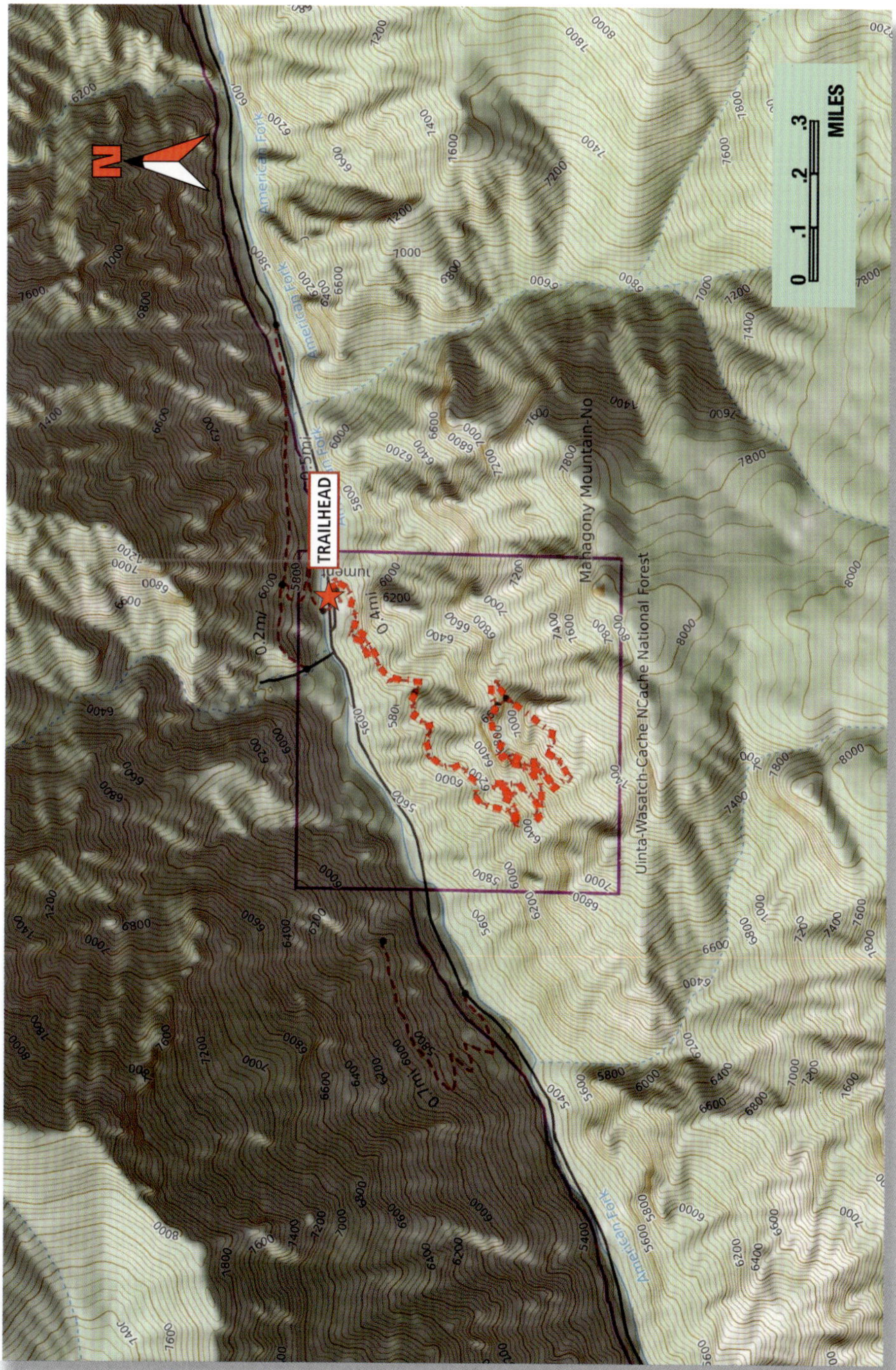

TIMPANOGOS CAVE TRAIL

Stalactites hang down from a solution cave in Timpanogos National Monument.

Soon you will see the 0.75 sign on your left. A pocket of trees, a bench, and some interpretive signs are found at 1.3 miles. Hear the call of the canyon wren and learn about animals that call the area home like rattlesnakes, rock squirrels, and mountain lions.

The trail makes another switchback and crosses the downhill trail you will take when you exit the cave. Continue right on the trail. If you have a large backpack or kid carrier, this is your chance to leave it in a storage box before entering the cave. The last chance bathroom is at 1.5 miles; there is no other chance to use a bathroom until you are back at the visitor center. Just a bit more climbing and you reach the top and the cave entrance. You made it!

The cave tour takes about one hour. You can explore three solution caves connected by man-made tunnels: Hansen Cave, Middle Cave, and Timpanogos Cave. There are many speleothems (cave features), including stalagmites and stalactites, soda straws, and popcorn. The cave features that resemble bacon and ice cream may make you hungry! You can also see the "Heart of the Timpanogos." The calcite "heart" is 5.5 feet tall and weighs approximately two tons.

After the one-hour cave tour, exit the caves and head back on the downhill trail, which connects with the main trail below the bathrooms at the storage box. Once you are back down the hill, stop by the visitor center for little hikers to pick up their Timpanogos Cave Junior Ranger badges. For some post-caving fun, an additional Junior Cave Scientist badge is available online at the National Park Service website.

Pleasant Grove Area

Utah's "City of Trees," the town of Pleasant Grove was once called Battle Creek after a battle between the Mormons and Ute Indians. The name was changed to Pleasant Grove to be more positive in nature and is based on a grove of cottonwoods that grow between Grove Creek and Battle Creek. It borders the Wasatch Mountains and is home to the longest running community festival in Utah- Strawberry Days held in June since 1921.

Trees line the trail to Battle Creek Falls.

Rank 3

24. Battle Creek Falls Trail

RATING	Seeker, due to elevation gain in a short amount of time
ROUND TRIP DISTANCE	1.1 miles out and back
ROUND-TRIP TIME	1–1.5 hours
ELEVATION CHANGE	333 feet (from 5,435 to 5,768 feet)
MAP	Trails Illustrated Wasatch Front North
NEAREST LANDMARK	Kiwanis Park
FEES	None
RESTROOMS	Seasonal vault toilets at Kiwanis Park
DOGS	Off leash OK
OPERATING HOURS	May 19 through September 3, 7 a.m. to 6 p.m.

COMMENT: This trail, named for a battle between the Ute Indians and the Mormon Settlers in 1849, has little shade, so bring plenty of water. The trailhead is rutted and rocky. Grab a stick in the beginning of the hike to help your little hiker get up the trail.

The trail is also popular with horses and mountain bikers, and you may see rapellers coming down the falls. You can walk directly into the falls. You can hike the trail in snowshoes or with spikes on your shoes during the winter. The falls are said to be stunning even when frozen. This hike is a part of the forest biome.

GETTING THERE: From Salt Lake City, take Interstate 15 south to Exit 275 for Pleasant Grove/Lindon. Turn left onto Pleasant Grove Blvd.; continue for 1.0 mile and turn right onto W 220 S St. After 0.5 mile, make a right onto State St. Take a sharp left onto s 100 E after 0.5 mile. Take that for 0.3 mile to E 200 S and make a right. The trailhead is on the right after 2.0 miles. There are plenty of parking spots as the trailhead shares a parking lot with Kiwanis Park.

THE ROUTE: This wide-open dirt trail begins to the right of Kiwanis Park. Gambel oaks line the trail. After 628 feet, you will see a metal piece of water diversion equipment buried in the ground, and shortly after, there is a black pipe. The sound of rushing water here is no doubt quite peaceful compared to the battle that was fought near the falls.

At 0.2 mile, the trail curves to the right. You may find some shade and butterflies here depending on the time of day. There is an erosion slide area on the right at 0.25 mile, and a rock outcropping at 0.3 mile that provides a shady spot to grab

Battle Creek Falls is popular for rappelling.

some water. Several rocks along the trail provide other good places for water stops. Squirrels scamper along this trail and up and down the trees.

Look left at 0.35 mile to see a tree that has bent and is growing across the stream on the left.

Take a break and enjoy the chance to dip your feet in the water on the left. The trail continues to climb with areas of shade starting just shy of 0.4 mile. The large rock at 0.4 mile on the right is popular for climbing and taking a break before the final push to the falls. Cross the bridge at 0.45 mile as the trail heads left. A little cavern on the left at 0.5 mile intrigues little ones, while water access can be found directly across on the right.

Scree fields on the left make the trail loose and rocky for the final approach up to the falls. At 0.55 mile you will see the falls on your right. It is a short descent to

There are plenty of natural hiking sticks to find along the trail to the falls

the falls, where lady bugs and wasps are common, especially in summer and fall. The 50-foot waterfall is fed by runoff from Mt. Timpanogos and a natural spring, so the strength of the falls depends on the time of year. One of the best parts about the falls is that it is easy to get into the spray. This is a perfect cool down spot after the hike up.

Before heading back to the trailhead, take a few moments to close your eyes and picture the battle between the Utes and the Mormons. Can you imagine navigating the terrain while trying to defend your people? Trace your steps back to the trailhead with the calming rush of the stream following you.

HISTORY IN HIKING

The battle at Battle Creek Falls occurred on March 5, 1849. Mormon militia led a pre-dawn attack on the Utes in the area of Battle Creek Falls. According to historians, a band of Indians was accused of stealing horses from Brigham Young's herd. Though word was received that the horses were not in fact stolen, the militia was nevertheless ordered to attack the Indians for killing cattle and other crimes.

Before the battle began, the Mormons gave the Utes the chance to surrender, but they refused. A Ute was killed and a few others injured. The Mormons again offered them the opportunity to surrender. Women and children were wounded by rocks the Mormons were throwing to move them out of their hiding places. After some time, the remaining Utes retreated and the battle was over. At least four Utes were killed, but the number may be higher. The town was called Battle Creek for many years before the settlers changed the named to Pleasant Grove.

BATTLE CREEK FALLS TRAIL

The Utah Valley from the Buffalo Peak Trail.

Provo Area

Along the Wasatch Front, Provo is the third largest city in the state of Utah. It is home to Brigham Young University (BYU). It was once called Timpanogots by the Timpanogos because of its rocky terrain. Its nickname is "The Garden City" because there are many gardens and orchards around the town. It lies in the Utah Valley.

The area provides a beautiful background for photo shoots.

Rank 3

25. Buffalo Peak to Squaw Valley Trail

RATING	Seeker, due to terrain and quick elevation gain
ROUND TRIP DISTANCE	1.0 mile out and back
ROUND-TRIP TIME	About 1 hour
ELEVATION CHANGE	300 feet (from 7,750 to 8050 feet)
MAP	Trails Illustrated Wasatch Front North
NEAREST LANDMARK	Provo Canyon
FEES	None
RESTROOMS	None
DOGS	Must be leashed
OPERATING HOURS	One hour before sunrise to one hour after sunset

COMMENT: There aren't many opportunities to summit a peak with just a 1.0 mile hike, but this is one of them. Part of the road to the trail is a dusty rutted drive, which just adds to the fun. The road is closed in winter and early spring due to snow, making this a late spring to early fall hike. There is no water access, so fill up before you head out on this hike. Be aware that this area is popular with hunters and ATVs. Horses and mountain bikes also use the trail. This hike is a part of the forest biome.

If you time your hike right, you can experience the beautiful yellows of the wildflower known as mule's ear. The fall brings reds, oranges, and yellows of aspens, maples, and oaks across the mountainsides.

GETTING THERE: From Salt Lake City, take Interstate 15 to Exit 272. Continue from the exit for 3.7 miles. Take the turnoff for I-189/Provo Canyon Rd. Head up Provo Canyon Rd. for 1.8 miles. Take a right at the Squaw Peak turn off, then wind your way up the canyon for 4.0 miles. Turn left at the T as you head toward Hope Campground. The road turns to dirt as you follow it for another almost 3.0 miles to a dirt parking lot on the left. Park at the lot on the right across from the "Protect Your Wildland Playground" sign.

THE ROUTE: Once you spot the sign and park, the trail is on your right. It begins at a gap in a wooden fence. Park as far on the right as you can.

From the start of the hike, you can see Buffalo Peak straight ahead. The trail climbs slightly uphill from the start. It is fairly wide but has obstacles like roots and

Buffalo Peak is one of the easiest summits in Utah for little hikers.

rocks. At 518 feet, the trail opens up from the shade of the trees to a meadow and views on the right of Mt. Timpanogos What a background!

Avoid short social trails along the hike on both sides that feature steep drop offs. The beautiful shade at the beginning of the hike fades and at 0.2 mile, you can see the summit of Buffalo Peak. Don't let that intimidate you or your little hikers because the trail switches back a bit, and you can take as many breaks as you need. Views continue on left of Utah Lake and Provo and Orem.

At 0.3 mile there is a fire pit area on the right that is also the trail connector for the hike extensions. Some tree cover begins again after the fire pit area, but the trail pops back out of the shade at 0.35 mile. There are interesting pines close to 0.4 mile on the left. The final push to the top is steep. Views continue on left of Utah Lake, Provo and Orem. A pine a little past 0.4 mile provides a shady spot for a quick swig of water. Just up the switchback are clear and amazing almost 360-degree views, including Squaw Peak and Rock Canyon.

The trail becomes loose rock as you continue. Good grip shoes are handy for the ascent and descent. Your little ones may be feeling the fatigue, but there is no need to rush to the top. There are little pockets of shade that provide great places to rest and take in the views. Take snack and water breaks, and enjoy this time as they work hard to get to the top. The rocks create almost natural steps as you reach the top of Buffalo Peak. The nice part about this summit is there is no exposure, making it safe for children.

The reds, yellows and oranges are vibrant in the fall near Buffalo Peak.

Jump in the air and give your hikers a high five for summiting a mountain! After you take some photos of their achievement, take in the panoramic views from the top. Utah Valley and Utah Lake can both be seen, making it possible to get lake, mountain, and city views. Head back to the trailhead.

HIKE EXTENSION: If you have older hikers, there are two hike extensions that make for a longer route to the summit. From the Little Rock Canyon Overlook, it is a 2.0 mile round-trip hike. Or park at the Squaw Peak Overlook parking lot for a 4.2-mile round-trip hike with a vertical gain of 1,350 feet, making this an Adventurer-rated hike.

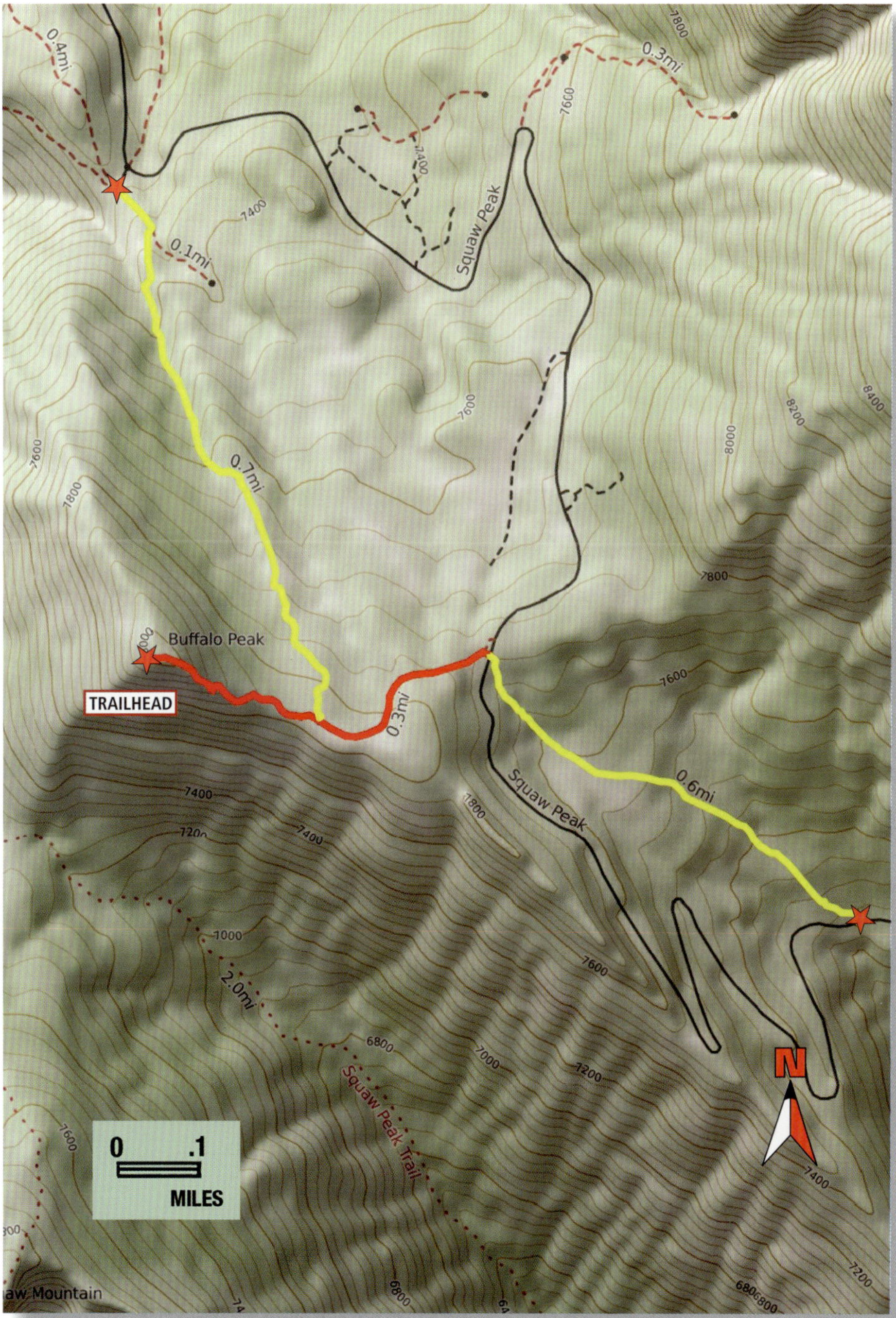

BUFFALO PEAK TO SQUAW VALLEY TRAIL

The Fifth Water Hot Springs bring many visitors to the Spanish Fork area.

Spanish Fork Area

Mountains surround the city of Spanish Fork with the city limits within Utah Valley and the Wasatch Mountains to the east. Mormon Pioneers first settled it in 1851. Its name is derived from two Franciscan friars who visited the area in the 1770s. Spanish Fork was the first Icelandic settlement in the U.S. and celebrates Icelandic Independence Day with a festival every June.

People enjoy dipping in the Fifth Water Hot Springs year round.

Rank 3

26. Fifth Water Hot Springs Trail/Diamond Fork Hot Springs Trail

RATING	Adventurer due to length
ROUND TRIP DISTANCE	4.75 miles out and back
ROUND-TRIP TIME	2.5-3 hours
ELEVATION CHANGE	575 feet (from 5576 to 6151 feet)
MAP	Trails Illustrated Wasatch Front North
NEAREST LANDMARK	Spanish Fork
FEES	None
RESTROOMS	Pit toilets
DOGS	Must be leashed
OPERATING HOURS	One hour before sunset to one hour after sunset

COMMENT: Fifth Water Hot Springs is also known as Diamond Fork Hot Springs. The trail is a part of the forest biome. One of the best features of this trail is the many shaded places to stop and sit on a log or rock and just listen to the water. Rattlesnakes are known to frequent this trail, so keep a careful eye. If you or anyone in your hiking group tends to get headaches or have trouble breathing from things like the smell of sulfur, you may want to skip this hike. Be aware that you may encounter nude bathers at the pools.

The gate to Diamond Fork Road is typically closed in the winter, adding a significant amount of mileage to the hike. So, this hike is best done from spring through fall, especially with smaller hikers. However, some people do use fat bikes or ski to the hot springs. The trail is also open to mountain bikes and horses. Don't forget a towel to dry off after a soak!

GETTING THERE: From Salt Lake City, take Interstate 15 south/I-80 east. Continue for over 40 miles and take Exit 257 B-A, US 6 E, in Spanish Fork. Continue on US 6 for 20 miles. Turn left at mile marker 184 onto Diamond Fork Rd. Before the turn you will see a utilities building on the left and a sign for Spanish Fork River Park on the right. Follow Diamond Fork Rd. for 9.0 miles to the trailhead, on the right. A sign marks Three Forks Trailhead, which is the start of the hike. About 15 cars can fit in the parking lot. Do not park on the street as you could get a ticket.

THE ROUTE: From the parking lot, head straight past the bathrooms and find a wooden sign with a map of the area. In case the dry erase arrow and note are missing from the map, head straight on the trail to get to Fifth Water Hot Springs. There is a bat house on the right as you begin a short climb at 0.14 mile. The creek runs on the right as the trail rolls through a canopy of trees, and wild berries and wildflowers line the trail.

At 0.65 mile, there is a wooden fence on the right protecting from the trail erosion at this location. You will exit the canopy at this point for a short while, but don't fret as the shade comes back at 0.75 mile. Be sure to look at the patterns on the rocks created over time. The trail continues to meander with nothing too steep. At 0.8 mile there is a rock resembling a mushroom on the right that looks similar to a hoodoo and just begs to be climbed.

Gambel oaks and pines continue to line the trail. As you make your way toward the hot springs, there are many fun rocks and trees to climb on the left. They also make for good spots to stop and grab water and some fuel. The waters of Sixth Water Creek continue on the right and offer plenty of places to splash some water on yourself.

At the 1.0 mile mark, there is more erosion fencing on the right. Shortly after the fencing, you will cross a somewhat rickety wooden bridge. This is the fork

The hot springs vary in temperature.

Enjoying the water with the "honey pot" in the background.
Photo: Kristin Mason

between Sixth Water Creek on the left and Fifth Water on the right. Fifth Water Creek flows on the right as the trail bends, all the way to the hot springs. At a fork at 1.25 miles continue straight. The trail becomes a bit uneven at 1.3 miles with a drop off and no fencing. At 1.5 miles, and continuing as you get closer to the springs, there are unmarked campgrounds on the right.

If you take a splash in the water before you hit the actual springs, you will notice that it gets warmer and clearer as you hike along. In the winter months, the water tends to be more blue and green than in the summer. You may begin to smell sulfur around the 2.0 mile mark. The smell often has to do with recent weather and the winds. At 2.2 miles, the trail bends to the right. There are several places to soak once you reach the first waterfall at 2.3 miles on the right. The warmest pool is located at the "honey pot." The water from the fall at the pot is much cooler than the water in the pool.

There are plenty of rocks to lean against to remove your shoes and stash your gear under while you soak. It's incredible to think that within the Uintas volcanic activity still exists in the form of the hot springs. Because the groundwater and still hot igneous rocks are interacting, use caution when entering the pools as some may be too hot, especially for younger children.

Spend some time unwinding at the pools and take in the spectacular scenery. Try moving from pool to pool. After you enjoy this unique experience, dry off and make your way 2.5 miles back to the trailhead.

FIFTH WATER HOT SPRINGS TRAIL/DIAMOND FORK HOT SPRINGS TRAIL

Park City Area

Twenty-five miles southeast of Salt Lake City, Park City was the home of the 2002 Winter Olympics. Two world-class ski resorts are located in Park City: Park City Mountain and Deer Valley Resort. It is a popular destination for Olympic fans, outdoor enthusiasts, hand crafted whiskey connoisseurs and foodies.

Outdoor recreation from soccer and golf to skiing and hiking make Park City a popular destination. *Photo: Heather Sims*

Rank 1

27. Cottontail Loop (Dutch Hollow Trail System)

RATING	Experimenter, due to easy terrain and short distance
ROUND TRIP DISTANCE	1.4-mile loop
ROUND-TRIP TIME	1 hour plus
ELEVATION CHANGE	207 feet (from 5,750 to 5,957 feet)
MAP	Trails Illustrated Wasatch Front North
NEAREST LANDMARK	Midway
FEES	$7 day use fee; Utah State Parks pass
RESTROOMS	Pit toilets
DOGS	Must be leashed
OPERATING HOURS	One hour before sunrise to one hour after sunset

COMMENT: The Dutch Hollow Trail System is a part of Wasatch Mountain State Park. Remember the rules of trail courtesy: bikes yield to hikers, and hikers and bikes yield to horses. There is no water access and very little shade, so come prepared. The trails are muddy after rain and during the spring runoff. Snowshoeing is popular in the winter. This hike is a part of the forest biome.

HOW TO GET THERE: From Salt Lake City, take Interstate 80 easttoward Cheyenne. Take Exit 146 for US 40 E toward Heber/Vernal. Keep right to continue toward US 189/US 40 E. Continue onto US 189/US 40 E to River Rd. Turn right onto River Rd., continue for 2.0 miles, and turn right onto Dutch Hollow Rd. There are over 20 spots in the lower parking lot, and there is an upper parking lot as well. Don't forget to display your state parks pass or receipt for the day use fee. The park entrance and trailhead are on the right.

THE ROUTE: There are almost 20 miles of trails within the Dutch Hollow Trail system. With mellow climbs and easy terrain, these trails are perfect for young hikers looking to log miles to prepare for bigger and harder hikes. Cottontail Loop is no frills, and there is no particular destination but the trailhead when you are done. There are carbonite signs along the trails, but grab a map and have a route planned beforehand. You can always add mileage or deviate from the original plan once you are hiking. Follow the main trail from the parking lot. A few hundred feet from the parking lot, there is a sign on the left for the Cottontail Loop. Continue on the wider trail as it switchbacks through the oak. The trail is rocky in spots. Pass a trail on the right just shy of 400 feet, and at 0.15 mile, head right to continue on the Cottontail Loop. You will see an open meadow on left with scrub oak on the right. The trail continues to slowly climb, but the elevation gain isn't very noticeable.

Birds of prey soar high above and wildflowers bloom in the meadow in late spring.

The trail flattens out a bit at 0.4 mile as it opens up on both sides. At the trail junction at 0.45 mile, take the left fork for the Sage Loop. Look back and left for views of Heber Valley.

The trail is still rocky in spots but fairly flat as it twists and turns in and out of the scrub oak. You will cross a maintenance road at 0.5 mile. There are some blind corners as you hike along, so listen for mountain bikers or horses, which could come from either direction.

There is another trail junction at 0.8 mile on the left; head left to stay on Sage Loop. At this point, the trail heads back toward Heber Valley, with continued views. Continue straight at the junction at 0.9 mile, where the trail opens up again. Wild grasses grow in the meadow. Purple and yellow wildflowers bloom. This is the perfect area for binoculars; try to spot wildlife from afar. Elk, bears, and cats reside in Wasatch Mountain State Park.

A Sage Trail sign at 1 mile on the left lets you know you're on the right track. Head straight and don't take the trail that heads left up the hill. There is a bike trail junction at 1.1 miles that crosses over Sage Trail on the right. Be sure to check for bikers coming down the hill, keeping in mind that they might be riding fast. Note the hand-written warning on the carbonite sign that for safety reasons hikers should not hike on this trail. Continue straight for the Sage Loop. This is a good place to stop for water and see if you can catch a biker careening down the hill with joy.

The Dutch Hollow Trails overlook Heber Valley.

The Dutch Hollow Trails are multi-use trails.

The trail is fairly flat as it moves through the open meadow. The Cottonwood Loop heads right at the 1.2 miles trail junction. Continue straight. The trail bends around and there is a park road on the right. A scenic footbridge on the right at 1.3 miles takes you to the park road. Continue straight and the trail leads to the farthest end of the parking lot.

On the Way Home

THE CRATER

Did you know that the only certified warm water dive location in the continental United States is in Midway, Utah? The Crater, a geothermal spring, is hidden within a 55-foot tall, beehive-shaped limestone rock. Located on the Homestead property, the water stays between 90 and 96 degrees. You can hike and soak on the same day! Be sure to book your visit ahead of time online. There are various packages and rental equipment is included.

The Crater

700 Homestead Dr.
Midway, UT 84049
(435) 657-3840
www.midwaycrater.com
Cost: $13–$27, depending on activity and day
Hours: Monday through Thursday 12:30 p.m. to 6:30 p.m.; Friday ad Saturday 10:30 a.m. to 6:30 p.m.; Sunday 10:30 a.m. to 4:30 p.m., with holiday closures

COTTONTAIL LOOP (DUTCH HOLLOW TRAIL SYSTEM)

Rank 4

28. Mid Mountain Trail

RATING	Wanderer, due to steepness
ROUND TRIP DISTANCE	2.8 miles out and back
ROUND-TRIP TIME	1–2 hours
ELEVATION CHANGE	315 feet (from 8,105 to 8,420 feet)
MAP	Trails Illustrated Wasatch Front North
NEAREST LANDMARK	Park City Resort
FEES	None
RESTROOMS	Within Park City Resort or possible portable toilets near singletrack
DOGS	Must be leashed
OPERATING HOURS	One hour before sunrise to one hour after sunset

COMMENT: This trail is very popular, so expect to see mountain bikers, other hikers, and trail runners. The trail is best enjoyed from June through October, between the snowmelt and the snowfall. There is no water access outside the resort area. This hike is part of the forest biome.

Locals recommend hiking this trail later in the day in the summer as mornings are usually crowded with mountain bikers. There is plenty of shade on this hike, mostly from aspens, making it more tolerable in the summer sun. Don't be surprised to be showered by the leaves on a windy fall day.

While the entire trail is 20 miles long, this hike is a shorter out and back that offers the best of this classic trail. In its full length, Mid Mountain connects Deer Valley, Park City, and Canyons ski resorts. The trail is singletrack and contains many roots.

GETTING THERE: From Salt Lake City, take Interstate 15 south. Take Exit 298 for I-215 E/Belt Route. Take Exit 2 off the Belt Route for I-80 toward Park City. Use the right two lanes for Exit 145 toward Kimball Junction. Turn right onto UT 224 S. After 5.8 miles, turn left onto Deer Valley Rd. At the traffic circle, take the first exit onto Marsac Ave. Almost 2.0 miles down the road, turn left onto Guardsman Connection and make another quick left onto Royal St. The Silver Lake Lodge is on the right. Parking at Silver Lake can be tough, but you are allowed to park on the road from May through November.

MID MOUNTAIN TRAIL

The chair lifts of Park City Ski Resort from the Mid Mountain trail. *Photo: Heather Sims*

THE ROUTE: From the parking lot, go past the Silver Lake Lodge. Turn right past the Silver Lake Express lift and walk down the hill to the bridge. Just under the bridge on the left the Mid Mountain Trail starts. Starting at the lodge offers the most gradual ascent, which makes it more manageable for kids.

The trail begins in aspens. At about 0.2 mile, you will see the Quincy chair lift below on the right. Just after this, the trail pops out of the trees and onto a fire road. Turn left up the hill and after about 50 feet rejoin the Mid Mountain Trail on the right. From here, you will start back into trees and cross the many ski runs. During late spring and summer, the wildflowers fill the ski run meadows with color. Stop on the ski runs and take in the view overlooking Park City and Summit County. Look up the hillsides as you cross the ski runs and you may see deer grazing. You may also see moose; be sure to give them plenty of space. Other animals living in the area include deer, elk, rabbits, coyotes, and even bears.

At 0.6 mile there is a small marked split in the trail with Mid Mountain on the upper left and Tour De Suds on the right. Stay on Mid Mountain and continue in and out of the trees on the rolling single-track. The trail has sections of shade and sections of exposure. As you climb, the trail crosses under chair lifts, and after 1.4 miles, it pops out on Highway 224 Hwy/Empire Pass. You can either cross the road for a longer hike or head back to Deer Valley the way you came. If you cross the road, the Montage Deer Valley Hotel is located after about another 300 feet. You can enjoy a meal there before heading back down.

Rank 4

29. PC Hill Trail

RATING	Wanderer, due to elevation gain and starting altitude
ROUND TRIP DISTANCE	1.3 miles out and back
ROUND-TRIP TIME	1–1.5 hours
ELEVATION CHANGE	518 feet (from 6,684 to 7,202 feet)
MAP	Trails Illustrated Wasatch Front North
NEAREST LANDMARK	Park City Resort
FEES	None
RESTROOMS	Seasonal portable toilets
DOGS	Off leash once on trail
OPERATING HOURS	One hour before sunrise to one hour after sunset

COMMENT: Throughout Utah, mountainsides have letters indicating city names and universities, including Brigham Young University and the University of Utah. There are 78 sets of hillside letters across the state, including the town of Park City. Touted as a must do hike for locals, the PC Hill Trail takes you to the hillside "PC" letters that can be seen from town. The concrete PC letters were a gift to the city from the PC High School senior class of 2004. While you look at the handprints and names, you can see the high school below.

There is no shade on this trail, so mornings or evenings are the best times in the summer, and spring and fall are ideal. This trail is also popular in the winter for snowshoeing. Bring plenty of water for your group, including any four-legged friends. This is a forest biome hike.

GETTING THERE: From Salt Lake City, take Interstate15 south/I-80 east toward Summit County. Take Exit 146 for US 40 east toward Vernal and Heber. Keep right to continue onto US 189/US 40 east. Drive almost 5.0 miles to Exit 4 Park City/Kamas. Turn right onto UT 248 west/Kearns Blvd. toward Quinn's Junction. Look for a road on the left just past Treasure Mountain Middle School. Turn left and follow the dirt road to the park at the end. There are plenty of parking spots.

THE ROUTE: This summit trail begins on the right side of the parking area opposite the soccer fields known as North 40. At the end of the parking lot and opposite the bridge that crosses the river, you can let your pooch off leash. Make sure dogs remain under voice command.

Views of Park City can be seen from the PC Hill Trail. *Photo: Heather Sims*

This hike begins climbing right away, with almost immediate views. The dirt trail is rocky in spots and is predominantly exposed single-track. Birds and chipmunks are frequently seen along the trail among the brush.

The trail has two main switchbacks. Breaks are encouraged to catch your breath and enjoy the scenery. The trail comes to a junction at 0.3 mile. Both trails have little offshoots that end up back on the main trail. Take the nameless left trail if you have kids older than three as it can be a little rocky. This trail has the advantage of views of Round Valley. For toddlers, keep straight to continue on the PC Hill Trail, with a fence line in front of you. Turn left when you meet the fence and head up the hill. Take the second left single-track route, which will bring you to the top. The trail gets rockier as you near your destination—the letters. There are two big boulders, and a new bench to take in the views. Kids will enjoy the wide-open space at the top to explore. Make sure to give them a high five at the top for reaching the letters and completing this iconic hike.

Look from right to left to see Canyons Resort, Iron Mountain, downtown Park City, and the Park City Resort. Look southwest for Bald Mountain. This west-facing trail has stellar sunsets. If you are in town for July 4th or in mid-September for the Autumn Aloft Balloon Festival, the top of PC Hill is the best view in town for fireworks and watching balloons.

Turn around and head back to the trailhead and take in the views again. Enjoy a picnic and some time at the fields before heading home. You can continue exploring by strolling through the Treasure Mountain Nature Preserve. The preserve is accessed via a path at the south end of the soccer fields, which heads toward the school buildings. The preserve has wetlands, and you may see herons, geese, and ducks.

The fall displays vibrant colors including the red of Gambel oak and the yellows from the cottonwoods. Skip some rocks and enjoy lunch or dinner under the shade. After playing in the water, or watching the falls from a distance, return the way you came.

PC HILL TRAIL

Rank 4

30. Round Valley Trails

RATING	Wanderer, due to starting altitude and elevation gain
ROUND TRIP DISTANCE	2.6 mile loop
ROUND-TRIP TIME	1–2 hours
ELEVATION CHANGE	208 feet (from 6,707 to 6838 feet)
MAP	Trails Illustrated Wasatch Front North
NEAREST LANDMARK	Park City
FEES	None
RESTROOMS	Pit toilets
DOGS	Off leash OK
OPERATING HOURS	One hour before sunrise to one hour after sunset

COMMENT: Round Valley is 700 acres of open space that has been preserved. Wildflowers, mountain mahogany, and scrub oak cover the sides of the trails. In the winter, 25 kilometers of Nordic trails are groomed. There are also designated snowshoe/hiking and fat bike trails. The views are quite different in the winter, but still breathtaking, if you choose to hike when the snow is falling.

Don't forget your furry friend on this trail, as it is one of the few trails where your pooch can run free (but note that voice control is required). There are several trails here that are popular for beginning hikers, trail runners, and mountain bikers, and great for kids, because of their short length and easy terrain. So expect to share the trail with bikes and possibly horses too. Remember that mountain bikes yield to hikers and horses, and hikers yield to horses. But don't assume that the bikers will follow the yield. Fortunately, this is a double-track hike, which makes yielding easier.

The Gambel oak surrounding the trail brings vibrant colors in the fall. Sagebrush also lines much of the trail. For the most part the trail is obstacle free with a few rocks and occasional debris from the surrounding vegetation. Beyond friendly dogs, moose can be seen along the trail, mostly in winter. Also expect to see rattlesnakes, birds of prey, coyotes, jackrabbits, and elk. There is no water access, so bring plenty, as this trail is exposed. Early or late in the day during summer, spring, and fall are the best times to enjoy this trail. These trails are also popular in the winter for snowshoeing, cross-country skiing, and winter hiking or running. This trail is part of the forest biome.

GETTING THERE: From Salt Lake City, take Interstate 80 east. Take Exit 146/US 40 east toward Heber/Vernal. Continue for 3.5 miles and then merge onto State Route 248/UT 248 via Exit 4 toward Park City/Ski Areas. Make a right onto Round Valley Drive. Shortly thereafter, you will see the Park City Dog Park at the Recreation Complex at Round Valley and Gilmore Dr. Park at the far end of the parking lot next to the soccer fields.

THE ROUTE: Cross the parking lot to Quinn's Junction Trailhead. Fill up your water bottles here if necessary. At the trailhead, take the middle double-track, named Fastpitch. This is the more scenic route. As you walk up the small hill, notice the top of Park City Mountain in the distance.

After 0.5 mile, there is a four-way junction. The trail on the right leads back to the trailhead along Hat Trick. The left trail is a route to the PC Hill Trailhead. Continue straight along Fastpitch. The trail system is well marked.

As you head down the hill, you will come across another intersection with the Fairways Hills Connector. If you head left, it leads into a neighborhood. By going right, you will head back to the trailhead and pass the National Ability Center. Remain on Fastpitch, heading straight up the hill behind the National Ability Center. You may

There is very little shade along the Round Valley Trails. *Photo: Heather Sims*

Enjoy a snack at this little picnic area. *Photo: Heather Sims*

see horses grazing, or there maybe a horse out on the National Ability Center horse trails. Look behind you to get a nice view of the PC Resort.

Just under another half a mile, there is a pond on your right and a large tree. The TC Connector path leads across a small wooden bridge over a stream to the tree. This is a great snack stop for the little ones. After finishing your snack, you can head back onto Fastpitch for another 0.3 mile. This leads to the Round Valley Trailhead parking lot. Before you reach the parking lot, you will see a bench on the right.

If your pooch hasn't had enough off-leash time, enjoy the dog park located at the trailhead/parking area. And your kids can burn off additional energy at the playground at the bottom of the Ability Way Trail.

HIKE EXTENSION: Beyond this beginner friendly hike, the trails around Round Valley extend for many miles. Continue on any loop to add more mileage. For example, turn left on a small connector to the junction of Matt's Flat and Ability Way. Depending on how far you want to go you can continue on the double-track about another 0.5 mile and take the left fork up Cammy's Trail to the bench for a spectacular view of Canyons Resort and Iron Mountain. This is an out and back and will add about another 1.0 mile to the walk. Alternatively, head back down Ability Way past the tree where you can stop for another snack and head back past the east side of the National Ability Center to the parking lot.

ROUND VALLEY TRAILS

Black Dragon Canyon is a part of the San Rafael Swell.

San Rafael Swell

The San Rafael Swell was formed about 60 million years go. Today, I-70 divides the swell into north and south. Pictographs and petroglyphs found along the sandstone walls show evidence that the area was once inhabited by Native Americans. A bill was put forth in 2018 to make the area a national monument called "Jurassic National Monument" by U.S. Representative John Curtis after a failed attempt in 2002 by the Utah Governor at the time Mike Leavitt.

Black varnish can be seen along the walls of Black Dragon Canyon.

Rank 3

31. Black Dragon Canyon Trail

RATING	Seeker, due to mostly flat terrain but longer length
ROUND TRIP DISTANCE	3.5 miles
ROUND-TRIP TIME	1.5–2 hours
ELEVATION CHANGE	207 feet (from 4,250 to 4,457 feet)
MAP	Trails Illustrated San Rafael Swell
NEAREST LANDMARK	Interstate 70, Spotted Wolf Canyon
FEES	None
RESTROOMS	None
DOGS	Must be leashed
OPERATING HOURS	One hour before sunrise to one hour after sunset

COMMENT: Named after the Dragon Pictograph on the canyon wall, the wide-open hike in Black Dragon Canyon is as mysterious as its name. The black varnish that covers the over 500-foot sandstone walls looks as if an angry dragon breathed fire all through the canyon. It's known mostly to locals because of its almost hidden location.

Beyond the pictographs and petroglyphs, be on the lookout the many animals that call the Swell home, from deer and bats to rabbits and lizards. Even pollywogs and frogs are known to find a home in the pools of water in the small basins, while eagles also frequent the area. Recent rain may cause small waterfalls on the canyon walls, which is a treat to see. Depending on the time of year, wild chrysanthemums may also be in bloom throughout the canyon, mainly in late summer. Plant life abounds in the spring and summer, covering the canyon walls and ground.

This is a multi-use trail. Jeeps, mountain bikers, dirt bike enthusiasts, and four-wheelers also enjoy the canyon. The canyon is prone to flash floods. Bring plenty of water on this hike. It's best enjoyed March through November due to the heat.

GETTING THERE: From Green River, take I-70 west for 13 miles. Turn north on the dirt road right after mile marker 147. After you turn off I-70, drive through the livestock gate and close it behind you. When you come to the T about 100 feet later, turn left. Then turn left at the Black Dragon Wash sign. Immediately after this left, there is a dirt parking area on the left at the no camping sign. It is best to park here and walk into the canyon. Note that you will have to cross the median to get back on eastbound 1-70.

Petroglyphs can be found in a few places in Black Dragon Canyon including the dragon in red on the right of this photo.

Because of the rough road conditions, only vehicles with high clearance should attempt to navigate the terrain. For the best directions, stop at the John Wesley Powell Museum in Green River for a hand drawn map or an area map.

THE ROUTE: To begin this out-and-back hike, head northwest down the Jeep road from the parking lot. The trail narrows and enters the canyon about 0.1 mile from where you parked. This part of the hike is often shaded, especially in the morning as the sun rises over the canyon walls, so you can find some shade in the heat of the summer.

As you head up the canyon toward the first set of petroglyphs and pictographs, the wash is wide. Rocks are easy to avoid for most of this hike. This trail is also called Black Dragon Wash because it is in the wash the entire time. Hiking with a pack or holding hands with your little hikers is easy while searching for evidence of past visitors or the dragon. Black varnish streaks across the reddish sandstone walls as the trail continues west. From the start of where the canyon narrows, you can test your echoes in this almost empty canyon, where sounds bounce off the canyon walls.

The first set of Barrier Style rock art is just beyond an overhang at 0.25 mile from the canyon start, about 200 feet up the wall. The art the canyon is named for is on the right side marked off with a brown Bureau of Land Management fence.

Some petroglyphs are hidden within the canyon.

Along with the winged "dragon," various other drawings and carvings are visible here, including what could be calendars and figures of animals that lived in the area.

A trail highlight is that you can climb right up to the drawings and see them up close. Unfortunately, vandals have used this opportunity to carve their names and marks into the wall, making some of the Native American carvings tough to decipher. There is debate about whether the early drawings were created by Fremont Indians and whether the rock art resembles a pterosaur. Regardless of its origins, the meaning behind the dragon-like figure on the wall still intrigues the minds of all who witness it.

Left of the fenced area, there is a cave at the top of the rockslide area. It is not noticeable from the trail, so many visitors do not know it is there. If your daredevil group wants to venture up to the cave, it will take some ducking, scrambling, and climbing skills. The cave is called the Dragon's Lair and is home to bats, as evidenced by the amount of guano found there. Headlamps are handy for exploring the cave.

The trail divides at several places past the drawings, but all of the routes join back up, making it impossible to get lost in the dry river wash. One route is often higher than the other making it easy to avoid any standing water if there was recent rain.

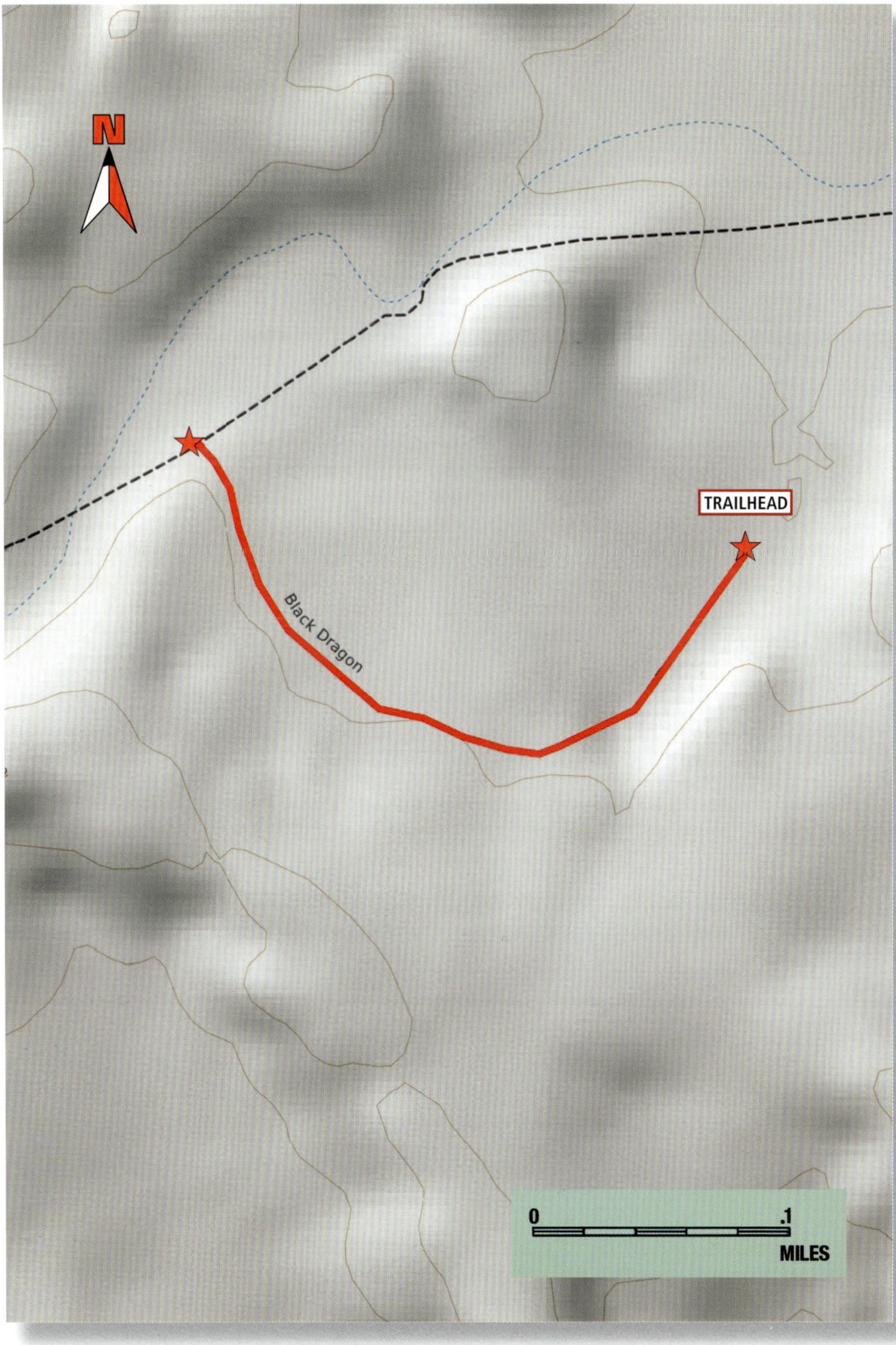

BLACK DRAGON CANYON TRAIL

Past the large area of pictographs and petroglyphs, the trail slowly gains elevation as you navigate past boulders, cottonwood, and juniper trees. The cottonwood leaves bring a warm yellow contrast in the fall to the continuous red walls of the canyon. More petroglyphs and pictographs decorate the canyon walls, so keep a keen eye.

Just shy of 2.0 miles, the canyon forks. Turn around at the fork and follow the same route back.

A BLM sign identifies the location of the Black Dragon and other art.

On the Way Home

JOHN WESLEY POWELL MUSEUM

Head to the John Wesley Powell Museum in Green River to learn about the rivers of the Southwest from the Colorado River to the Green River. Learn about war hero Major John Wesley Powell's journey through the uncharted waters in 1869 to map out unknown territory. Children will delight in the dinosaur bones and full dinosaur skeletons in the basement. Adults will enjoy reading about the expeditions and seeing replicas of expedition boats from the 1800's. Temporary exhibits highlight art that is often for sale.

John Wesley Powell Museum
765 E. Main St.
Green River, UT 84525
(435) 564-3427
johnwesleypowell.com
Admission: Adults $6, children 5 through 12 $2, families $15
Hours: Summer, Monday through Saturday, 9 a.m. to 7 p.m.; Sunday noon to 5 p.m.; winter, Tuesday through Saturday 9 a.m. to 5 p.m.

Goblin Valley State Park

Searching for cattle, cowboys were said to be the first to discover Goblin Valley. Hite Ferry boat owner Arthur Chaffin came to the area in the 1920s looking for a more direct route between Green River and Caineville. Part of the San Rafael Desert, the valley formations were created over 170 million years ago from part of an inland sea. As more people came to see the Mars-like landscape, the desire to protect it grew, and it became a state park on August 24, 1964. Goblin Valley is one of few places in the world with such a large amount of hoodoos.

The Valley of the Goblins is said to look like the surface of Mars.

Rank 2

32. Curtis Bench Trail

RATING	Searcher, due to length
ROUND TRIP DISTANCE	2.1 miles
ROUND-TRIP TIME	1–1.5 hours
ELEVATION CHANGE	96 feet (from 4,961 to 5,057 feet)
MAP	Trails Illustrated San Rafael Swell
NEAREST LANDMARK	Goblin Valley State Park Group Campsite Picnic Area
FEES	$13 day use fee for cars; Utah State Parks pass
RESTROOMS	At group campsite
DOGS	Must be leashed
OPERATING HOURS	7 a.m. to 10 p.m. year-round

COMMENT: The Curtis Bench Trail is a mix of desert grass and sand that runs above the Valley of the Goblins. Mostly singletrack, the trail is wide enough for walking side by side with no obstacles. If you have happened to see the movie *Galaxy Quest*, some of the scenery showcased in the movie can be seen from this trail.

This trail offers the best view of this unique landscape without crowds of people. Because of the arid desert environment, there is not much vegetation in the valley, so there is no shade on this hike. Bring plenty of water and lather on the sunscreen as you look out for bobcats, rabbits, and lizards that call the scrub brush area home. This desert biome trail is best hiked in the morning or evening if visiting in the summer months. Fall, spring, and winter are less crowded times to hike this trail, and the weather is also more favorable. Taking a souvenir from the trail is forbidden!

What little vegetation that can survive the desert climate can be seen in spurts along the trail, from Mormon tea to various cacti. But don't expect these plants to provide any shade on this wide-open trail unless you are a lizard or jackrabbit. In fact, don't be alarmed if a small green or brown guy scurries quickly past your feet on this trail. Most Goblin Valley animals, from the kit fox to the kangaroo rat, are nocturnal, so a track or two may be the most you will see of them on this hike during the day. You might spot a snake track; they like to hide near the larger rocks that dot the trail. The rocks make good places to stop, but watch your feet.

GETTING THERE: Goblin Valley is located 50 miles southwest of Green River. From Green River, head west on Interstate 70. Take Exit 149 onto Highway 24 and head south for about 24.0 miles until you see the park turnoff (also the Temple Mountain turn off). Take the park turn off and continue on the paved road for 12.0 miles to the park entrance. From Hanksville, take Hwy 24 to the Temple Mountain/Goblin Valley junction. Make a left and follow the paved road 12.0 miles to the park entrance.

Once in the park, follow the road until you hit a T. Make a right at the T and continue to the campsites on the left. There is a parking lot close to the group campsite.

THE ROUTES: Beginning at the Entrada Canyon Trailhead at the Group Campground picnic area, the Curtis Bench Trail follows the Entrada Canyon Trail for 0.2 mile before reaching a gravel service road and breaking off. Look straight and to the right on the service road to see the brown sign designating the Curtis Bench Trail. Alternatively, you can park in the lot at the top of the service road that also serves as a parking lot for the Wild Horse Mesa Mountain Bike Trail. The trailhead for Curtis Bench will now be on the left of the parking lot. Starting here, will cutoff 0.2 mile each way.

At this point, the Curtis Bench Trail runs parallel to and above the Entrada Canyon Trail. As you continue on the wide-open trail, you can see many of the

The Curtis Bench Trail offers 360-degree views of the valley.

The Three Sisters as seen from the Curtis Bench Trail.

trademark formations of Goblin Valley; the panoramic views include Three Sisters and other landmarks such as the Wild Horse Butte and the Henry Mountains.

Don't forget to look in every direction for something new to see. The Curtis Formation, the gray-green hued rock layer that lies above the layers of Entrada sandstone (for which the trail was named), can be viewed from the trail. The contrast between the red of the Entrada and gray and green of the Curtis Formation is striking.

The trail is well established and marked with cairns. The terrain rolls and crests, reaching its high point at 0.75 mile. Around the 0.85 mile mark, you will see a cut-off trail on the left that leads down to the valley. Continue straight to stay on the Curtis Bench Trail. The trail continues south with slight elevation changes and ends at a brown End of Trail sign. There is an outcropping here with a grand view. As you return to the campground, don't miss the best chance to see the four main rock formations that make up Goblin Valley: Summerville, Morrison, Curtis, and Entrada.

CURTIS BENCH TRAIL

Rank 3

33. Entrada Canyon Trail

RATING	Seeker, due to uneven, narrow terrain, lack of shade, and distance
ROUND TRIP DISTANCE	2.1 miles
ROUND-TRIP TIME	1.5 hours or more
ELEVATION CHANGE	158 feet (from 4,906 to 5,028 feet)
MAP	Trails Illustrated San Rafael Swell
NEAREST LANDMARK	Goblin Valley State Park Group Campsite Picnic Area or Observation Point
FEES	$13 day use fee for cars; Utah State Parks pass
RESTROOMS	Vault toilets at Observation Point and pit toilets near group campsite
DOGS	Must be leashed
OPERATING HOURS	7 a.m. to 10 p.m. year-round

COMMENT: The 2.1 mile out-and-back Entrada Canyon Trail is a narrow trail through Entrada sandstone wash and the desert biome. Parents carrying children in packs can navigate through it safely, but the narrowness makes it difficult at times to walk side by side with children. Most of the goblins along this trail cannot be viewed from any other vantage point in the park, making it a unique experience. The walls of sandstone will swallow you as you continue past the hoodoos. At any point, you can climb to higher ground for a better viewpoint if you feel you have lost the trail.

The little holes in the canyon walls make great places to rest, have a snack, and maybe find a little shade as there is none to be had on the trail. Bring plenty of water as it warms up fast on this trail. It may be tempting to collect a rock or two, but it is prohibited within the park.

GETTING THERE: Goblin Valley is located 50 miles southwest of Green River. From Green River, head west on Interstate 70. Take Exit 149 onto Highway 24 and head south for about 24.0 miles until you see the park turn off (also the Temple Mountain turn off). Take the park turn off and continue on the paved road for 12.0 miles to the park entrance. From Hanksville, take Hwy 24 to the Temple Mountain/ Goblin Valley junction. Make a left and follow the paved road for 12.0 miles to the park entrance.

The Entrada Canyon Trail takes you below the hoodoos for a unique view.

Once in the park, follow the road until you hit a T. Make a left at the T and follow the road past Three Sisters and other goblin formations until you reach Observation Point. The stairs to the valley are to the right of the picnic shelter.

THE ROUTE: Beginning at the Group Picnic Campsite. The trail reaches a dirt service road at the 0.2 mile mark. (You can cut off 0.2 miles each way by starting at the parking lot off the service road that is also the start of the Wild Horse Mesa Mountain Bike Trail. Or start at Observation Point instead of the campground, heading northwest. Turn around at the service road or at the group campsite. This road is where the Curtis Bench Trail splits off and becomes its own trail and is also the start of the Wild Horse Mesa Mountain Bike Trail. Continue on the Entrada Canyon Trail down the somewhat steep hill and into the canyon. Don't be alarmed if a Frisbee or two passes near your head at this point as the trail passes under a disc golf course above the canyon walls. The trail narrows at this point as you parallel Goblin Valley Road.

There are many offshoots created by rain wash, so be sure to follow the brown arrow signs noting the direction. From 0.3 mile to the 1.0-mile mark, there are also numerous cairns to help you stay on course. As you continue on the trail, you might feel small under the hoodoos towering 10 to 15 feet above.

Running ahead, the offshoots make wonderful places to hide and scare each other. As you meander through the canyon, note the shapes the goblins might resemble and how they change in appearance from each angle.

The terrain continues to turn and twist as you make your way past the hoodoos, which become more numerous as you continue toward Observation Point. The trail gets more difficult to follow from the 0.75 mile mark until the turnaround point.

There are many places to hide along the Entrada Canyon Trail.

Just continue to follow the brown signs and cairns. The trail ends at 1.05 miles after a steep, narrow incline up to Observation Point.

Take a break at Observation Point by enjoying a snack in the shade of the picnic shelter before heading back to the trailhead. Watch how the hoodoos change shape as you view them from the opposite direction as you retrace your sandy steps back to the starting point.

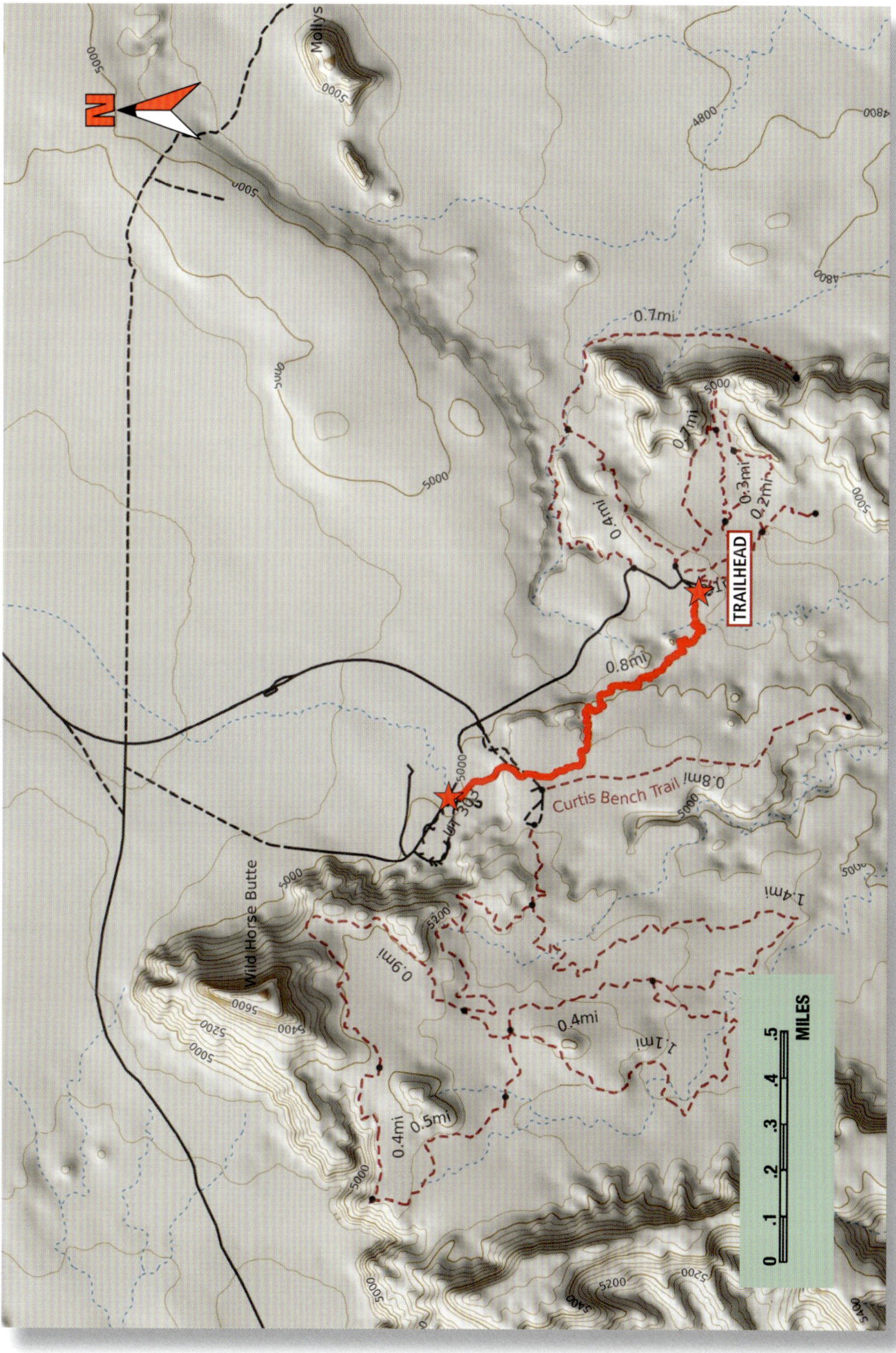

ENTRADA CANYON TRAIL

Rank 2

34. Valley of the Goblins Trail

RATING	Searcher, due to short distance, and low elevation gain
ROUND TRIP DISTANCE	About 1.0 mile, depending on the route
ROUND-TRIP TIME	1.0 or more hours
ELEVATION CHANGE	65 feet (from 4,892 to 4,957 feet), depending on specific route
MAP	Trails Illustrated San Rafael Swell
NEAREST LANDMARK	Observation Point
FEES	$13 day use fee for cars; Utah State Parks pass
RESTROOMS	Vault toilets at Observation Point
DOGS	Must be leashed
OPERATING HOURS	7 a.m. to 10 p.m. year-round

There is no specific trail through the Valley of the Goblins.

Children love to run and hide amongst the hoodoos.

COMMENT: While this hike is named the Valley of the Goblins and the park website and brochure state that there are three valleys, it is really one valley that can be divided into three geographical areas: upper (Valley 1), middle (Valley 2), and lower (Valley 3). Valley 1 is where the trail begins at Observation Point. Most visitors tend to spend their time in this area because the farther you venture, the more remote it becomes. Valley 2 becomes more remote at a low ridge (no signage) approximately 0.5 mile from Observation Point, depending on your route. Valley 3 is more than 1.0 mile from Observation Point and is secluded, with a mix of small and large goblins within the wash. There is no shade in this desert biome, so bring water and wear sunscreen. Spring, fall, and winter are ideal times to visit the park. If visiting in summer, plan to visit early or later in the day.

Erosion continues to change the landscape through rain and the freeze and thaw of winter. The alien planet scene in the *Galaxy Quest* movie was filmed in the park, and thanks to the movie production, roads that were once gravel are now paved.

GETTING THERE: Goblin Valley is located 50 miles southwest of Green River. From Green River, head west on Interstate 70. Take Exit 149 onto Highway 24 and head south for about 24.0 miles until you see the park turn off (also the Temple Mountain turn off). Take the park turn off and continue on the paved road for 12.0 miles to the park entrance. From Hanksville, travel along Hwy 24 to the Temple Mountain/Goblin Valley junction. Make a left and follow the paved road 12.0 miles to the park entrance.

Once in the park, follow the road until you hit a T. Make a left at the T and follow the road past Three Sisters and other goblin formations until you reach Observation Point. The stairs down into the valley are to the right of the picnic shelter.

THE ROUTE: The best part about a hike through the Valley of the Goblins is that there is no set route. It's a virtual playground for kids, who can delight in creating their own paths, and climbing and hiding among the goblin-shaped hoodoos.

Often said to look like Mars, the three valleys can be delineated by ridges and washes. There are no set trails here, but you can see the most frequent routes visitors have taken by the beaten down paths. Head in any direction to find something new to see and explore, but scope out a few landmarks as it can be easy to get lost on the valley floor.

Valley 1 begins as you descend the stairs from Observation point to the right of the covered picnic area. Wide open and vast, this is where most visitors prefer to explore. Dogs can run free here, just like the people enjoying the varied landscape. Depending on your route, about 0.50 mile from Observation Point and Valley 1 is Valley 2, which looks different than the first. The goblins stand much taller, and this is where you will find the Goblin's Lair, a canyoneering slot canyon where you may request a day permit for rappelling. Valley 3 is over 1.0 mile from Observation Point. It is remote and frequently visitor free, if you are looking for solitude. The topography here is much like a mix of Valleys 1 and 2 with the addition of side canyons.

Stop and have lunch at the picnic area at Observation Point, or if your adventurers are eager to explore, eat among the goblins. There is no shade among the goblins, so carry plenty of water and put on another layer of sunscreen before descending the stairs into Goblin Valley.

Movie buffs may enjoy re-living scenes from the Star Trek spoof movie *Galaxy Quest*. Playing flashlight tag and seeing the valley under night skies is also a treat, especially if you camp in the park. Stargazers will especially enjoy a trip into the valley at night because there are approximately 10.0 miles of light free skies. This makes it one of the darkest night skies in the world, according to the National Park Service's Night Sky Team.

HISTORY IN HIKING: What is a hoodoo?

Sometimes referred to as an earth pyramid or fairy chimney, a hoodoo is a thin and tall spire of rock. Hoodoos vary in thickness and height and typically form within formations of either volcanic or sedimentary rock including limestone dolomite and mudstone. They are created by the weathering and erosion of rock especially from ice and rain.

Spires and pinnacles are created by weathering and erosion as well. They are individual rock features that stand alone and often are pointed at the top. The top of spires and pinnacles is often made from mudstone, the softest rock.

VALLEY OF THE GOBLINS TRAIL

The Vermillion Cliffs of Zion National Park.

Zion National Park

On November 19, 1919, Congress established Zion as a national park. In 1956, the Kolob section of the park was officially added. Vermillion cliffs and valleys surround this national park originally named Mukuntuweap, meaning "straight canyon" in Paiute, by John Wesley Powell in 1892. Over 4 million visitors come to see the massive sandstone walls of Zion Canyon every year.

The trail to Lower Emerald Pools begins with a bridge.

Rank 2

35. Lower Emerald Pools Trail

RATING	Searcher, due to little elevation gain, and distance
ROUND TRIP DISTANCE	1.2 mile loop
ROUND-TRIP TIME	1–1.5 hours
ELEVATION CHANGE	70 feet (from 4,275 to 4,345 feet)
MAP	Trails Illustrated Zion
NEAREST LANDMARK	Zion Lodge
FEES	Private vehicle $30; Zion annual pass; National Parks pass
RESTROOMS	Public restrooms available in the Zion Lodge
DOGS	Not allowed
OPERATING HOURS	24 hours

COMMENT: The hike to the lower and middle pools is paved. With assistance, the lower pools can be reached with a wheelchair or stroller. The trail may be sandy in spots due to frequent winds that blow through the canyon. This hike is best from March to November, depending on weather. While it may be tempting to bath in the water near the waterfalls, this is prohibited. Make sure to fill up your water bottles before you head out. Zion is a part of the desert biome, with hot temperatures in the summer and fairly mild temperatures through the winter.

GETTING THERE: From Salt Lake City (307 miles) and Cedar City, Utah, (57 miles) take Interstate 15 south. Take Exit 27 and turn left on State Route 17 south for six miles. Make a left on Route 9 east in La Verkin. Continue on Route 9 for twenty miles into Zion National Park.

From Las Vegas, Nevada, (163 miles), Mesquite, Nevada, (80 miles), and Saint George, Utah, (40 miles) take Interstate 15 north. Take Exit 16 and turn right on State Route 9 east. Continue on State Route 9 east through La Verkin and into Zion National Park.

With limited parking in the park, free shuttle services run from February through November, depending on weather. No private vehicles are allowed into Zion National Park from April through October, unless you have a red permit because you are staying at the Zion Lodge.

THE ROUTE: From the Zion Lodge parking lot, cross over the road. Head over the bridge that crosses over the Virgin River (don't miss a photo opportunity here). At the end of the bridge there is a trailhead sign on the right. Follow the wide paved

The hike to Lower Emerald Pools runs along the Virgin River.

path along the Virgin River as it climbs slowly through the canyon. Cottonwoods and other trees provide shade for most of the hike. Water seeps from the walls, creating hanging gardens and shelves of moss and as you make your way north. Columbines, shooting stars, and other flowers grow along the canyon walls.

Depending on the time of year you visit, butterflies may join you in flight as you meander toward the falls. Chipmunks, bighorn sheep, and deer are often seen on the uneven slopes of the black walls that surround the trail. The ever-friendly squirrels may come to your feet looking for a snack. While your little hikers may think the begging is cute, don't feed the wildlife.

As you get closer to the pool, the trail begins to bend away from the river. There are two waterfalls near the lower pool. Unless you are visiting at the height of spring snowmelt, the waterfalls may be only a trickle, depending on recent weather. If there is enough flow, you may also be able to walk underneath the falls or feel their spray. The paved part of the trail becomes hard packed or loose red dirt and sand close to the falls, which are behind a metal railing.

After the falls there is a short, steeper climb up stairs to the Lower Emerald Pool, which is named for its deep green color due to algae on the rocks at the bottom of the pool. Lower Emerald Pool and the falls are fed from both Heaps and Behunin Canyons. Expect to see pond-skittering insects skimming the spring-fed ponds. Note that visitors are no longer allowed to enter the pools.

There are offshoot paths on the right side as you make your way to the pools, and on the left when you head back, that hikers use to cool off in the river below. Follow the trail back the Zion Lodge and trailhead. The sandstone continues to amaze as it towers over you from the opposite direction.

HIKE EXTENSION: This hike can be extended 2.0 miles to continue to the middle pool, and 2.5 miles to the upper pool. The hike rating changes to Wanderer because

There is another chance for a bridge view as the Lower Emerald Pools Trail heads back to the trailhead.

of the slippery rocks, steeper terrain, and the elevation gain. Another option is to branch of on the Kayenta Trail at the Lower Emerald Pool and return to the Zion Lodge via the Grotto Trail. Or take the shuttle once you reach the Grotto shuttle stop. The Kayenta Trail is not paved and requires more technical hiking.

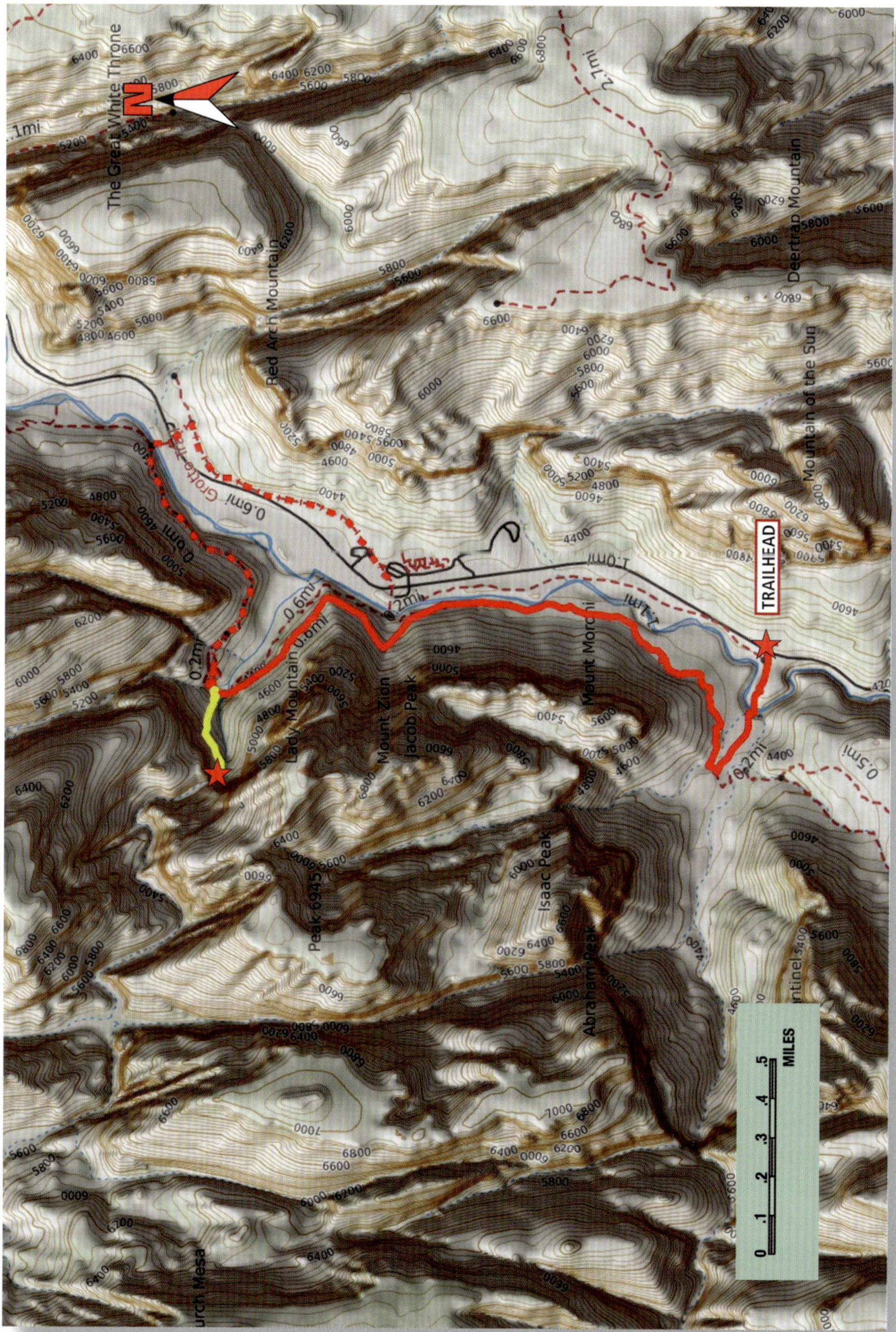

LOWER EMERALD POOLS TRAIL

Rank 2

36. Riverside Walk Trail

RATING	Searcher, due to easy terrain
ROUND TRIP DISTANCE	2 miles out and back
ROUND-TRIP TIME	1–1.5 hours
ELEVATION CHANGE	60 feet (from 4,437 to 4,497 feet)
MAP	Trails Illustrated Zion
NEAREST LANDMARK	Temple of Sinawava
FEES	Private vehicle $30; Zion annual pass; National Parks pass
RESTROOMS	Full restrooms, water access, and showers
DOGS	Not allowed
OPERATING HOURS	24 hours

COMMENT: Previously known as the Gateway to the Narrows, this path is stroller and wheelchair friendly. Some spots on the paved wide path may be sandy due to frequent winds that blow through the canyon. Use the public transportation system (available to the last stop at the Temple of Sinawava). The Riverside Walk is the most popular hike in Zion with an estimated 2,500 to 3,000 visitors a day in peak months. Expect larger crowds as the day goes on and a wait for shuttles. The closer to dusk you are on this hike, the more likely it is to see animals, including wild turkeys and people-friendly squirrels. Resist the urge to feed them no matter how cute they are! This hike is best in late spring through fall. Fall brings amazing colors from Fremont cottonwoods that shade the hike. This hike is a mix of wetland and forest.

Hanging gardens and weeping walls adorn the canyon walls while bubbling water pools line both sides of the trail. Columbine, moss, and other plant life cascade, down the canyon walls. Water flows through holes in the massive rock faces.

GETTING THERE: From Salt Lake City (307 miles) and Cedar City, Utah, (57 miles) take Interstate 15 south. Take Exit 27 and turn left on State Route 17 south for six miles. Make a left on Route 9 east in La Verkin. Continue on Route 9 for twenty miles into Zion National Park.

From Las Vegas, Nevada, (163 miles), Mesquite, Nevada, (80 miles), and Saint George, Utah, (40 miles) take I-15 north. Take Exit 16 and turn right on State Route 9 east. Continue on Route 9 east through La Verkin and into Zion National Park.

With limited parking in the park, free shuttle services run from February through November, depending on weather. No private vehicles are allowed into

The Riverside Walk Trail is also known as the Gateway to the Narrows. *Photo: Heather Sims*

Zion from April through October unless you have a red permit because you are staying at the Zion Lodge.

THE ROUTE: After filling up your water bottle at the water filling station, follow the signs from the trailhead parking lot on the left side for Riverside Walk. The path is fairly flat as it meanders through the shade of the numerous cottonwood trees. The Virgin River, one of the last undammed rivers in the West, flows on the left, while massive rock formations rise on the right.

The paved trail rolls along without any real notice of elevation change as it narrows. With so much to look at, the mile to the beginning of the Narrows goes by quickly. The 2,000-foot cliff walls make you feel even smaller as they tower over you. As you spend more time on the Riverside Walk, you can truly begin to understand why Zion's earliest visitors considered this place so sacred.

Don't skip the interpretive signs along the path explaining the unique conditions that allow so many micro and riparian habitats. Learn about the Zion Rock snail, which is only found in the Narrows. Keep your ears open for the sounds of canyon tree frogs.

Several benches along the trail offer perfect spots to take in the beauty of the area. While there are access points along the trail to dip the feet in the river, don't miss the opportunity to wade in the Narrows where the Riverside Walk Trail ends. If you want to get away from the crowds, there is a sand and dirt path that walks the length of the river.

The sandy start of the Narrows offers a great picture taking opportunity. Depending on the water levels, kids may enjoy sand and water play before returning back the way you came. As you wait for the shuttle post-hike, don't forget to look across the parking lot to see the Red Pulpit on the other side of the road.

HISTORY IN HIKING

Called the Holy Desert, Zion National Park was originally named Mukuntuweap, meaning "straight canyon" in Paiute, by John Wesley Powell in 1892. Over 10 years later, President William Howard Taft signed a proclamation in 1909 creating Mukuntuweap National Monument to protect the area. Mormon settlers, who called the area home, referred to the area as Zion, based on their concept of heaven and the hill in Jerusalem where the City of David sits. The newly created National Park Service changed the name to Zion in 1918. Historian Hal Rothman concluded that the name change was based on the idea that an Indian or Spanish name that was difficult to pronounce could prevent people from visiting. On November 19, 1919, Congress established Zion as a national park. In 1956, the Kolob section of the park was officially added.

In 1916, Ogden Utah Methodist Minister Frederick Vining Fisher toured the park, naming many of the geological features with names that are still used today. The sandstone peaks known as the Court of Patriarchs were named for Abraham, Isaac, and Jacob, all patriarchs found in the Old Testament.

Standing over 2,000 feet high, the Great White Throne (once referred to as the Temple of Aeolus) was also named by Fisher. He said, "Never have I seen such a sight before. It is by all odds America's masterpiece. Boys, I have looked for this mountain all my life but I never expected to find it in this world. This mountain is the Great White Throne." The 5.0-mile Angels Landing hike there is so steep at the top that Fisher proclaimed no one but an angel could land on the top; hence the hike's name.

Other landmarks within the park bearing religious names include the Temple of Sinawava, the Altar of Sacrifice, and the Watchman, which guards the southern entrance. Powell named the East and West Temples. After a visit in 1922, Stephen Johnson named the mountain west of Angel's Landing Cathedral Mountain. Other biblical references in the park include resurrection moss, which is moss that can turn from a dark brown/black back to green with just a few drops of water.

RIVERSIDE WALK TRAIL

The sun sets in Bryce Canyon.

Bryce Canyon National Park

Named a national park February 25th, 1928, Bryce Canyon National Park has the largest concentration of hoodoos on the Earth. It is named after Mormon pioneer Ebenezer Bryce who had a homestead in the area in the 1850s. Despite the name, it is actually a series of bowls (amphitheaters). The elevation at the rim varies from 8,000 to 9,000 feet. It is estimated that 1.5 million people visit Bryce Canyon National Park every year. Maybe you will be one of the lucky visitors that see a Utah Prairie Dog in the only national park where prairie dogs exist.

Bryce Canyon National Park has the largest concentration of hoodoos on the Earth.

Rank 1

37. Mossy Cave Trail

RATING	Experimenter, due to easy terrain and shorter length
ROUND TRIP DISTANCE	1 mile plus (varies if you hike up to Turret Arch)
ROUND-TRIP TIME	1 hour
ELEVATION CHANGE	93 feet (from 6835 to 6926 feet) (varies if you hike up to Turret Arch)
MAP	Trails Illustrated Bryce Canyon
NEAREST LANDMARK	Turret Arch, Mossy Cave
FEES	None
RESTROOMS	Pit toilets
DOGS	Not allowed
OPERATING HOURS	24 hours

COMMENT: This hike is a part of the "I hiked the Hoodos" program, which challenges visitors to Bryce Canyon to hike at least 3.0 miles of specially marked trails. Program participants take rubbings of the survey markers or pictures of themselves at the markers and obtain a special reward from the visitor center.

The trail can be slippery and icy in winter. Sections can also be slippery during the summer due to recent weather and the flow level of the falls. This hike is considered forest biome, but the hoodoos make it seem more like a desert biome hike.

There is virtually no shade on this trail after the sun rises over the hoodoos, despite the tall pines towering above. This trail offers easy access for seeing hoodoos. For hoodoo viewing, it's a good alternative to hiking all the way down the canyon on the Queen's Garden or Navajo Loop Trails inside Bryce Canyon National Park. The dolomite hoodoos on this trail are stronger than the traditional limestone hoodoos, but all will eventually crumble due to erosion. Be grateful to experience them before Mother Nature runs its course.

GETTING THERE: The Mossy Cave Trailhead is located outside of Bryce Canyon National Monument on Highway 12. Park about 4.0 miles east of the Hwy 12 and Hwy 63 junction off of HWY-12. It is just over 3.0 miles west of Tropic. Look for a pullout on the west side of the road where you will find the trailhead parking lot and bathrooms. There are 15 to 20 parking spots that tend to fill up early, especially in the heart of visitor season-summer.

MOSSY CAVE TRAIL

The falls on the Mossy Cave Trail.

THE ROUTE: From the parking lot, follow the wide and easy trail straight up to the cave and falls. As you gain elevation, don't miss the chance to observe the hoodoos above you. Water flows on the right and can be heard from the parking lot. It's easy to get to the water's edge to cool off on hot days.

At around 0.1 mile you will cross the first of two bridges. Be sure to look up as you can get a peak at Turret Arch among the trees. The trail to the arch may be closed for restoration. The water is now on the left, and you may spot ducks here. At 0.25 mile, you will cross a second bridge, and the trail begins to climb again. Right after the crossing, there is a nondescript trail on the right that leads to the right side of the falls. If you continue up the hill, you will catch a good view of the falls from the left.

The cutoff for the falls and Mossy Cave is at 0.3 mile. If you are participating in the Hoodoo program, find the spot to make your rubbing. Head left and up the hill to the cave. In the winter months, giant icicles hang from the cave's overhang. Because the cave gets very little sun, the icicles can sometimes last until June. Visitors may even see a mix of moss and icicles. Note that you cannot go into the cave, so moss and icicle viewing must be done from a distance. This is a shelter cave with the grotto shaped by an underground stream.

By going right (north) a short distance, the trail will lead you to a waterfall. The many side/social trails may be tempting, but stay on the main path to protect the area. The small waterfall runs over a lip of dolomite and limestone. It typically flows between late spring and October. Be sure to stop and take in the views from every angle as well as the soothing sounds of trickling water, the reds and oranges of the hoodoos, and the scent of pine trees. This trail delights the senses in many ways. Return the way you came after exploring the area.

Rank 4

38. Queen's Garden to Navajo Loop Trail

RATING	Wanderer, due to length and elevation changes
ROUND TRIP DISTANCE	2.9 mile loop
ROUND-TRIP TIME	2–3 hours
ELEVATION CHANGE	8,015 feet at Sunrise Point; 7,400 feet low point
MAP	Trails Illustrated Bryce Canyon
NEAREST LANDMARK	Sunrise Point
FEES	Private vehicle $30; Bryce Canyon annual pass; National Parks pass
RESTROOMS	Restrooms and drinking water are available May through October at the Bryce Canyon General Store
DOGS	Not allowed
OPERATING HOURS	24 hours

COMMENT: Four major rock formations can be seen from this loop, including the Queen's Garden, Queen Elizabeth, Thor's Hammer, and Gulliver's Castle. Look east to see the Navajo Mountains. This hike is a part of the "Hike the Hoodoos" program at Bryce National Park, which challenges visitors to Bryce Canyon to hike at least 3.0 miles of specially marked trails. Participants take rubbings of the survey markers or pictures of themselves at the markers and obtain a special reward from the visitor center. The Queen's Garden to Navajo Loop passes through the forest biome but has hints of desert biome throughout.

This route is a good alternative to the steeper Wall Street Trail. There are places on the Navajo Loop where the terrain is steep, but the trail is wide. March through November is the best time to hike this trail. Without many trees, most of the hike has little shade, and snow on the trail tends to melt fast. Sage lizards and great horned lizards are frequent visitors on the trail. The trail tends to get busier as the day goes on.

GETTING THERE: From Interstate 15 south, take Exit 95/UT 20 and travel east. UT 20 becomes US 89 and later turns into UT 12. Continue east on UT 12 to UT 63. Head south on UT 63 to Bryce Canyon National Park.

Thor's Hammer is one highlight of the Queen's Garden Trail.

From I-15 north, take Exit 16/UT 9. Head east on UT 9 through Zion National Park to US 89. Take US 89 north to UT 12. Turn east on UT 12 and continue to UT 63. Follow UT 63 south to Bryce Canyon National Park.

The shuttle system runs to and from this trailhead. The parking lot at the trailhead fills up quickly, so the shuttle is a better choice.

THE ROUTE: The Queen's Garden Trailhead begins on the south side of Sunrise Point, east of Bryce Lodge. The Queens Garden Trail is the easiest way to descend to the bottom of the canyon. Visitor center signs proclaim that this is the best 3.0-mile hike in the United States. This loop hike brings you up close and personal with the hoodoos you can see from above on the Rim Trail.

From the shuttle stop at Sunrise Point, continue on the paved trail (the Rim Trail) for 0.1 mile. At the rim, look for the Queens Garden sign and follow the trail to Sunrise Point, where a sign points down to the descent into the canyon. Use caution here because there are steep spots as you head down with drop offs on each side. Keep children closer to the middle of the trail because the edges of the trail can be loose.

At 0.5 mile, there is a sign for Queen's Garden and a horse trail. Head right to continue on the Queen's Garden Trail headed toward the Navajo Loop. Less than a minute later, you will reach a fork. Make a hard right to stay on the trail.

QUEEN'S GARDEN TO NAVAJO LOOP TRAIL

Just past the fork, you will walk through a man-made tunnel into the Queen's Garden. Walk past formations that resemble royalty as you continue through two more tunnels. Just after the third tunnel a short trail on the right leads to the Queen Victoria hoodoo. People believe that the forms at the base resemble statues of the monarch sitting on her throne in London overlooking her garden. A man-made divide helps hikers pass through two hoodoos as the trail continues.

Heading south toward the Navajo Loop Trail junction, there is a bench under a rock overhang serves as a perfect spot for taking a drink and snack break. Test your echo while you are here. The pines on both sides offer some of the little bit of shade on the trail in this area.

At 0.8 mile, the Queen's Garden Trail hits the junction with the Navajo Loop. Continue on the Navajo Loop. Before you begin the switchbacks, a short trail on the right leads to the Two Bridges viewing point. The 10 or so switchbacks to the top of the trailhead and Sunset Point are where the most elevation gain occurs (approximately 500 feet). The switchbacks are walkable for children, but they may need some breaks as you head out of the hoodoos. As you climb the switchbacks, Thor's Hammer comes into view. The trail ends at the overlook for Sunset Point.

The Hoodoos bring a magical feel to the Queen's Garden Trail.

Rank 1

39. The Rim Trail

RATING	Experimenter, due to fairly flat, paved, and wide trail
ROUND TRIP DISTANCE	1.0-mile round-trip from Sunset Point to Sunrise Point; 11.0 miles round-trip if you hike the full trail
ROUND-TRIP TIME	30 minutes
ELEVATION CHANGE	24 feet (from 8000 feet to 8024 feet from Sunset Point to Sunrise Point)
MAP	Trails Illustrated Bryce Canyon
NEAREST LANDMARK	Sunset Point or Sunrise Point
FEES	Private vehicle $30; Bryce Canyon annual pass; National Parks pass
RESTROOMS	Vault toilets at Sunset Point
DOGS	Must be leashed and only allowed between Sunset Point and Sunrise Point
OPERATING HOURS	24 hours

COMMENT: This trail is paved between Sunset Point and Sunrise Point, making it ADA accessible and a good beginner hike for little ones. Both strollers and wheelchairs can navigate this trail. It follows the outer rim of Bryce Canyon, also known as the eastern rim of the Paunsaugunt Plateau, and offers fantastic scenery in a short amount of distance. You may even see a prairie dog or two as Bryce Canyon has the largest population of prairie dogs in the nation. Because of its higher elevation, mornings and evenings can be quite cool. The Rim Trail passes through the forest biome.

This mostly flat trail is the most popular trail in the park because of the minimal elevation gain and the views of many area landmarks. This trail is great to visit during sunrise, sunset, and at night, for amazing stargazing and night photography. You might encounter bats while viewing the Milky Way. This is also a popular hike if visiting the park in the winter months, Expect to see crowds on this trail at all times of the day. If you want serenity, the morning hours are usually the most quiet. There is also a dirt trail along the canyon rim, but it runs quite close to the canyon edge. The paved trail is definitely the better choice for little ones getting their hiking legs.

GETTING THERE: From Interstate 15 south, take Exit 95/UT 20 and travel east. UT 20 becomes US 89 and later turns into UT 12. Head east on UT 12 to UT 63. Head south on UT 63 to Bryce Canyon National Park.

Bryce Canyon as seen from the Rim Trail.

From I-15 north, take Exit 16/UT 9. Head east on UT 9 through Zion National Park until you reach US 89. Take US 89 north to UT 12. Turn east on UT 12 and continue to UT 63. Follow UT 63 south to Bryce Canyon National Park.

The visitor center is 1.0 mile inside the park. You can start this hike from the shuttle stop at either Sunrise Point or Sunset Point. There is a parking lot at both the Sunset Point and Sunrise Point Trailheads. The Sunset Point Trailhead is the busiest in the park because of its proximity to so many trailheads, and it tends to fill up early every morning.

THE ROUTE: From Sunrise Point just east of the Bryce Canyon Lodge, the paved trail heads south toward Sunset Point. As you head south, keep an eye out for Bristlecone Point, the Bryce Amphitheater, and the Queens Garden. The trail follows the rim of the canyon from point to point. As you look across the landscape you can spot other popular Bryce Canyon trails, including the Queens Garden Trail and the Navajo Loop. On clear days, you can see the Escalante Mountains by looking east.

The trail is smooth pavement making it easy for young hikers. Wooden benches along the path provide perfect spots to stop and take it all in. Chipmunks scurry across the path and the bright blue Steller's Jays can be seen fluttering from tree to tree. This is a hike where you can take your time marveling at the largest concentration of hoodoos on the Earth. You can see the marvels of what weather and erosion can do to a landscape over time. At one time the now exposed roots of the more than a hundred year old limber pines that line the trail were once under ground.

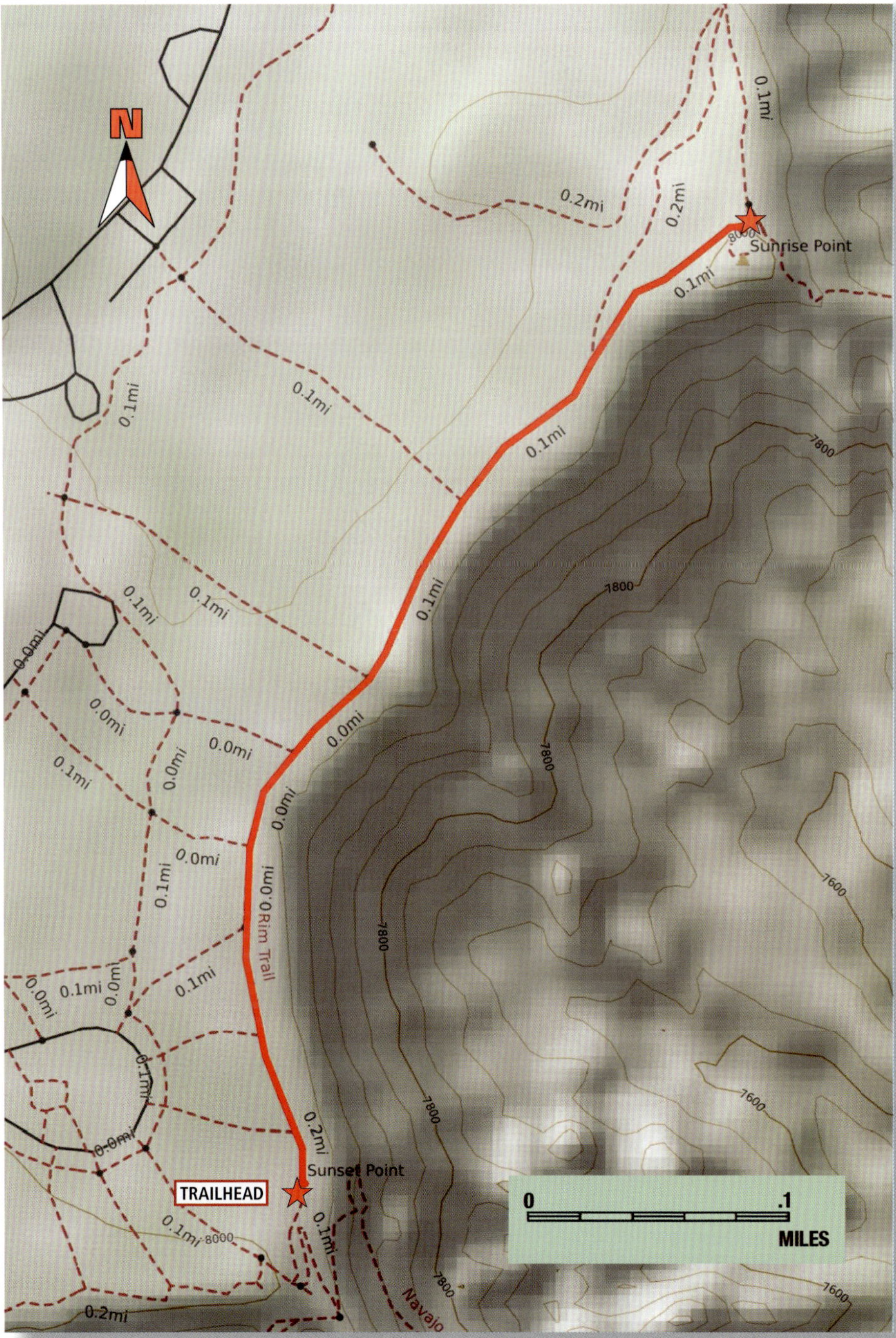

THE RIM TRAIL

Enjoy the area they refer to as the "Silent City," as it silently erodes away, a predicted two to four feet per century. Head back the way you came keeping an eye out for Thor's Hammer and the top of the Wall Street slot canyon as you look into the amphitheater.

HIKE EXTENSION: From Fairyland Point to Bryce Point, the Rim Trail is a total of 5.0 miles each way. Since this is an out and back hike, you can add as much mileage on it as you want to extend your hike. Be aware that the hike is not ADA accessible or stroller friendly beyond the path between Sunrise Point and Sunset Point. Dogs are not allowed beyond those points either. The trail rating becomes an Adventurer rated trail due to the length.

On the Way Home

THE LODGE AT BRYCE CANYON

Don't miss the opportunity to catch a meal at the Bryce Canyon Lodge Restaurant. Note that the restaurant is typically not open from November to the end of March. Dining is first come, first served. The restaurant is also located at a shuttle stop.

Open since 1925, the lodge serves breakfast, lunch, and dinner. You can choose from a breakfast buffet or menu items including the Grand Staircase Breakfast Burrito and the Fairland French Toast. Lunch is a large buffet with hot and cold dishes including the lodge's famous elk chili. The menu includes game meats and vegetarian dishes. The wines and beers are Utah-based. Kids menu items include traditional favorites. Menu items are locally sourced, as much as possible, and focus on healthy dining.

Rustic decor includes historical photos of the lodge and Bryce Canyon National Park. Staff is available for tips on hikes and other activities in the park. A gift shop features Bryce Canyon National Park merchandise, local artwork, and sundries including snacks and beverages. There is also a coffee shop and pizza restaurant in the lodge. Don't forget those National Parks stamp books, as the lodge is a historical site.

The Lodge at Bryce Canyon
Bryce Canyon National Park
Bryce, Utah 84764
(435) 834-8700
www.brycecanyonforever.com/dining
Prices: $6 and up
Hours: Breakfast 7 a.m. to 10 a.m.; lunch 11:30 a.m. to 3 p.m; dinner 5 p.m. to 10 p.m.

Kodachrome Basin State Park

Kodachrome Basin State Park is a unique desert biome landscape with spires of different heights. It is believed that the area was once similar to Yellowstone National Park, with thermal pools and hot springs. These were covered by sand that over time eroded and weathered to become the 67 monolithic spires found throughout the park. It was established as a state park in 1962 and got its name from the National Geographic Society based on Kodachrome film.

Sixty seven monolithic spires can be found throughout Kodachrome Basin State Park.

Rank 2

40. Grand Parade Trail

RATING	Searcher, due to fairly flat terrain but longer distance than a beginner hike
ROUND TRIP DISTANCE	2.0-mile loop, including box canyons
ROUND-TRIP TIME	1 hour, plus time to explore box canyons
ELEVATION CHANGE	31 feet (from 5,795 to 5,850 feet)
MAP	Trails Illustrated Grand Staircase, Paunsaugunt Plateau
NEAREST LANDMARK	Kodachrome Basin State Park
FEES	$8 per vehicle; Utah State Parks pass
RESTROOMS	None
DOGS	Must be leashed
OPERATING HOURS	6 a.m to 10 p.m., year-round

COMMENT: This trail is open to hikers, cyclists, and horses, but only foot traffic is allowed in the box canyons. After rain or snow, the trail can be quite muddy. The wash areas tend to freeze in the winter, making the trail slippery in spots. With the lack of shade, this hike is best in spring and fall or early summer mornings. Wildflowers bloom in late spring.

The trail is mostly exposed, but there are sections where the Utah juniper and pinyon pines offer pockets of shade. Lizards scurry amongst the Indian paintbrush and other desert vegetation. Birds of prey may circle over the box canyons searching for their next meal.

GETTING THERE: From UT 12 turn south onto Cottonwood Canyon Rd./Kodachrome Basin 9, the Cottonwood Canyon Scenic Backway. The paved road runs through Cannonville. Continue straight at the Skutumpah Rd. junction at 3.0 miles. At 7.5 miles, turn left to stay on the pavement to the entrance of Kodachrome Basin State Park. From the entrance, continue north on the main park road for 0.6 mile. The signed parking area for the Grand Parade and Panorama Point Trails is on the right. The parking lot fits about 15 cars, depending on the number of RV's or other larger vehicles.

THE ROUTE: This red sand trail begins from the parking lot for the Grand Parade Trail and Panorama Trail and travels along the floor of Kodachrome Basin. The trail is fairly wide open and obstacle free. It heads east from the parking lot toward the box canyons.

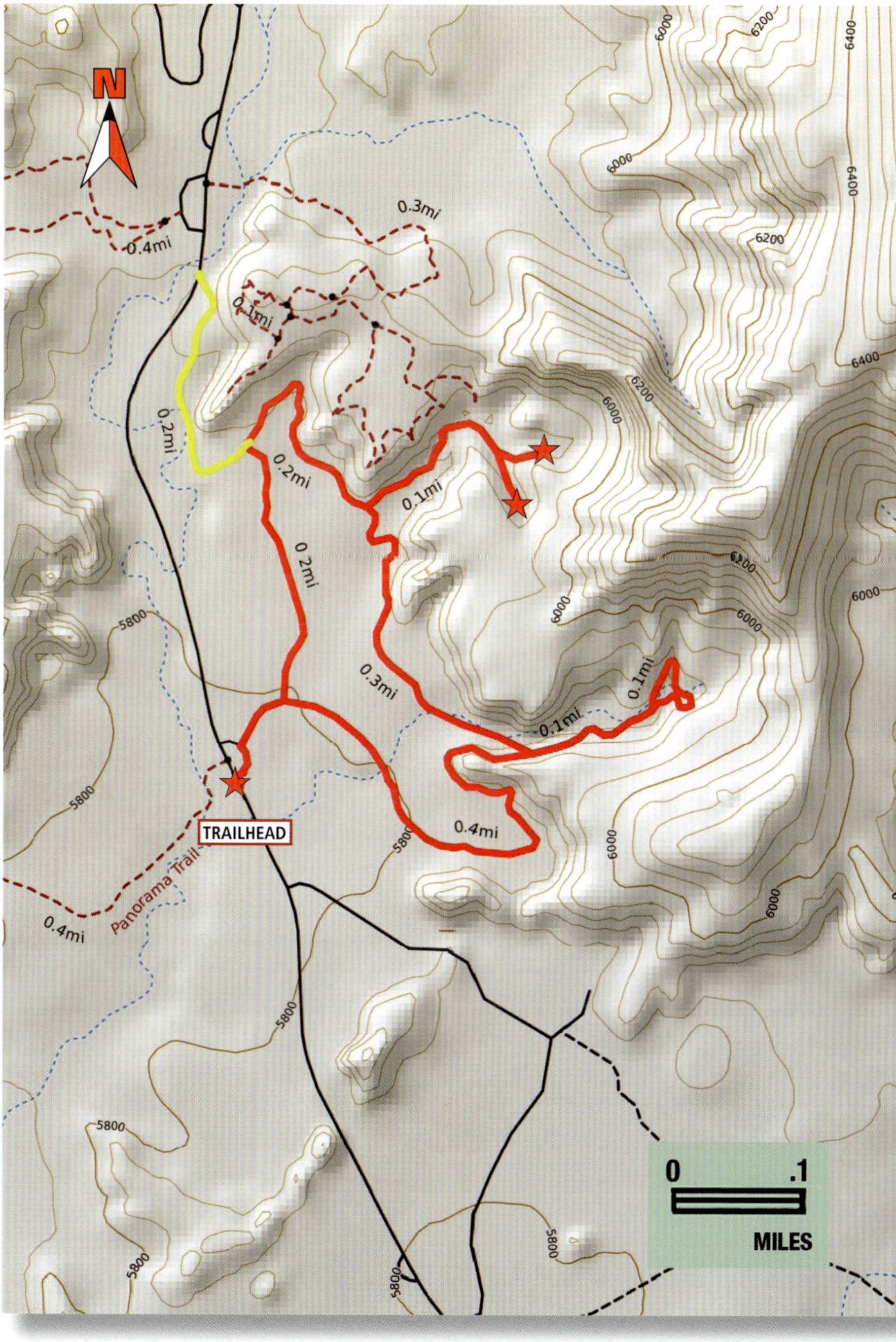

GRAND PARADE TRAIL

A spire along the Grand Parade Trail in Kodachrome Basin State Park.

Less than 0.2 mile from the parking lot, turn right at a fork to follow the trail counterclockwise. Brown arrows and trail markers help keep hikers, bikers, and horseback riders on the right path. The trail leads down into a wash that may contain water. The trail passes sand pipes of many sizes as it makes its way closer to the red cliffs symbolic of Entrada.

Be careful to stay on the path to not disturb the fragile cryptobiotic soil surrounding the trail, especially near the sand pipes, including Dinosaur Spire, which is one of the most popular named features in the park. The pipes and other rock features are very delicate, so enjoy them from a distance. The trail offers numerous opportunities for taking photos.

At about a 0.5 mile, there is a spur trail to the first box canyon that heads right. There is also a brown sign on the left designating the trail. The terrain is uneven here, so small adventurers may need some help with navigating. The potential for water crossings is high in the box canyons, and there is always a risk of flooding. At the park entrance, ask the rangers about the risk of flooding, and explore only if you know there is no potential risk.

There are no designated paths in the box canyons. You can follow other footprints to minimize the impact on the soil. At 1.0 mile, the second box canyon is on the right. Here, the spur trail for the canyon crosses a ravine that may hold water and the designated trail ends again. Follow footprints again to explore the second canyon and return to the main loop trail. The trail wanders in and out of the wash before reaching a fork at 1.5 miles. Head left at the fork and continue following the path.

As you head around the loop, you may be able to see The Red Stone Cabins and Store on the right. A rock geyser towering over 50 feet into the air highlights the end of your grand parade around the floor of Kodachrome Basin. At the trail junction around 1.8 miles, head left to return to the parking lot.

41. Panorama Point Trail

RATING	Seeker, due to length and some uneven surfaces
ROUND TRIP DISTANCE	3.0 miles with 6.0-mile option
ROUND-TRIP TIME	1.5–2 hours
ELEVATION CHANGE	153 feet (from 5,683 to 5,836 feet)
MAP	Trails Illustrated Grand Staircase, Paunsaugunt Plateau
NEAREST LANDMARK	Kodachrome Basin State Park
FEES	$8 per vehicle; Utah State Parks annual pass
RESTROOMS	None
DOGS	Must be leashed
OPERATING HOURS	6 a.m to 10 p.m., year-round

COMMENT: The National Geographic Society contacted the Kodak Company in 1949 for permission to name the park Kodachrome Basin State Park, which tells you something about its splendor. This is a multi-use trail with mountain bikers, hikers, and even stagecoach tours. Expect to see bikes on the entire route, but the stagecoach tours only travel the first mile. There is no shade on this hike, so it is best hiked in the early morning or evening in the summer months. The best times to hike here are April through June and September through November. After rain and snow, the trail can be quite muddy, and the wash areas tend to freeze in the winter making the trail slippery in spots.

Most wildlife is nocturnal, so you might only see lizards and birds. Mountain lions, mule deer, rattlesnakes, and kangaroo rats are common in the park. Ravens, golden eagles, and two types of jays are also park dwellers. An occasional pinyon pine or Utah juniper dot the landscape, but do not provide any shade. The chimneys and spires vary in color from reddish to white. The pink crags in the distance provide a stunning backdrop to Panorama Point. The towering red walls take on the look of fire as the sun begins to lower behind the horizon.

GETTING THERE: From UT 12 turn south onto Cottonwood Canyon Rd./Kodachrome Basin 9, the Cottonwood Canyon Scenic Backway. The paved road runs through Cannonville. Continue straight at the Skutumpah Rd. junction at 3.0 miles. At 7.5 miles turn left to stay on the pavement to the entrance of Kodachrome Basin State Park. From the entrance, continue north on the main park road for 0.6 mile. The signed parking area for the Grand Parade and Panorama Point Trails is on the

Panorama Point offers incredible views of Kodachrome Basin State Park and the surrounding area.

right. The parking lot can fit about 15 cars depending on the amount of RV's and other larger vehicles.

THE ROUTE: The trail to Panorama Point is fairly flat but has some loose sandy terrain. Recent rain may make the trail surface a bit unstable and uneven. Generally, it is easier to hike in the middle of the trail where the sand is more packed down. Depending on recent weather, there may be a few easy water crossings.

The trailhead begins on west side of the parking lot after you cross over the main park road. There is no shade on this trail, so begin your hike with plenty of water. Watch for horses and bikers.

From the start, you can see the white and reddish spires that make this trail and state park unique. They depict the geologic history of the Colorado Plateau in the layers of rock from the Carmel Foundation on the bottom to the Tropic Shale at the top. As the trail heads a bit north, you will walk through a ravine that may contain water. If the ravine is dry, your shoes will begin to collect red sand. The trail bends west over the red sand terrain. Be on the lookout on the right for the Fred Flintstone Spire.

At 0.3 mile there is a trail junction. If you head right, you will begin the full loop around the Panorama Trail, or continue left to Panorama Point. This part of the trail has distant views all around but lacks up-close features.

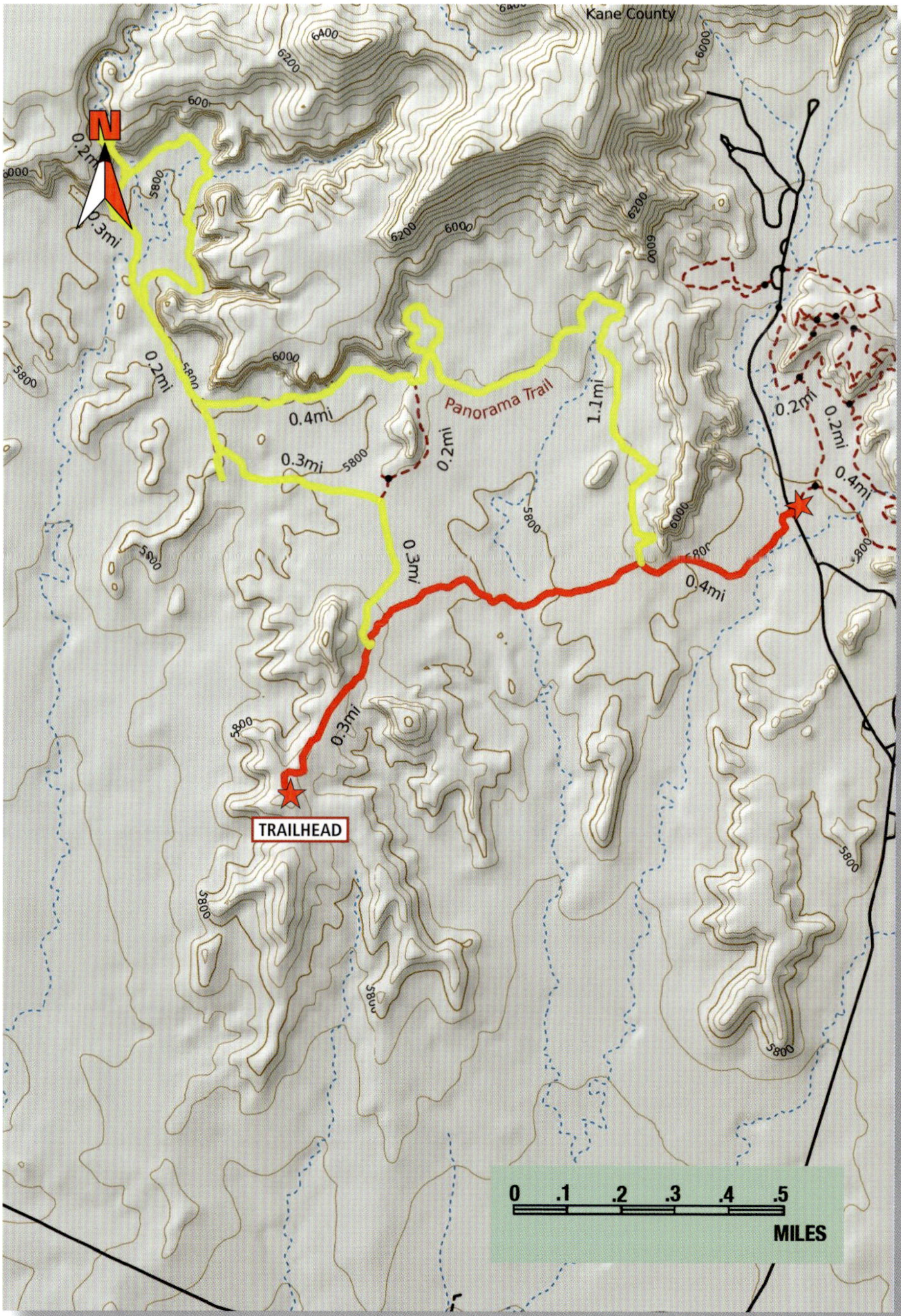

PANORAMA POINT TRAIL

The trail remains pretty flat with an occasional small rise as you walk toward the Panorama Point junction at 0.9 mile. If you head right, the trail completes the full 6.0-mile route. Head left at the wooden sign that says Panorama Point. This is the start of the most difficult part of the hike, with steep loose terrain and little mounds. Small hikers may need a steady hand to help them up and down. Butt sliding is encouraged on the way down. You earn your view here.

Once you reach the high point on the trail, look west for the white and pink cliffs of Bryce Canyon. To the south is Grand Staircase-Escalante National Monument. Don't miss the opportunity to get a photo featuring the wooden Panorama Point sign in the background. What a view for a snack break or even a meal!

After enjoying the view, begin your descent to the main trail. This is a great place for kiddos to get some windmill arms going as they run down the hills. When you hit the junction for the point, head right and follow the trail back to the trailhead.

TRAIL EXTENSION: This can be turned into an almost 6.0-mile hike that visits many park jewels. The extension will likely take up most of the day with all of its sites, including the Secret Cave and the Hat Shop. The recommended route for the full loop is counter-clockwise. The trail rating changes to Adventurer now due to length.

Extending your hike to six miles on the Panorama Point Trail allows you to see interesting features including the Hat Shop.

Rank 1 Rank 3

42. Shakespeare Arch/ Sentinel Trail

RATING	To Arch, Experimenter, due to length and terrain; full loop including Sentinel Spire, Seeker, due to terrain change
ROUND TRIP DISTANCE	1.0 mile out and back to Shakespeare Arch, or 1.7-mile loop
ROUND-TRIP TIME	45 minutes to 1.5 hours
ELEVATION CHANGE	260 feet (from 5,850 to 6,110 feet)
MAP	Trails Illustrated Grand Staircase, Paunsaugunt Plateau
NEAREST LANDMARK	Kodachrome Basin State Park
FEES	$8 per vehicle; Utah State Parks annual pass
RESTROOMS	None
DOGS	Must be leashed
OPERATING HOURS	6 a.m to 10 p.m., year-round

COMMENT: This wide red sand trail climbs up and down with little overall elevation change. It is relatively free from rocks, making it popular with trail runners. Brown trail signs make the trail easy to follow. Make sure to not disturb the fragile cryptobiotic soil surrounding the trail. The exposed trail is known for lizards as well as rattlesnakes. Utah juniper and pinyon pines line the trail as well as rabbit brush and Mormon tea. Ravens, eagles, and other raptors may circle above the arch and pipes in search of a kangaroo rat or jackrabbit for their next meal. Many of the animals in the park are nocturnal.

There is no shade on this hike, so go in early morning or evening in the summer months. The best times to visit are April through June and September through November. After rain and snow, the trail can be quite muddy, and the wash areas tend to freeze in the winter, making the trail slippery in spots. There are two options for this trail: a 1.0-mile easy round trip out and back to the arch, or a 1.7 mile loop with more difficult terrain. This is a desert biome hike.

GETTING THERE: From UT 12 turn south onto Cottonwood Canyon Rd./Kodachrome Basin 9, the Cottonwood Canyon Scenic Backway. The paved road runs through Cannonville. Continue straight at the Skutumpah Rd. junction at 3.0 miles. At 7.5 miles, turn left to stay on the pavement to the entrance of Kodachrome Basin State Park. From the entrance, turn right onto the gravel road shortly after leaving the visitor center. Follow the gravel road for approximately 0.7 mile. Turn right at the sign for Shakespeare Arch. It is another 0.7 mile to the trailhead. The trail may be rutted, especially after rain. In most cases, you do not need a four-wheel-drive vehicle to navigate. The parking lot fits approximately eight cars.

THE ROUTE: The secluded trail begins to the south/southwest of the parking lot. The suggested direction for the trail is counterclockwise. The trail is wide open and travels up and down through some washes that may contain water. You may have to open and close a fence/cattle gate. It is easy to unhook the chain if needed. An overlook on the right is worth a stop at around the 0.25-mile mark. It is a short spur trail designated by a brown sign showing a camera. The overlook provides views of Kodachrome Basin and Grand Staircase. After stopping there, continue on the main trail to Shakespeare Arch at 0.4 mile, which is denoted by a brown Bureau of Land Management sign. Shakespeare Arch is the only natural arch in the park. It remained a secret until a ranger searching for a coyote den discovered it in 1976. If you visit under cloud cover, the arch blends in very well with the Entrada layers that surround it, making it hard to see.

You can turn around at the arch or continue to complete the full 1.7-mile loop. If you decide to take the slickrock cutoff trail to complete the loop, it becomes more strenuous with a steep pitch. If you continue, the trail leads behind both Shakespeare Arch and Sentinel Spire and continues up and down. It gets tight in some places making it a bit difficult if you're wearing a hiking backpack. Evening hours offer fun shadow play along the trail.

Continue counterclockwise and just around the corner from Shakespeare Arch, you will see the Sentinel Spire, a white and khaki colored sedimentary pipe. If you have novice hikers or little ones in your group, extra time and caution may be necessary here as the terrain becomes uneven due to erosion. You may notice a spot where a future arch might be forming on the left side.

The trails in Kodachrome Basin are sandy.

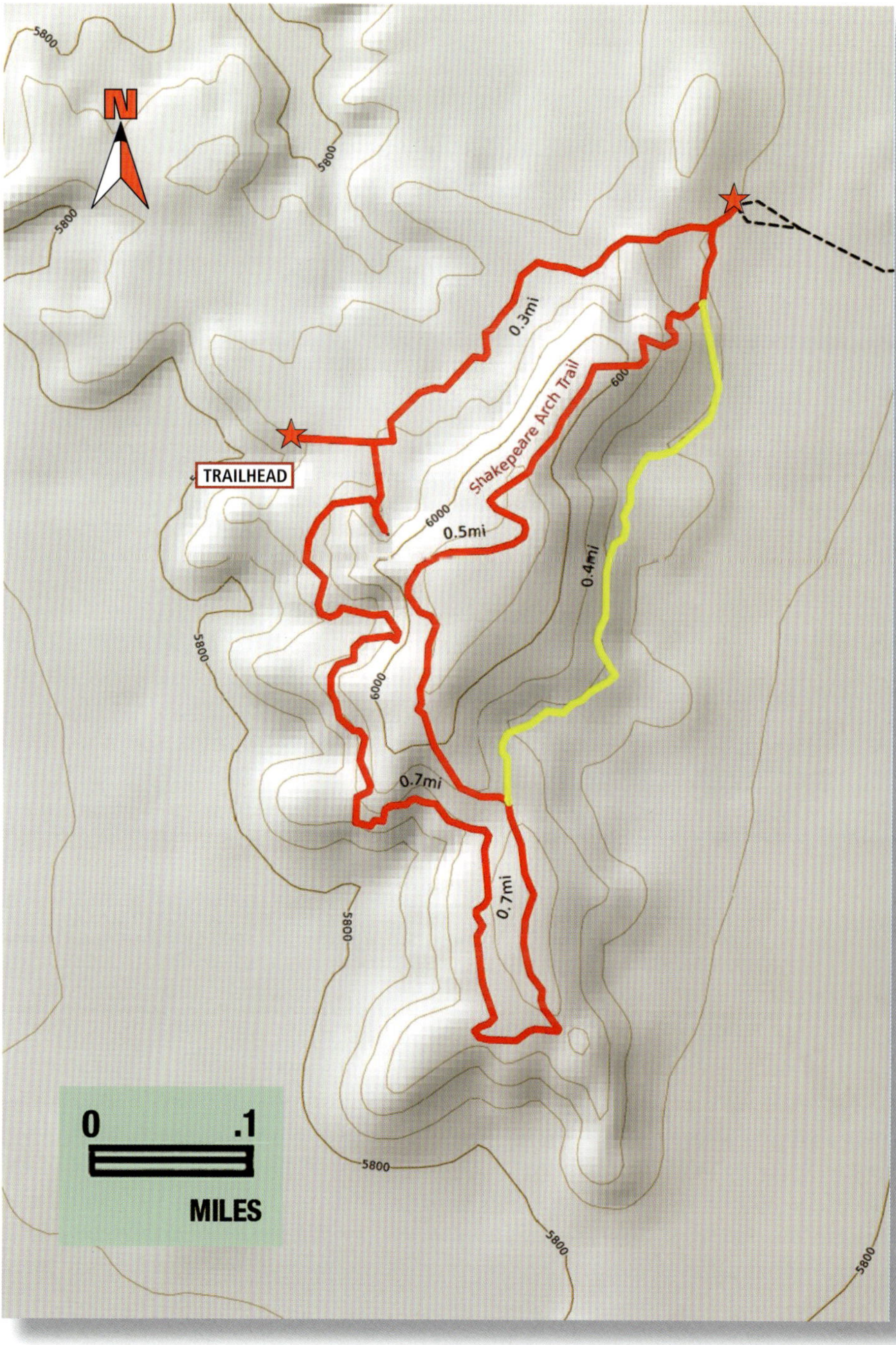

SHAKESPEARE ARCH/SENTINEL TRAIL

Shakespeare Arch amongst the Entrada Sandstone.

The trail widens again, leaving the up-close views of Entrada sandstone. The overlook just shy of the 1.0-mile mark offers almost 360-degree views. Parts of the Grand Staircase and white streaks of gypsum really stand out against the red of the sandstone.

At approximately 1.0 mile, there is a brown sign indicating the slickrock cutoff trail junction. Head left for the slickrock cut off or straight for the loop. The slick-rock route is quite an adventure. Little hikers may need a butt boost to get started. Steps help navigate up and over the slope. The trail takes you above the Sentinel Spire. The views from here are not obstructed; Cottonwood Rd., Kodachrome Basin, the Grand Staircase-Escalante, and the parking lot and trailhead are all visible. The trail makes two large drops down and moves opposite the arch with views to the west. It switchbacks to the north of the mesa. A slope leads down back to the main route close to the trailhead.

If you avoid the cutoff trail and take the mellower loop, continue right at the trail fork. You will see more vegetation than rock as you continue back to the trail-head. It offers many of the same views as the trail cut off, but from a lower point.

Escalante Area

The city of Escalante is named after Franciscan missionary Silvestre Vélez de Escalante. A push was made to turn the area including the Escalante River and the canyons into a national park before World War II. However, it wasn't until 1996 that The Grand Staircase-Escalante National Monument was established. It is said to be the last part of the lower 48 states to be cartographed.

The Grand Staircase-Escalante National Monument was established in 1996.

Rank 2

43. Devil's Garden Trail

RATING	Searcher, due to steep slopes
ROUND TRIP DISTANCE	0.5 to 0.75 mile, depending on route
ROUND-TRIP TIME	1 hour plus
ELEVATION CHANGE	5,243-foot low point, with little elevation gain
MAP	Trails Illustrated Grand Staircase, Paunsaugunt Plateau
NEAREST LANDMARK	Hole in the Rock Rd., Seep Flats
FEES	None
RESTROOMS	Vault toilet
DOGS	Must be leashed
OPERATING HOURS	6 a.m to 10 p.m., year-round

COMMENT: Not to be confused with the more famous Devil's Garden hike in Arches National Park (also featured in this book), this hike has no set path. Some refer to the area as a mini-Goblin Valley and may enjoy the solitude of this place compared to Bryce Canyon. This trail is generally accessible year-round, but snow falls in the area during winter. Recent weather may make the dirt road to the trail impassable. There is no cell service or water access at the trailhead. Don't forget to pack a picnic to enjoy at one of the picnic tables. Devil's Garden is an example of the desert biome.

GETTING THERE: From Escalante, head east for about 5.0 miles on Highway 12. Make a slight right onto Hole in the Rock Rd. (signed). Check the road conditions with the Bureau of Land Management (BLM) before driving on this road. The road is not paved and may be rough and rutted, so it is best traveled with a high clearance vehicle. The road may also have pools of water that have to be navigated, and cows roam the roadside. Follow the road for 12.0 miles. A Devil's Garden sign on the right designates the right turn toward the trailhead. The trailhead is on the left after about 0.3 mile.

THE ROUTE: Some of the best trails, especially for kids, are the ones with no set path. Devil's Garden lets you choose your own path, walking, running, or even skipping from formation to formation.

Resembling a land where imaginary goblins and fairies might roam, the BLM designated this site as an Outstanding Natural Area. Three layers of Entrada sandstone are visible: the reddish Gunsight Butte Member, the multi-color Cannonville

The Devil's Garden is a playground for adults and children.

Member, and the white and yellow of the Escalante Member (the most common layer in the area). Informative signs at the trailhead explain how the hoodoos, arches, and other features of the 640-acre area were created over time.

There are plenty of formations to scramble upon, some easy and some steeper. Younger children will need spotting when climbing up and down the formations. Devil's Garden is an excellent place to play a game of hide and go seek with its 200-plus acres to explore.

The two most popular features of the garden, Metate Arch and Mano Arch, are side by side. Said to be named after stone tools, they are about 0.1 mile from the parking lot, depending on your route. You can walk right under the arches for perfect picture-taking opportunities. Three hoodoos that stand next to each other (and somewhat resemble the Three Sisters formation in Goblin Valley) are sometimes referred to as the Three Cockatoos. Also be on the lookout for Gnome Rock, the Marching Trolls, and the Four Wise Men formations.

Be prepared for a lack of shade, except from some rocks among around the sparse and varied vegetation. The desert vegetation is fragile, so make sure little ones don't trample it while exploring.

Two hundred plus acres of hoodoos create a playground.

The Three Cockatoos in Devil's Garden.

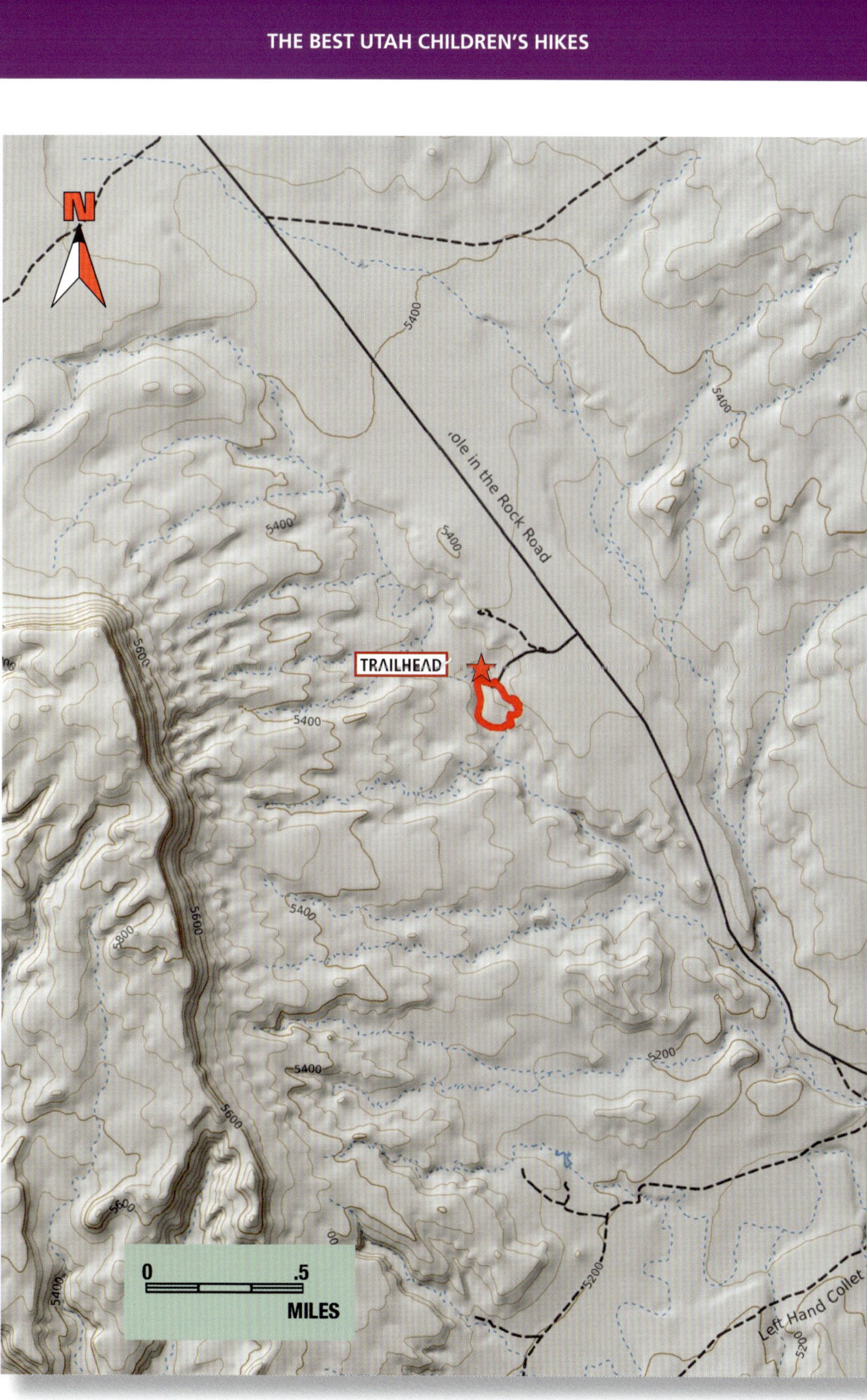

DEVIL'S GARDEN TRAIL

Rank 6

44. Lower Calf Creek Falls Trail

RATING	Adventurer, due to distance and sandy sections
ROUND TRIP DISTANCE	6.5 miles
ROUND-TRIP TIME	3.5–5 hours
ELEVATION CHANGE	298 feet (from 5340 to 5512 feet)
MAP	Trails Illustrated Grand Staircase, Paunsaugunt Plateau
NEAREST LANDMARK	Calf Creek Recreation Area and Campground
FEES	$5 day use fee
RESTROOMS	Pit toilets with seasonal closure
DOGS	Must be leashed
OPERATING HOURS	24 hours

COMMENT: Named for the pens of calves in the area in the 1800s and 1900s, this trail is a mix of sand, slickrock, and Navajo sandstone. Wildflowers dot the landscape from late spring through the summer. Caterpillars hang from the trees in the spring before transforming into butterflies. Cactus plants line the trail as well as common reed and boxelder. A wild turkey or two are known to roam this area along with mountain lions, bighorn sheep, and elk. Condors, falcons, and other birds of prey fly high above. The red desert tortoise and tiger salamanders can be seen near the water's edge.

Expect some deep sand at places, making shoe dumping necessary for little ones. Water is available seasonally at the picnic grounds, but it must be treated, so bring plenty. Wear sun-protective clothing, bring sunscreen to reapply throughout the hike, and pack a towel for after you cool off in the falls. Download a trail guide before your trip or pick one up at the trailhead (seasonal availability) to learn about features, flora, and fauna, and other interesting trail facts. Although the trail is sandy like most desert hikes, the ecosystem is forest biome. This trail can be hiked year round

GETTING THERE: From Escalante, head east on UT 12 for approximately 15.0 miles. The trailhead and campground are on the left. From Boulder, drive approximately 11.5 miles south on the Burr Trail Rd. to UT 12. Take UT 12 west for 9.3 miles. The trailhead and campground are on the right. The parking lot holds about 25 cars. Pay the day use fee to the campground host or place the envelope in the collection area.

THE ROUTE: From the parking lot, hike about 0.2 mile on the paved road. The trailhead is on the left. The trail heads to the north and slowly climbs up and down sec-

The trail to Lower Calf Creek Falls is sandy.

tions of sand and rocks known as the Kayenta Formation. Views of the Haymaker Bencher are off to the right as you keep heading north toward the falls. The rock turns to sand and vegetation grows in abundance on the sides of the trail. Because of the dense vegetation, especially from spring to fall, you will likely be able to hear the creek but not see it for the beginning portion of the hike.

The first of a few washes appears at about 0.25 mile. The trail is generally easy to follow, but the wash area may be a bit confusing as you climb out of it, so pay attention. Before you reach 1.0 mile, you will climb through a second wash. After 1.0 mile, you will see as well as hear Calf Creek flowing on the right. Now the trail opens up a bit from the Navajo sandstone walls. Look for a beaver pond in the creek after you crest a short hill.

As you meander closer to the falls, access to the creek becomes easier. Waterfowl can be seen cooling off in the water, and various species of trout, including rainbow, swim in the creek. Signs of beavers, from tooth marks to various dams, are visible along the waterway.

Trail marker 5 points out the first set of granaries used by the Fremont Indians. It is hard to distinguish them from the canyon's rock walls. Into another wash, a promontory on the left notes the sudden changes in rock from Kayenta to Navajo sandstone. At approximately 1.4 miles, at marker 9, look for a pictograph painted in red of three Fremont Indians in full headdress holding hands. To find the pictograph, look at the west wall of the canyon; the panel is near the light colored sand-

Lower Calf Creek Falls flows year round.

stone in the lower section. A large fin almost breaks the wall into two sections. Look left of the desert varnish to see the panel.

Below the pictographs is evidence of beaver ponds. The trail climbs quickly to a point where the ponds come into full view. The trail is now closer to the creek where water dwellers can be seen. A second granary denoted by marker 10 was also used by the Fremont Indians and can be seen on the east cliff across the creek. At one time, farmers grew crops along the creek banks, including famous Boulder watermelons. There are no signs of these crops today, but there are still signs of old cattle grounds including old fence lines just shy of the 2.0-mile mark.

LOWER CALF CREEK FALLS TRAIL

Vegetation now becomes more abundant and replaces the browns, reds, and oranges of the sand and rock for the green of oaks and occasional pines, among other tree varieties. The dense trees offer much needed shade. Several large rocks along the trail offer spots for dumping shoes and having a snack break. You will encounter deeper and longer sections of sand closer to the falls. At about the 3.0-mile mark, you may see a glimpse of the falls on the right among the cottonwoods and other trees. The sandy trail passes through a marsh-like area with vibrant green reeds.

The falls are approximately 126 feet high and flow year round. The sandstone rock behind the falls is often yellow and green from algae. In winter, the water is quite cold and the spray from the falls is perfect for a little bit of cool down. The area around the falls can be windy. Because the falls face southeast, the area is shaded most of the day. This is a perfect spot for lunch or dinner before heading back to the trailhead. After enjoying the falls, return the way you came.

On the Way Home

KIVA KOFFEEHOUSE

Don't miss a chance to grab a cup of joe or hot cocoa, or some breakfast or lunch, at the Kiva Koffeehouse in the Grand Staircase. Open seasonally, the views of the Kiva and the Grand Staircase area are breathtaking from the circular windows or the outside patio. The Koffeehouse resulted from the vision of artist and engineer Bradshaw Boman. He conceived the idea in 1990, but it took until 1998 for the building, made of natural local materials including pine logs and sandstone, to be completed. The Koffeehouse serves fresh pastries, and made from scratch soups, teas, juices, and coffee drinks. You can even rent a cabin for an overnight stay.

Kiva Koffeehouse

Highway 12, mile marker 73.86
P.O. Box 130
Escalante, UT 84726
(435) 826-4550
www.kivakoffeehouse.com
Hours: Open seasonally Wednesday through Monday from April through October, 8:30 a.m. to 4:30 p.m.

Capitol Reef National Park

Capitol Reef takes its name from sandstone domes that resemble capitol buildings and the reef like cliffs that create travel barriers. Originally a national monument established in August of 1937, visitor access did not begin until 1950 when it was open to the public. Its status as a national park was established in 1971. The park is over 240,000 acres and includes its main formation the Waterpocket Fold—the largest exposed monocline in North America.

Capitol Reef National Park is a national park not to be missed.

Rank 1

45. Sunset Point Trail

RATING	Experimenter, due to short distance and minimal elevation gain
ROUND TRIP DISTANCE	0.7 mile
ROUND-TRIP TIME	30 minutes–1 hour
ELEVATION CHANGE	26 feet (from 6,355 to 6,381 feet)
MAP	Trails Illustrated Capitol Reef
NEAREST LANDMARK	Capitol Reef National Park
FEES	None
RESTROOMS	No
DOGS	Not permitted
OPERATING HOURS	One hour before sunrise to one hour after sunset

COMMENT: Capitol Reef takes its name from the sandstone domes that resemble capitol buildings and the reef-like cliffs that create travel barriers. This trail is in the desert biome. Despite its beauty, this area isn't as popular as nearby Bryce Canyon National Park.

As its name implies, sunset is a particularly busy time here. Note that the trail can be difficult to follow, especially when navigating with headlamps. Steep drop offs make it essential for staying on trail and watching small hikers.

GETTING THERE: From the Capitol Reef National Park Visitor Center, head west on Highway 24 for 2.5 miles. At the top of the hill, turn left and stay left past the Panorama Point sign. It is about 0.8 mile to the end of the dirt road and the trailhead. Parking shouldn't be a problem at the Goosenecks parking area, but note that the road to the trailhead can be bumpy, especially after recent rain.

THE ROUTE: From the Goosenecks parking area, head east on the Sunset Point Trail. There will be a sign made of rock on the right denoting the direction of the trail.

There are views of the Waterpocket Fold to the west and to the east from the very start. In fact, this trail offers one of the best places in the area to see the unique layers of rock from as young as Cretaceous (80 million years old) to Permian (270 million years old). Even black volcanic rocks can be found near the Fremont River.

Sunset Point is beautiful all times of the day. *Photo: Heather Sims*

The trail has a bit of a rocky start, but it isn't too challenging. The slight elevation the trail gains overall is mostly at the beginning. Make sure to stay on the trail to not disturb the fragile cryptobiotic soil.

At about 0.17 mile, roughly the halfway point, there is a bench on the right where you can take in the Waterpocket Fold. Pinyon pine and other desert vegetation line the trail but provide no shade. Lizards are abundant. Bats, ringtails, bighorn sheep, and mule deer along with over 200 species of birds make their homes in the fold.

At 0.25 mile the trail crosses a ridge, with Sulphur Creek Canyon below. This area has a steep drop off, so use caution with footing and hold little hikers' hands. Sulphur Creek contains the oldest rock layers in the Capitol Reef area, White Rim sandstone and Kaibab limestone.

When you reach Sunset Point at 0.35 mile, there is a second bench. The rocks at this eastern point resemble pancakes because of their flatness. The Waterpocket Fold extends south. Looking out, a dense area of trees helps to set off Miners Mountain and Boulder Mountain. If it is a clear day, you can see the Henry Mountains to the east rising up from the area of Lake Powell. They may be capped with snow.

If you visit during sunset, the reds and oranges of the landscape glow, providing the best light for photo opportunities. The Waterpocket Fold bursts in multiple colors from rust and tan to the green of the pockets of vegetation. The Fremont River flows below. You may even be able to see the goosenecks in the

The Waterpocket Fold can be seen along the Sunset Point Trail. *Photo: Heather Sims*

river that give the area its name. Whether you take in the view during the day or at sunset, spend some magical moments before heading back the short distance to the trailhead.

HIKE EXTENSION: The Goosenecks Trail begins from the same parking lot and is a short 0.2 mile hike offering additional opportunities for views, especially of the Sulfur Creek Goosenecks when it's a good water year. Don't forget to stop at Panorama Point for more landscape photo opportunities.

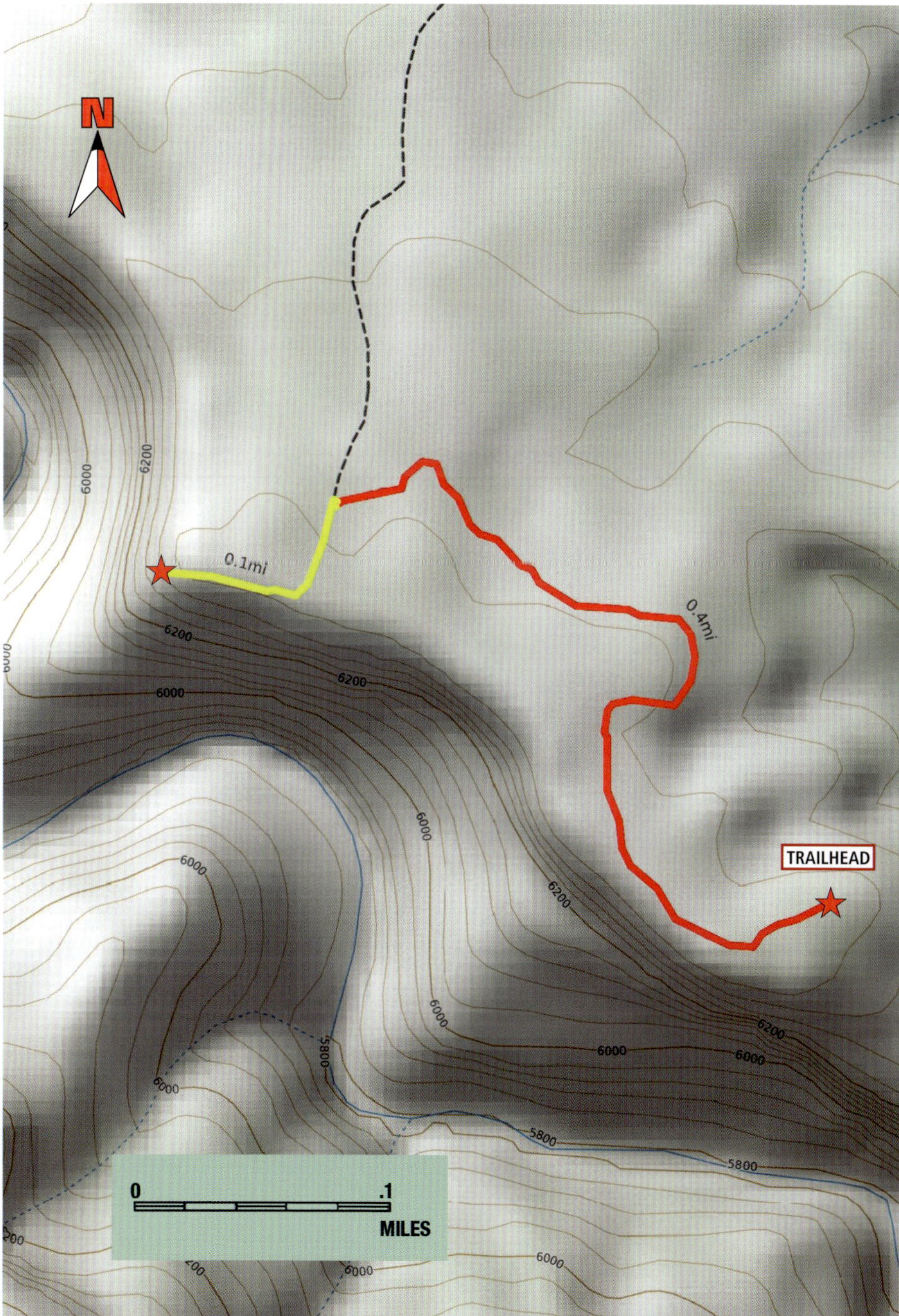

SUNSET POINT TRAIL

Rank 4

46. Cohab Canyon Trail

RATING	Wanderer, due to distance and elevation change
ROUND TRIP DISTANCE	3.4 miles
ROUND-TRIP TIME	2–3 hours
ELEVATION CHANGE	575 feet (from 5,380 to 5,955 feet)
MAP	Trails Illustrated Capitol Reef
NEAREST LANDMARK	Capitol Reef Visitor Center
FEES	Private vehicle $15; National Parks pass
RESTROOMS	Pit toilets at trailhead
DOGS	Not allowed
OPERATING HOURS	24 hours

COMMENT: Legend says that Mormon polygamists in Fruita used Cohab (cohabitation) Canyon to hide their wives after the Edmunds Act, which banned polygamy, was passed in the late 1800s. Whether you believe the tale or not, the rock formations, including a mushroom-shaped hoodoo and the Cohab Canyon Arch, as well as the side canyons, seem like good hiding spots.

This out-and-back trail has virtually no shade, so consider that when planning when to hike and how much water to bring. Views of the Fruita Cliffs and hidden canyons are among the highlights of this hike. Make sure your shoes are tight for the uneven footing caused by roots and rocks. This trail is an example of the desert biome because of the lack of precipitation and extreme temperatures. Winter provides an opportunity to see the canyon in a different way.

GETTING THERE: Head east from the Capitol Reef National Park Visitor Center on Highway 24 for 1.9 miles. The Hickman Natural Bridge Trailhead and parking lot are on the left. There are about 15 parking spots at the trailhead, but they fill up quickly because this is the trailhead for two popular hikes.

THE ROUTE: The trail for Cohab Canyon begins at the Hickman Bridge Trailhead parking lot. If you are with little hikers, you may want to stop at the overlook and not descend all the way to the Fruita campground. An alternative route starts across from the Fruita Campground area and goes out and back from that starting point.

From the parking lot, head left and cross Hwy 24. On the right, after a guardrail, you will see a brown sign heading to the right and up. The trail is rocky but wide as it switchbacks up into the canyon. Slow and steady is the pace you want

Looking down at the Fruita Campground along the Cohab Canyon Trail.

to take. There are some views, but power lines and road noise mark the beginning of this hike from this starting point. At about 0.37 mile the trail levels off. A small overhang may provide a bit of shade for grabbing a quick drink. At 0.4 mile there is a nice viewpoint as the road noise disappears, followed by a short footbridge.

There is a Fruita Overlook sign about a half-mile down the trail. Hikers will find pockets of shade here. A little more than half a mile in, there is a wooden sign. Continue right here toward the campground. The trail drops down and becomes soft sand and slickrock. Cairns dot the landscape to help show you the way. If you head left, the trail leads to the Frying Pan area of Cassidy Arch and Grand Wash.

At 0.7 mile the canyon opens up and offers a fun playground area to take a break, climb the slickrock, and jump over the potholes that may contain water.

As the trail heads down away from the slickrock, it enters some wash at 0.79 mile. At the fork in the wash at 0.93 mile, continue right (left leads to a box canyon). At the 1.0-mile mark there is another box canyon on the left. If time or curiosity permits, you can explore any of the box canyons. Look for birds resting in holes known as the Cohab Canyon Beehives, which are caused by water erosion. You may also see bighorn sheep and deer along this hike or within the park boundaries.

The trail continues through the wash. At 1.09 miles, a sign on the right indicates a National Park Service (NPS) study of endemic and rare plants. Look left to see another box canyon to explore. Soon after the NPS study sign, the trail begins to climb out of the wash. The rocks at 1.22 miles make for a good place to hide and surprise someone, or to catch your breath and enjoying a break. At 1.25 miles, there

Views from the top of the Waterpocket Fold from the Cohab Canyon Trail.

is a rise to views of Fruita, the Fruita Campground, and the Gifford Homestead belonging to one of the first families to settle in the town of Fruita. This is the top of the Waterpocket Fold. The views here are panoramic and breathtaking.

You can turn around here at 1.3 miles or continue down the switchbacks to the campground. Going to the campground is longer hike for a total of 1.7 miles, or 3.4 miles round-trip. As you return back to the Hickman Bridge Trailhead parking lot, you will have full views of Capitol Dome.

COHAB CANYON TRAIL

Rank 3

47. Hickman Bridge Trail

RATING	Seeker, due to elevation changes and uneven surfaces
ROUND TRIP DISTANCE	2.0 miles
ROUND-TRIP TIME	1.5–2 hours
ELEVATION CHANGE	575 feet (from 5,380 to 5,955 feet)
MAP	Trails Illustrated Capitol Reef
NEAREST LANDMARK	Capitol Reef Visitor Center
FEES	Private vehicle $15; National Parks pass
RESTROOMS	Pit toilets at trailhead
DOGS	Not allowed
OPERATING HOURS	24 hours

COMMENT: The Hickman Bridge is a 133-foot natural bridge made of Navajo sandstone. Grab a trail brochure at the trailhead to locate 18 things to see on the hike, including a smaller bridge known as Nels Johnson Bridge and the remains of a Fremont pit house. This trail has virtually no shade, so consider that when planning when to hike and how much water to bring. The trail features panoramic

The trail up to Hickman Bridge begins with some stairs.

Hickman Bridge blends into the background.

sunsets. The lighting on the bridge tends to be better in the morning for photo buffs. This trail is in the desert biome.

GETTING THERE: Head east from the Capitol Reef National Park Visitor Center on Highway 24 for 1.9 miles. The Hickman Natural Bridge Trailhead and parking lot are on the left. There are about 15 parking spots at the trailhead, but they fill up quickly because this is the trailhead for two popular hikes.

THE ROUTE: From the parking lot, head to the right begin the hike to Hickman Bridge. A large stone sign points in the direction of the beginning of the trail. The Fremont River runs on the right of the trail for 0.2 mile, providing peaceful background music as it hugs the sandstone wall. Then the trail begins to switchback as you climb stairs and leave the Waterpocket Fold.

You will come to a dirt trail to the right. Take this short spur trail east for about 80 feet to see the standing ruins of a Fremont pit house and granary. This spot is noted in the trail pamphlet. Return to the trail and continue up and at 0.3 mile, you will reach the Rim Overlook/Navajo Knobs Trail junction. A brown wooden sign points you toward the bridge. Hike to the left to continue onto Hickman Bridge. Look over the canyon, almost straight ahead, to see Pectol's Pyramid, named after Ephraim Pectol, one of the pioneers in facilitating national monument status for Capitol Reef in 1937. Also look east for views of Capitol Dome, named for its resemblance to the dome on the Capitol in Washington, D.C.

Depending on the time of year you visit, wildflowers may dot the side of the trail here, mixed in with other vegetation. Cottonwoods blaze yellow in contrast to the red rocks in the fall. Chipmunks and lizards and are common wildlife seen on the trail. At the half mile mark, the trail drops into a wash and becomes a mix of sandstone and sand. Cairns will help guide you as well as other hikers, because this is one of the most popular trails in the park. Note that the slickrock areas before the bridge can be slippery, especially after recent rainfall.

At 0.7 mile on the right, you will encounter Nels Johnson Bridge. Once a pothole, this bridge is named after the first European American settler who settled in the Capitol Reef area in 1880. It's unique for its location and the fact that it isn't high in the sky like most arches. Take a break in the shade underneath the sandstone before crossing under the bridge.

At about 0.8 mile there is a brown trail sign that explains the loop around the bridge. If you plan to hike the full loop, counterclockwise is the recommended direction. If you bypass the loop, head right across some slickrock for 0.2 mile until you see Hickman Natural Bridge.

To continue the loop after passing under the bridge, look for the hard to see path that heads left around a bend. You will cross a small drainage area before the trail leads to a vantage point for the Fremont Gorge and the Fremont River Valley area. The trail continues left and descends a short way back to the trail loop junction. You may have to try several angles and vantage points to get a good photo of the bridge. Morning is best for taking photos of the 125-foot high bridge with a 133-foot span.

Refuel in the shade under the bridge before heading back down to the trailhead. If you didn't take the short spur trail to the ruins on the way up to the bridge, consider doing so as you head back to the Fremont River and watershed.

On the Way Home

GIFFORD HOMESTEAD

After a tough day of hiking, stop by the Gifford House to refuel with an amazing homemade fruit pie. You can also purchase homemade goods from local artists and tradesman including rugs, soap, and replicas of tools that the Mormon pioneers used. Polygamist Calvin Pendleton built the original homestead in 1908. The Giffords are recorded as the last residents of the homestead and the third owners and lived at the residence for over 40 years until 1969, raising sheep and cows and growing their own food.

Gifford Homestead
HC 70, Box 15
Torrey, UT 84775
(435) 425-3791
www.nps.gov/care/learn/historyculture/giffordhomestead.htm
Hours: March 14 through October 31 (may vary with weather), from 8 a.m. to 5 p.m. (there may be extended hours in summer).

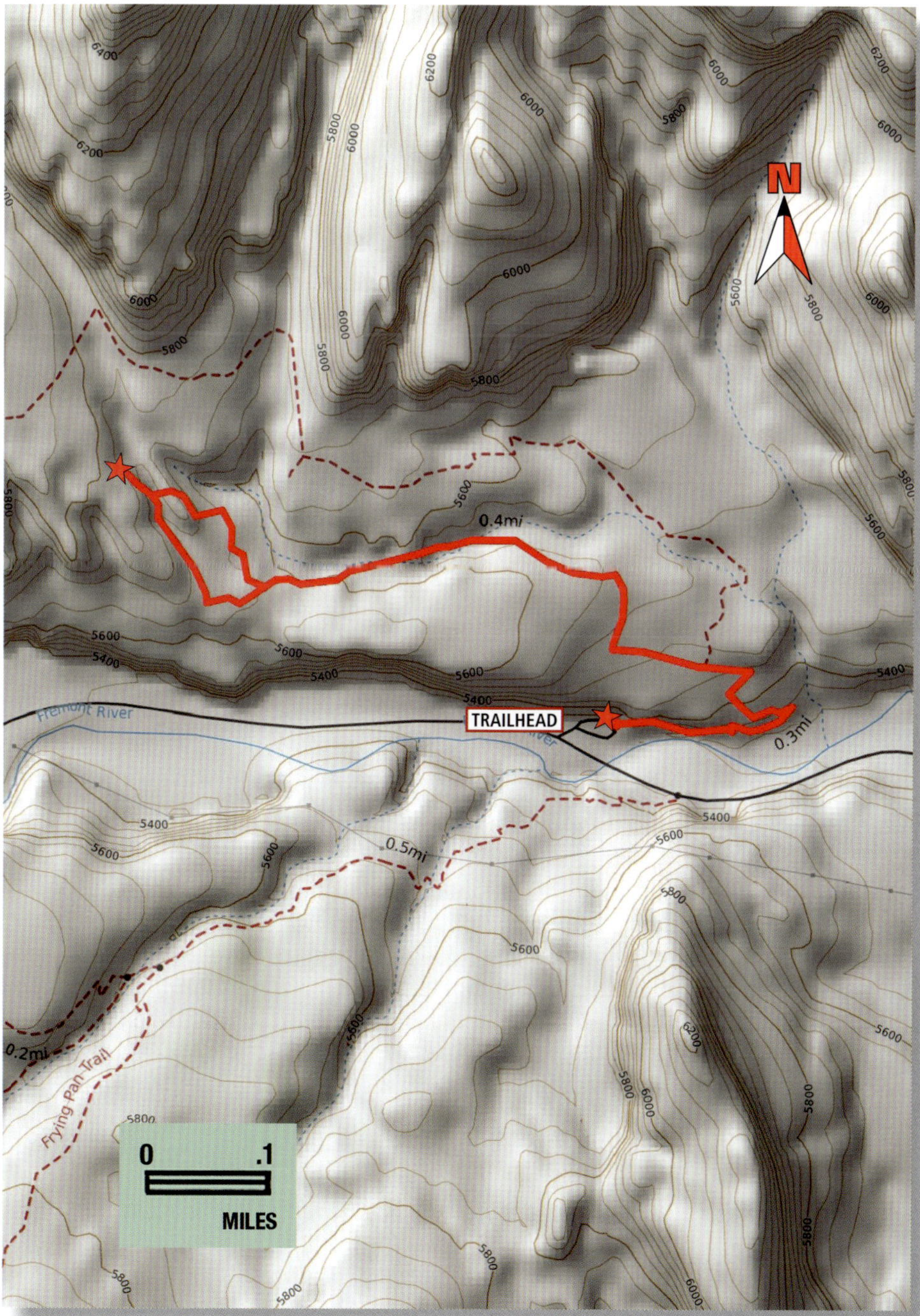

HICKMAN BRIDGE TRAIL

The Vernal area is known as "Dinosaurland."

Vernal Area

Vernal, Utah, is referred to as "Dinosaurland" for the abundance of dinosaur trackways and bones that have been found in the area. Established in 1876, it was one of the only cities in Utah not settled by Mormons. It is a part of the Uintah Basin. Don't forget to stop by and see Dinah the Pink Dinosaur that serves as a town welcome sign on the east side of the city.

Red Fleet Reservoir in Red Fleet State Park.

Rank 3

48. Red Fleet Dinosaur Track Site

RATING	Seeker, due to uneven surfaces, steep descents, and terrain
ROUND TRIP DISTANCE	2.0 miles out and back
ROUND-TRIP TIME	1–2 hours
ELEVATION CHANGE	136 feet (from 5,616 feet to 5,867 feet)
MAP	Trails Illustrated Dinosaur National Monument
NEAREST LANDMARK	Red Fleet State Park
FEES	None
RESTROOMS	Pit toilets at trailhead (may be closed in winter)
DOGS	Must be leashed
OPERATING HOURS	One hour before sunrise to one hour after sunset

COMMENT: This trail is best hiked during early spring, late summer, and fall when water levels are lower and the most tracks will be exposed. The tracks are best viewed in the morning or late afternoon into the evening when the sunlight is not directly overhead. Snow and ice will cause very slippery conditions on this slickrock trail during late fall through early spring. Pick up a copy of the Red Fleet State Park Dinosaur Track booklet or find it online and read about the numbered posts along the trail. Red Fleet State Park is part of the desert biome.

Bobcats, river otters, and even badgers call the Red Fleet State Park area home. Bald eagles frequent the area in the winter while hawks, owls, and osprey can be seen year round. Keep a keen eye out for the shy but beautiful mountain bluebird. If you downloaded the park trail guide, be sure to stop at the numbered posts to experience all that this unique landscape holds from the Red Fleet Formation and patches of desert varnish to native grasses and wildflowers that peak early spring through fall. But remember to leave rocks, plant life, and habitats undisturbed for the next visitors to enjoy.

GETTING THERE: The Red Fleet Dinosaur Track Site Trailhead is off Highway 191 about 12.0 miles northeast of Vernal. Take Hwy 191 north past the main park entrance road for Red Fleet State Park. About a mile down the road, there will be a brown Red Fleet Dinosaur Track sign on the right. You will also see the Simplot Vernal Mine site on the left at the turn. Take a right (the road may be called Donkey Flat

Painted dino tracks lead the way to the real tracks along the waterfront.

Rd. on GPS). The trailhead and bathrooms are on the right about 2.3 miles down the road. There is a small parking lot that fits about five cars.

THE ROUTE: The trailhead begins from the parking lot off Donkey Flat Rd. Right from the start, you begin to climb slick sandstone. The trail continues to alternate between rock and sand as you follow the painted black dinosaur tracks, the numbered posts, and the trail directional signs. Don't worry if you get a bit off trail as the signs, posts, and painted dinosaur tracks will guide you back.

At about 0.25 mile you will find a trail junction sign for the Dinosaur Track Trail and the Flat Rock Trail. Follow the Dinosaur Track Trail to the left and continue

Measure your own feet to see how they size up to the dino tracks.

toward the reservoir, which is sometimes referred to as "Little Lake Powell." The trail continues to roll between juniper trees, Nugget sandstone, and brush.

Close to the 1.0-mile mark, post 17 denotes that you have reached the trackway. As you reach the shoreline, the rock trail gets steeper, with an approximate 30-foot drop off. This trackway is said to be one of the best dinosaur trackways in Utah and the United States; there are several hundred tracks and seven trackways near the shoreline, created 200 million years ago by the three-toed theropods and the eubrontes.

Both natural casts and true tracks can be found in the Nugget sandstone. Some of the tracks are more obvious in the light than others. Signs along the slickrock shoreline help to identify track position. You can really see the scale of just how large these dinosaurs were when placing your own foot side-by-side for comparison. After exploring the tracks, retrace your dinosaur steps back to the trailhead.

RED FLEET DINOSAUR TRACK SITE

The sun sets quickly in Red Fleet State Park.

On the Way Home

GEORGE S. ECCLES DINOSAUR PARK

Don't miss the opportunity to visit the Utah Field House of Natural History when in Vernal. Off Main St., children and adults enjoy hands on fossil digs, dinosaur bones, and exploring the rich history of the Uinta Basin. A children's lab area contains books and puzzles along with dinosaur models. Three full dinosaur skeletons, including a complete stegosaurus, are a treat. The museum isn't all dinosaurs. Fossilized leaf prints, plant life, and animals are a must see in the Eocene exhibit area. Take a step through time with the thorough display of rocks and rock formations. Special exhibits change throughout the year but typically feature the environment and geology of the area.

Utah Field House of Natural History
235 E. Main St.
Vernal, UT 84078
Admission: Adults $7; children 6-12, $3.50; children 5 and under free
Summer Hours: (Memorial Day through September 3), 7 days a week 9 a.m. to 7 p.m.
Fall Hours: (September 3 through September 30, 7 days a week 9 a.m to 5 p.m.
Winter Hours: (October through March), Monday through Saturday 9 a.m. to 5 p.m. (closed Sundays)
Spring Hours: (March through Memorial Day Weekend), 7 days a week 9 a.m. to 5 p.m.
(435) 789-3799
https://stateparks.utah.gov/parks/utah-field-house

Dinosaur National Monument

Bordering Colorado and Utah, Dinosaur National Monument was named a monument in 1915 by President Woodrow Wilson to protect the dinosaur fossils discovered by Earl Douglass and his crew in 1909. Over 300,000 visitors a year comes to this part of the Uinta Mountains to see the fossils, tracks and bones themselves.

Views of the Green River can be seen from the Fossil Discovery Trail.

Rank 3

49. Fossil Discovery Trail

RATING	Seeker, due to easy trail and minimal elevation gain that can be skipped
ROUND TRIP DISTANCE	2.4 miles
ROUND-TRIP TIME	1.5–2 hours
ELEVATION CHANGE	235 feet (from 4,767 to 5,002 feet)
MAP	Trails Illustrated Dinosaur National Monument
NEAREST LANDMARK	Dinosaur National Monument Quarry Visitor Center
FEES	$20 per car day pass; Utah State Parks pass; National Parks pass
RESTROOMS	Flush toilets with sink, water fountains in visitor center
DOGS	Not allowed
OPERATING HOURS	Monument is open 24 hours; visitor center is open year-round, but hours vary by season, and it is closed for major holidays

COMMENT: The out-and-back Fossil Discovery Trail features three fossil areas. It is sometimes called the Geology Trail. The National Park Service states that this trail is very slippery when it is wet. Note that some areas of the park may be closed in winter due to weather. Some areas of the trails may also be closed for restoration, so check in advance to see about closures. The Quarry Exhibit Hall hours vary, so plan accordingly.

Grab a trail brochure at the visitor center or sign up for a ranger-led tour if you visit during the summer. The trail is sometimes referred to as the Geology Trail and is considered to be in the desert biome. Dinosaur National Monument was designated as an International Dark Star Park in April 2019. Since it is open 24 hours a day, think about hiking this trail at night with headlamps to do some star gazing, too.

GETTING THERE: From US Highway 40 in Jensen, take UT 149 north about 7.0 miles to Dinosaur National Monument. The trailhead is located at the Dinosaur National Monument Quarry Visitor Center.

THE ROUTE: Start at the Dinosaur National Monument Quarry Visitor Center. The trailhead is left of the visitor center entrance. Be sure to bring sun protection and water because this trail receives full sun exposure. As you head down the sandy

There are three fossil areas on the Fossil Discovery Trail.

trail, keep your gaze to the left, as the beginning of the hike is not very scenic. You will cross a bridge and the road that leads to the Quarry Exhibit Hall.

After a slight climb, at 0.5 mile there is a boulder on the left featuring "Classic Vernal Style" petroglyphs created by Fremont Indians. The petroglyphs show human-like figures. Petroglyphs are rarer in this area than in other parts of Utah. While you are encouraged to touch the dinosaur bones on the trail, do not touch the petroglyphs, because oils in human hands can damage these works of art.

Just past the petroglyphs the trail turns left (north) as it heads into the canyon toward the quarry. On the left you will pass a side trail that leads west to see Mowry shale, where there are fish scale fossils. Back on the main trail, turn left into the canyon. About 0.25 mile farther, after you crest a hill, the Morrison Formation is marked with a sign. The hike to the formation has rock steps. This area showcases over 10 species of dinosaur bones in their natural state that Earl Douglass found in 1909. You can also see small pieces of other fossils. Many of the fragments are marked with arrows and dots to help visitors locate them.

After the Morrison Formation, the trail continues to the left toward the Stump Formation and the trail's end. At the trail split go left and up the hill to the trail's end, or keep straight for the Stump Formation. The short Stump Formation offshoot continues north to an area that features marine fossils from both an ocean

The climb up the stairs to the Quarry Exhibit Hall is worth the huff and puff.

and river environment. Ripple marks are visible across the sedimentary rocks from years of ocean waves.

The trail ends at the top of the hill at the park service road. Don't skip the hill or you will miss quite a view of the Green River and surrounding area. There is also a surprise at the top that the true dinosaur lover won't want to miss. Before you turn around, be sure to hike a bit up the road to see the Quarry Exhibit Hall that features 1,500 dinosaur bones, some that you can even touch.

During summer, a tram is available from Quarry Exhibit Hall back to the Quarry Visitor Center. Some visitors choose to do this hike one way during the hot months by starting at the Quarry Exhibit Hall and finishing at the Quarry Visitor Center. It is about 0.5 mile down the road if you don't take a tram. Hiking back on the road is not recommended during summer because of the high volume of traffic.

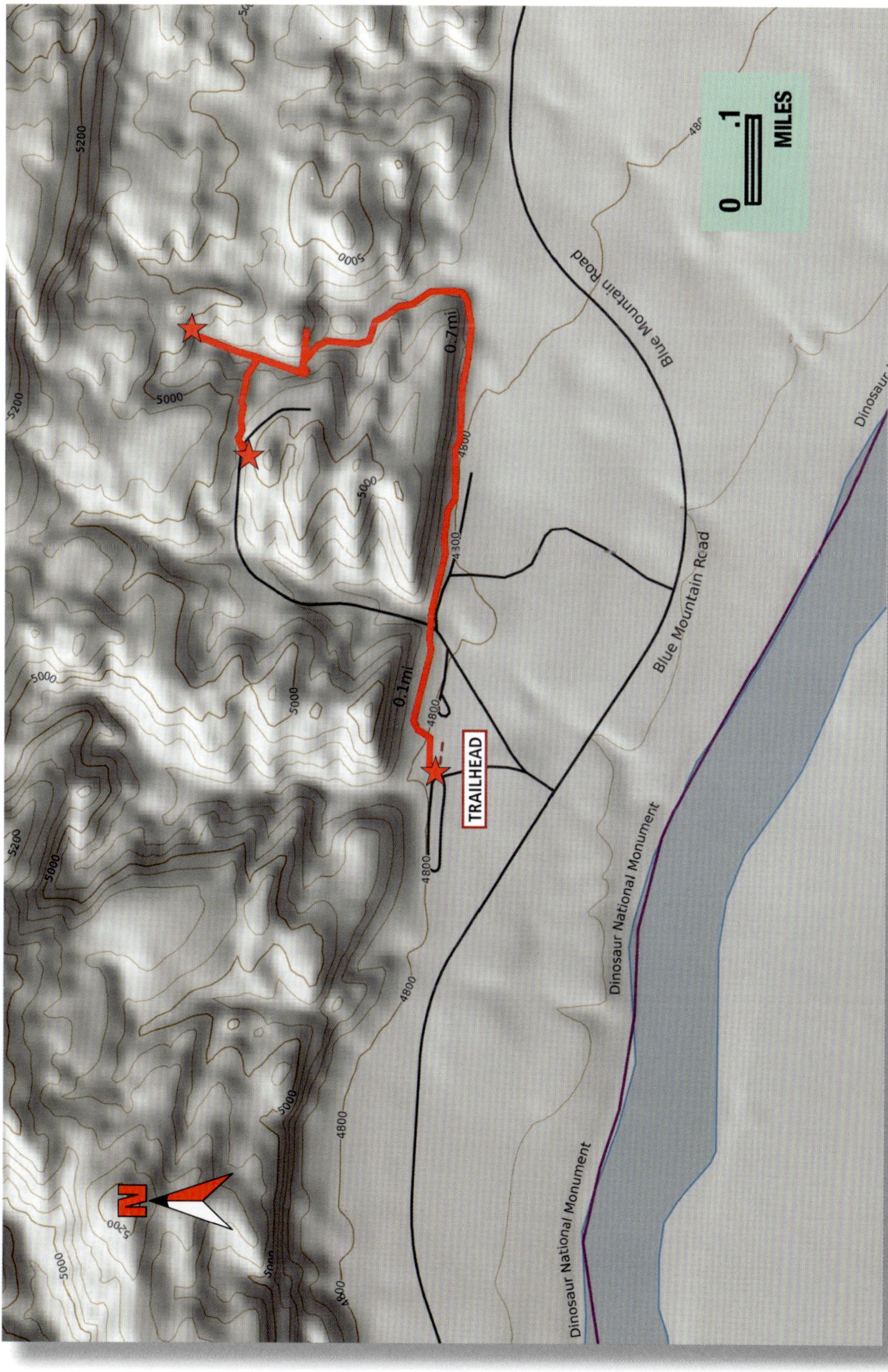

FOSSIL DISCOVERY TRAIL

The "Little Narrows" is a fun short slot found in Pioneer Park.

St. George Area

Located near the Arizona border in the southwestern part of Utah, St. George is a year round destination for tourists. Named the fastest growing metro area in the U.S the town lies within the Mojave Desert. First inhabited by the Anasazi and Paiute, it was later founded as a cotton mission in 1861 under the Apostle Erastus Snow. Once president of The Church of Jesus Christ of Latter- Day Saints Brigham Young originally called the town Dixie as recognized by the Dixie Rock located in Pioneer Park. It was later changed to St. George after Mormon Apostle George A. Smith.

The sand in Pioneer Park offers a perfect play place.

Rank 1 Rank 3

50. Pioneer Park Trail

RATING	Experimenter to seeker, depending on route
ROUND TRIP DISTANCE	Varies based on routes you take
ROUND-TRIP TIME	1 hour plus
ELEVATION CHANGE	3,091 foot low point; elevation gain depends on the route
MAP	Trails Illustrated St. George
NEAREST LANDMARK	Dixie Rock
FEES	None
RESTROOMS	Pit toilets and water fountains
DOGS	Must be leashed
OPERATING HOURS	7 a.m. to 10 p.m.

COMMENT: This area is one of the best free places to visit when in St. George. There are 52 acres for kids and adults to explore. Don't miss the old pioneer cabin, or "Boy Scout Cave." If you climb Dixie Rock (also known as Sugarloaf), on clear days you can see the town of St. George and even parts of Zion National Park. Bouldering is very popular in the park as well as mountain biking. There is not much shade, but there is water access near the bathrooms. The various picnic tables are perfect for taking a rest or enjoying a picnic. The various deep areas of sand within the park are great spots for sand play. This park highlights the features of the desert biome.

GETTING THERE: From Interstate 15, take Exit 8/St. George Blvd. Continue west and turn north onto 1000 east, then turn west onto Red Hills Parkway. Continue about 0.8 mile to the park. There is a parking lot on both the north and south side of the road. You can find additional parking about 0.25 mile west on Red Hills Parkway.

THE ROUTE: There are designated trails within Red Cliffs Desert Reserve area, but you can just make your own route to explore Pioneer Park. There is plenty of slickrock to climb and sand for digging. If you visit from March through October, you may ask yourself if you saw a rock move; more than likely, the "rock" was a desert tortoise, which are often seen in the area.

Climb Dixie Rock for city views. The simplest route is to pass the gazebo and head northwest from the parking lot. You will scramble and hike through some rocks and pass one canyon area. When you reach the second canyon running east to west, take it in a westerly direction. The canyon ends rather quickly. At the end,

There is plenty of exploring to do in Pioneer Park.

there are some steep carved steps on the right. Take your time navigating these steps (younger children will most likely need help). At the top of the steps, walk across the steel footbridge to Dixie Rock. Take in the incredible views but be mindful of the steep drop offs. Return the way you came and continue to explore other areas of the park. A local tradition is to climb to the top of Dixie Rock at night to experience the "St. George Ocean." If you lay flat on your back on the rock and raise your head to look at the red flashing lights of the Bloomington Hills area, the city lights look like stars and the night time sky appears to be the ocean.

The Boy Scout Cave, a historic pioneer cabin, is north of the main parking lot for Pioneer Park. The easiest way to locate the cave is to look up and north for the iron safety railings and a chimney on the rocks above. The cave is below the railings.

Visitors to Pioneer Park enjoy rock scrambling and bouldering.

Kids will enjoy exploring the cave. This spot is popular for bouldering, especially in the morning or evening.

"The Red Crack" or "Little Narrows" is a very small-scale introduction to slot canyons. Small children can sometimes fit through it without having to climb sideways. Adults have to squeeze through the slot, which is about nine inches at its narrowest. The most common way is to begin at the bottom and go up. Young children may need help climbing out.

On the Way Home

RED HILLS DESERT GARDEN

Opened in spring 2015, the Desert Garden is the first desert conservation garden in Utah. Just north of Pioneer Park, the garden is close to five acres. The area features a garden with over 5,000 plants, prehistoric dinosaur tracks, a stream with endangered and native fish, and a replica slot canyon. The paved trail through the gardens is ADA accessible. To see the fish, you need to head through the faux slot canyon. There are benches throughout the garden.

Red Hills Desert Garden
375 Red Hills Pkwy.
St. George, UT 84770
(435) 673-3617
https://redhillsdesertgarden.com
Admission: Free
Hours: Monday through Saturday 9 a.m. to 6 p.m.

PIONEER PARK TRAIL

The scrambling never ends in Snow Canyon State Park.

The moon begins to rise over Snow Canyon State Park.

Snow Canyon State Park

Named after the Mormon settlers Erastus and Lorenzo Snow, Snow Canyon State Park was named a state park in 1958. It includes several interesting geological features including sand dunes and lava tubes. Geographically, it is located at the confluence for the Colorado Plateau, Great Basin and Mojave Desert. It was originally named Dixie Park and is the site for many Hollywood films including *Jeremiah Johnson* and *Butch Cassidy and the Sundance Kid*.

Snow Canyon State Park is named after Mormon settlers Erastus and Lorenzo Snow.

Rank 3

51. Petrified Dunes Trail

RATING	Seeker, due to uneven surfaces
ROUND TRIP DISTANCE	1.2 miles
ROUND-TRIP TIME	1 hour
ELEVATION CHANGE	161 feet (from 3,481 to 3,642 feet) depending on route
MAP	Trails Illustrated St. George
NEAREST LANDMARK	Snow Canyon State Park
FEES	$6 per vehicle; Utah State Parks pass
RESTROOMS	Pit toilets are available at the Upper and Lower Galoot Picnic Areas
DOGS	Not allowed
OPERATING HOURS	6 a.m. to 10 p.m.

COMMENT: This out-and-back desert biome trail passes petrified dunes that were created by sand cemented into rock over 200 million years ago. The dunes and sandstone outcrops are perfect for climbing.

The 360-degree views of the area are breathtaking. Lava flows, sandstone cliffs, and the best view of Snow Canyon can be seen from the trail. Piano rock—a black rock area that resembles a mini piano—can also be seen from the trail. *Butch Cassidy and the Sundance Kid*, *The Flintstones*, and *Jeremiah Johnson* were filmed in this park. See if you recognize any of the landscapes from these movies.

GETTING THERE: From Interstate 15 south, take Exit 10/Washington. Turn right at the ramp and make a quick left at the light onto Bluff St. Continue for 5.0 miles to the intersection of Bluff St. and SR 18. Go through the light and continue on Snow Canyon Parkway for 3.5 miles until you reach the park entrance.

From I-15 north take Exit 6 onto Bluff Street. Head north on Bluff St. and turn left on Snow Canyon Parkway. Continue on Snow Canyon Parkway for 3.5 miles until you reach the park entrance.

From the south, the trailhead and small parking lot are on the left. From the north, the trailhead parking lot is on the right. If the parking lot is full, you can also park at the Upper Galoot Picnic area or the Lower Galoot Picnic Area, which have restrooms.

THE ROUTE: From the trailhead, head south/left onto the Petrified Dunes Trail. If you go right, you will be on the Butterfly Trail or Lava Trail. At the start, the trail

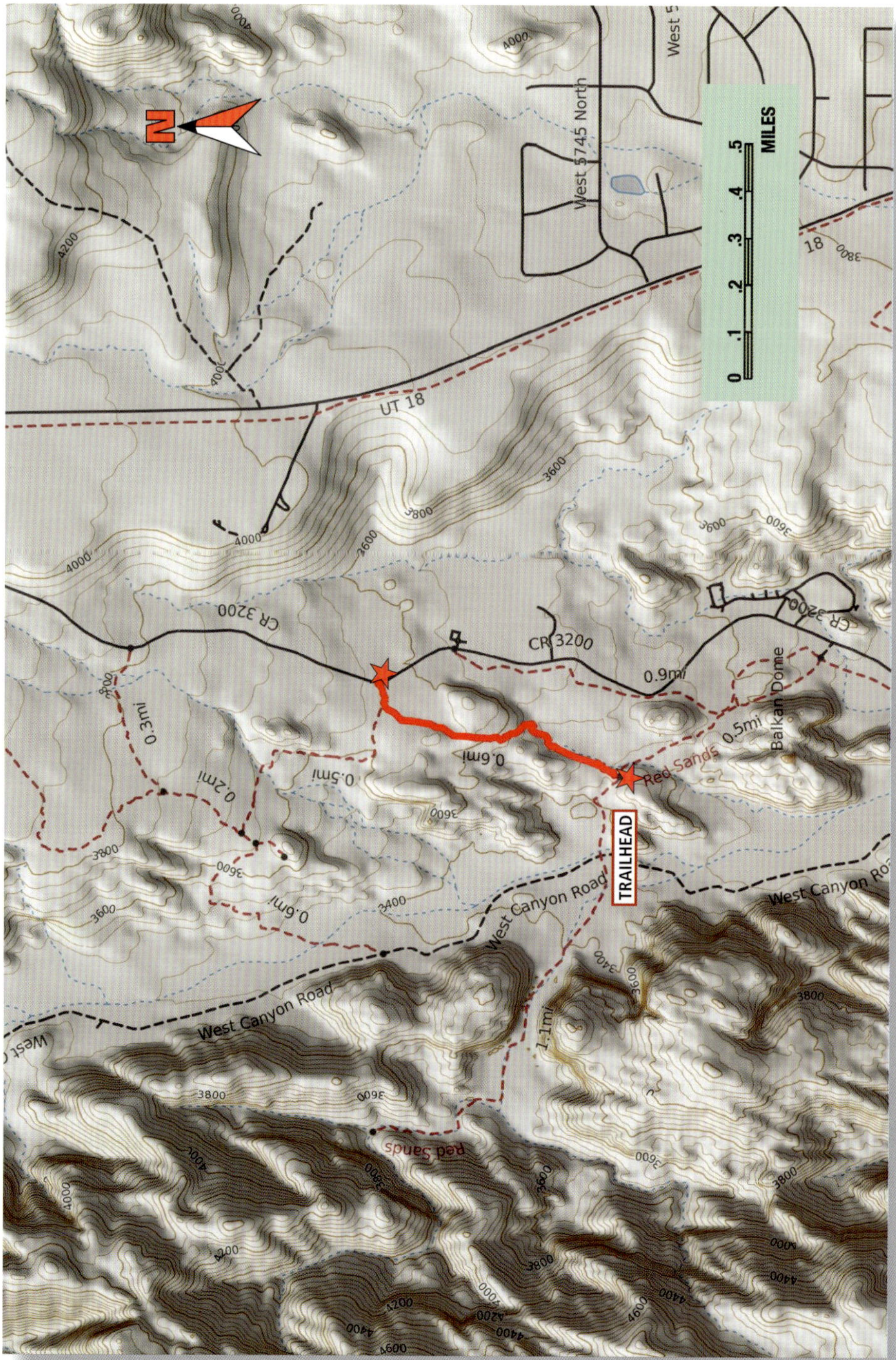

PETRIFIED DUNES TRAIL

The dunes offer a place to run and explore for visitors to the park.

is fairly open and flat with no shade. The red sand gets deeper as you approach the dunes. You will soon reach an area of trees and vegetation, the only shaded spot on the trail before you reach the dunes.

A brown arrow sign on the left signals to follow the trail through some deep sand and onto the dunes. It can be difficult to follow the trail once you reach the dunes; don't be discouraged if you get off trail as you can explore the dunes as you wish. Small children will most likely need help climbing and scrambling around the dunes. Pools of water collect in various potholes eroded in the sandstone (these also make good hiding places when dry if you can get flat enough). Vegetation grows among the petrified dunes.

Within the dunes, you may be lucky to see some Moqui Marbles. These are marble shaped rocks made up of iron oxide. These marbles are similar to ones found on Mars, known as Mars Blueberries. Don't sneak one into your pocket to bring home, because rock collecting is prohibited.

The trail ends at the sign for the Three Ponds/Red Sands Trail and the Hidden Pinyon Trail. Head back the way you came to return the trailhead. Take a different route on the dunes to see if you can spot anything new.

Rank 4

52. Red Sands Trail/ Three Ponds Trail

RATING	Wanderer, due to distance and sandy terrain
ROUND TRIP DISTANCE	3.5 miles
ROUND-TRIP TIME	2–3 hours
ELEVATION CHANGE	110 feet (from 3,400 to 3,510 feet)
MAP	Trails Illustrated St. George
NEAREST LANDMARK	Snow Canyon State Park
FEES	$6 per vehicle; Utah State Parks pass
RESTROOMS	Flush toilets with sink; water fountains across the main road at the Snow Canyon State Park Campground
DOGS	Not allowed
OPERATING HOURS	6 a.m. to 10 p.m. daily

COMMENT: Red Cliffs, which are said to be redder than the cliffs in Red Rock Canyon near Las Vegas, mix with white sandstone and evidence of past lava flows along this hike. The first half of the hike is through more compact sand. As you head closer to the canyon, the sand gets deeper. Be prepared to stop and dump the shoes a time or two on one of the larger rocks that surround the trail.

You may be lucky to spot one of the areas most popular reptiles, the Gila monster. Be aware that the Gila monster is poisonous. The nocturnal kit fox may be seen as the sun sets. Antelope squirrels are common on the trails of Snow Canyon State Park.

The trail rolls along as you navigate past the petrified dunes. If you are visiting during the peak wildflower season from late March to early May, cactus flowers and lilies also bloom along the trail. Depending on what time of year you visit, there may be water pools. More than likely the pools will not contain water; hence the recent change of trail name to the Red Sands Trail. But many park maps and signs still name the trail Three Pools. The park receives very little snow despite its name (it is named after the Utah leaders Erastus and Lorenzo Snow). This trail is best hiked in spring, fall, and winter, because of the high summer temperatures. It is a part of the desert biome.

GETTING THERE: From Interstate 15 south, take Exit 10/Washington. Turn right at the ramp and then make a quick left at the light. Continue for 5.0 miles to the intersection of Bluff St. and SR 18. Go through the light and continue on Snow Canyon Parkway for 3.5 miles until you reach the park entrance.

The Red Sands Trail follows along the dunes.

From I-15 north, take Exit 6 onto Bluff St. Head north on Bluff St. to Snow Canyon Parkway and continue on Snow Canyon Parkway for 3.5 miles until you reach the park entrance.

THE ROUTE: This out-and-back trail begins from the parking lot at the trailhead for the Hidden Pinyon Trail and the Three Ponds/Red Sands Trail.

Head northwest from the parking lot. In a few minutes, views of the Balkan Dome will be on the left. Around the 0.1 mile mark the paved Whiptail Trail joins the Three Ponds/Red Sands Trail for a short while. After the Whiptail Trail splits off to the north, the trail becomes a bit rocky for a short time.

There is a second junction around 0.2 mile on the right for the Hidden Pinyon Trail. This trail runs close to the Red Sands/Three Ponds Trail. At this point, the trail climbs slightly and there are some lava rocks to navigate for a short time. The lava rocks can be sharp and are easy to trip on. Little ones need to use extra caution here.

At close to 0.4 mile, a brown Bureau of land Management sign with a map points you straight to continue on the Red Sands Trail. The Hidden Pinyon Trail goes to the left. You will reach a junction with the Petrified Dunes Trail to the right at around 0.5 miles, which is the high point of the trail. Continue straight to the pools.

The Hidden Pinyon Overlook Spur is at 0.8 mile from the start of the hike. This is a very short overlook trail of 0.1 mile, but it offers spectacular views. The trail soon enters the wash area, and the sand becomes thicker. Try to focus on the views. Follow the sign for the correct path through the north-to-south running wash.

You'll cross over the West Canyon Rd. at about 1.0 mile and continue on the trail for another 0.75 mile until you reach the pools. At this point, the trail begins to run parallel to a horse trail. Look for signage again to stay on trail. Black lava rocks contrast the red sand trail, as you get closer to the canyon and the pools.

RED SANDS TRAIL/THREE PONDS TRAIL

Views of Pictograph Mountain—best known as the predominant peak in *Butch Cassidy and the Sundance Kid*—dominate the landscape. Trudge through the drainage area, now full of deep red sand, toward the pools at the edge of the Red Mountains. The wash runs west for about 0.5 mile before it turns north and becomes narrow. Black desert varnish streaks across the 400-foot Navajo sandstone walls and there is more evidence of black lava flows in this area. The canyon area offers the best chance of any shade on this trail, but there are plenty of places to stop and rest.

Only the first pothole pool is visible from the trail. Depending on how much water it contains, you may not be able to access the two farther pools by climbing through the first; you might have to scramble above the notch to see them. Frogs are frequent visitors to the pools when they contain water. After a cool-down in the pools (if you are lucky), follow the trail in the opposite direction back to the trailhead. An alternative route back is to take the Hidden Pinyon Trail from where the trails intersect. If you didn't take the time to take the short overlook spur trail on the way out, don't miss it on the way back.

On the Way Home

SNOW CANYON STATE PARK SAND DUNES

Don't miss the opportunity to play in one of the largest state park sandboxes in the United States while at Snow Canyon State Park. Bring sand toys and a Frisbee for a fun day at the "beach." Pack sunscreen, water, blankets, or towels, and a picnic lunch or dinner, to enjoy a few hours of playtime. Be on the lookout for holes (hole building is the most popular activity here) and little sticker bushes that may poke your little ones' feet. The sand can be super hot, especially in summer afternoons, so plan your visit accordingly

There are two places to park. The first and smaller lot along the park road takes you right to the dunes. A second gravel lot north of the south entrance/exit is for the south picnic area and contains bathrooms. From the south picnic area, you must hike roughly 0.5 mile round-trip. Reptile and animal tracks can often be seen in the deep red sand.

Snow Canyon State Park Sand Dunes

1002 N. Snow Canyon Rd.
Ivins, UT 84738
(435) 628-2255
https://stateparks.utah.gov/parks/snow-canyon
Admission: $6 per vehicle; Utah parks pass
Hours: 6 a.m. to 10 p.m. daily

Moab Area

A mecca for mountain bikers, hikers and off-road enthusiasts, Moab is an adventure seekers playground. Home to two national parks and one state park, thousands and thousands of visitors flock to the area. Over thirty movies and twenty TV shows have filmed in Moab. There is debate on where Moab got its name. Some think it was from the first postmaster William Andrew Pierce from a biblical reference while others historians believe it is derived from the Paiute word moapa or mosquito.

Moab is a playground for hikers, mountain bikers and other outdoor enthusiasts.

Rank 4

53. Corona Arch Trail

RATING	Wanderer, due to elevation change, Moki steps, and ladders
ROUND TRIP DISTANCE	3.0 miles
ROUND-TRIP TIME	2 hours
ELEVATION CHANGE	480 feet (from 3,990 to 4,470 feet)
MAP	Trails Illustrated Moab
NEAREST LANDMARK	Gold Bar Campground
FEES	None
RESTROOMS	One pit toilet near the campground
DOGS	Must be leashed
OPERATING HOURS	One hour before sunrise to one hour after sunset

COMMENT: While the mileage and elevation gain isn't substantial, this hike requires scrambling across slickrock, climbing a ladder, and using a cable aid to climb to the arches. You will also have to cross live railroad tracks with no warning lights or gates. There is virtually no shade on this hike, and there is no access to water. Therefore, visit during spring, fall, or early mornings in the summer. This is desert bighorn sheep lambing ground, so keep dogs leashed. Poop bags are available at the trailhead. Corona Arch and Bootlegger Canyon are examples of the desert biome.

Slickrock dominates the majority of the hike, which is slippery if wet. Several potholes in the rock collect water after rain. Cactus and juniper line the trail growing in the cryptobiotic soil. Be sure to look up on the canyon walls for rock climbers. With Moab's typically mild weather, this hike is accessible year round.

GETTING THERE: From Moab, take 191 north for 4.0 miles. Turn left (south) on Utah 279/Potash Rd. Travel southeast on Utah 279 for just shy of 10.0 miles. Turn right into the parking lot for the Corona Arch Trailhead. There are approximately 35 parking spots.

THE ROUTE: From the parking lot, begin with a short climb headed east. Shortly thereafter, there is Bureau of Land Management (BLM) fencing to protect bighorn sheep. At 0.1 mile, sign in at the BLM Register. The railroad tracks are right after the BLM fencing.

An old roadbed bends to the east as the trail meanders through some wash and up to a bench. As you head into Bootlegger Canyon, follow the cairns and green paint marks. The trail descends into the canyon. A set of safety cables and footholds

The varied terrain to Corona Arch makes this trail fun for all ages.

chiseled into the rock help with the steep slope. Go slow and steady with little hikers here.

At 0.75 mile, a field of about 50 cairns comes into view. From here, you can see both Bowtie Arch on the left and Corona Arch on the right. This is a good place to stop for a water break. If the ladder and Moki steps will be too much adventure for your hikers, this is a good place to turn around.

Beyond the field of cairns, the trail leads left to a set of Moki steps carved into the sandstone with handrails and cables. Navigating this section of trail is the most difficult part. Kids might want to crawl up and butt scoot down.

After the steps, the trail leads to a six-foot metal ladder bolted into the slickrock on the left. Slowly climb the ladder to the top of the bench where a twisted juniper tree sits. High fives are now in order as you have completed the most challenging part of this route. Keep hiking across the bench toward Bowtie Arch. Be mindful of the steep drop offs to the right of the trail. Keep little hikers left toward the canyon walls to be safe.

There are lots of lizards closer to Bowtie Arch. A pothole type arch, Bowtie Arch has water that trickles through it during periods of heavy rain. After admiring this arch, continue to Corona Arch. It is easier to access Corona Arch going lower on the slickrock. Some people say Corona Arch resembles Rainbow Bridge, and it is sometimes called "Little Rainbow Bridge."

Corona Arch has a 105-foot opening.

You may encounter lizards as you get closer to Bowtie Arch. Take in the views, and lie down and look at the arch from underneath. Return the way you came enjoying the delightful views of Bootlegger Canyon and the Colorado River as you descend slowly back to your car.

TRAIL EXTENSION: Look left for signs of a sand trail at around the 0.5-mile mark where the main trail levels off. This sand trail is not signed. It leads to Pinto Arch, a pothole arch. This is a grade-3 climb and adds an additional 1.0 mile to the hike. The trail to Pinto Arch changes from sand to rock, as you get closer to the arch. Just below the arch is an expansive section of desert varnish and moss. The level of difficulty of the trail changes to a Pathfinder.

HISTORY IN HIKING: The Difference Between Arches and Bridges

Utah is said to be home to over 800 arches and bridges. There are four main types of arches and bridges: pothole, freestanding, cliff, and natural bridges. Pothole arches are created when water collects in a natural pot-type hole. Continued weathering causes the water to cut through the sandstone. Eventually a hole is created from the erosion. Natural bridges are arches that are located near stream channels or streams. Cliff arches are arches on the side or next to cliffs and rock walls. To be an arch, light has to flow through it. Freestanding arches are sometimes referred to as windows; these arches stand alone without fins, cliffs, or rock walls for support.

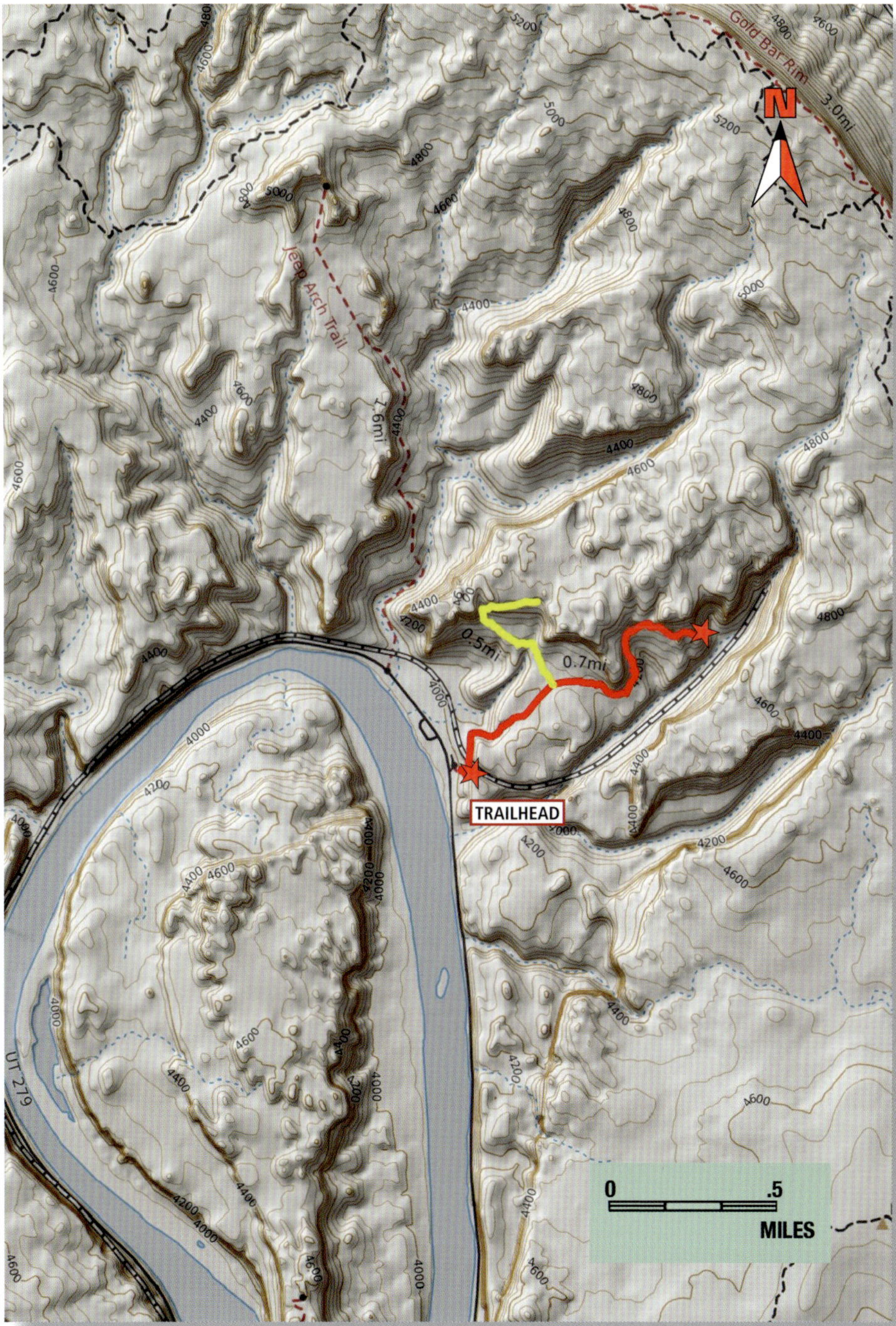

CORONA ARCH TRAIL

Rank 4

54. Grandstaff Canyon to Morning Glory Bridge Trail

RATING	Pathfinder, due to water crossings and trail length
ROUND TRIP DISTANCE	4.7 miles
ROUND-TRIP TIME	2.5 hours
ELEVATION CHANGE	300 feet (from 3,981 to 4,281 feet)
MAP	Trails Illustrated Moab North
NEAREST LANDMARK	Moab
FEES	None
RESTROOMS	One pit toilet
DOGS	Must be leashed
OPERATING HOURS	One hour before sunrise to one hour after sunset

COMMENT: According to the Bureau of Land Management, Morning Glory Bridge is the sixth largest natural bridge in the United States, spanning 243 feet. Until recently, this trail was called Negro Bill Canyon and many maps still carry that name. The canyon is named after black prospector and rancher William Grandstaff, who raised cattle there in the late 1800s.

Popular with rapellers, the Morning Glory Bridge Trail is a sand trail, but the sand is not deep. There is poison ivy on the trail, and you may see a sign at the beginning of the hike noting one of its locations. You will more than likely experience multiple water crossings on the trail, some more difficult than others. The trail has both sections of shade and sections of full exposure. This trail is a part of the forest biome and can be enjoyed year round.

GETTING THERE: From Moab, head east on Scenic Byway 128. The road follows the Colorado River. Around 3.0 miles down the byway, you will reach the Grandstaff Trailhead and parking lot on the right. There are 25 to 30 parking spots at the trailhead.

THE ROUTE: This out-and-back trail begins with a short hill and then rock steps. At 0.15 mile the trail turns to slickrock. One section may be wet and slippery, so look left to follow an alternative and drier route. At 0.35 mile there is a cave on the left. Shortly after the cave at 0.45 mile, you may find a government wilderness study book that you can add your name to. Look for birds of prey soaring above the cliff walls.

Morning Glory Bridge is popular with rapellers.

The trail continues to follow a stream to the right as you make your way to the bridge. You can get to the stream on the right for a snack break, or dip your feet to cool down. Dogs can splash around here. Brown wooden signs or plastic signs on trees keep you on the right path. The Navajo sandstone cliff walls are surrounded by forest with diverse trees, plants, and grasses, including pine, cactus, Mormon tea, and Utah juniper berry.

A little past the 0.5 mile mark you will find the first of about a dozen stream crossings; look for a rock outcropping and rock wall to left marking the spot. Several water crossings occur one after another.

About 0.75 mile in, the trail heads through a wash area that may contain water. Just shy of a mile, the trail becomes rocky and features rock stairs. The large rocks are a great spot to have a water or snack break. The trail begins to meander through the forest with nice shade cover before it heads back up against the rocks.

Beyond the 1.0 mile mark, the trail becomes slickrock and butts up against a rock wall on the left and a stream on the right. This is a perfect place to test your rock skipping skills. At 1.25 miles there is another water crossing with an overhang, and shortly after, another stream crossing that can be navigated a few ways. The stream is now on the left.

The stream crossings continue as the stream bends and twists. Be sure to stay on the main trail. You will pass a side canyon that heads to the right. Keep on the main trail as it bends to the left. Just past 1.5 miles the trail climbs. This rocky section boasts some elevation gain but is very manageable as it heads towards a wide canyon area. At 1.75 miles, navigate rock steps that lead the trail down and closer to the water.

The various water crossings along the trail are perfect places for skipping rocks.

After a few more stream crossings you will reach the Y in the canyon just shy of the 2.0-mile mark. The trail now climbs up and to the right (look for the brown sign and cairns) as you climb to Morning Glory Bridge. As you explore the bridge, see if you can see or hear the water that streams out from the face of the rock. Return the way you came to the trailhead. Don't forget to be on the lookout for poison ivy.

On the Way Home

MOAB ROCK SHOP

Don't skip a visit to the Moab Rock Shop when you are in town. The shop features fossils, rocks and minerals from around the world. They even have a large selection of rocks and fossils prevalent in Utah. This is the perfect place to spend a few of those piggy bank dollars! You can even find flyers at many of the restaurants or local motels/hotels to bring in and get your own piece of dinosaur bone.

Moab Rock Shop
600 N Main St.
Moab, UT 84532
(435) 259-7312
https://moabrockshop.com/
Hours: 8:30 a.m. to 10 p.m. daily except closed on Thanksgiving and Christmas

GRANDSTAFF CANYON TO MORNING GLORY BRIDGE TRAIL

The Island in the Sky section of Canyonlands.

Ranger created cairns keep hikers on the right track along the trails.

Canyonlands National Park

President Lyndon Johnson's first declared Canyonlands as a national park on September 12th, 1964. The park contains four districts all divided by rivers: Island in the Sky, The Needles, The Maze and then the Colorado and Green rivers as well. Mesas, canyons, and pinnacles make up the 337,598 acres. Over 700,000 people visit the park each year.

A haze over Canyonlands National Park.

Rank 2

55. Grand View Point Trail

RATING	Searcher, due to minimal elevation change
ROUND TRIP DISTANCE	2.0 miles
ROUND-TRIP TIME	1.5 hours
ELEVATION CHANGE	80 feet (from 6,190 to 6,270 feet)
MAP	Trails Illustrated Canyonlands
NEAREST LANDMARK	Grand View Point Overlook
FEES	$25 a day; National Parks pass; Southeast Utah Parks pass
RESTROOMS	Pit toilets
DOGS	Not allowed
OPERATING HOURS	24 hours

COMMENT: This trail follows the rim of the canyon. It is wide and stays back from the edge, but keep younger hikers close because the drop offs are very steep. This is a nice hike for kids looking to move up in distance because it is relatively flat. The views are more than enough to keep older kids intrigued. This hike offers what many call the best view of the Island in the Sky. Spring and fall are ideal times to hike this trail because of the lack of shade. Sagebrush, Utah pine, and wildflowers including desert princess plume line the trail. Sunrise, sunset, and pre- or post-thunderstorms offer the best light and drama for photo seekers. The Grand View Point Trail crosses over the desert biome. The Grand View Point Trail can be enjoyed year round.

GETTING THERE: From Moab, head north on S. Main St./UT 191 north. Turn left onto UT 313 and follow it for almost 15.0 miles. Stay straight onto Island in the Sky Rd., which turns into Grand View Point Rd. a little after 3.0 miles. Take Grand View Point Rd. for 3.0 miles to the entrance of Canyonlands National Park. From the Island in the Sky Visitor Center, drive 6.25 miles south on the Main Island Rd. At the junction of Upheaval Dome Rd./Grand View Rd., bear left toward Grand View Point. Continue for 6.0 miles, past White Rim Overlook, to the Grand View Overlook and trailhead. The parking lot is large and has spaces for RVs, but it fills up quickly and you may have to wait for a space.

THE ROUTE: The trail begins at the parking lot on a paved section that is ADA accessible to the viewpoint. Rock stairs on the right lead down from the overlook to the beginning of the path's route along the rim of the canyon. Past the stairs, the trail becomes a mix of relatively flat sandstone, slickrock, and red sand. Potholes line the early landscape and may contain water.

GRAND VIEW POINT TRAIL

Navigating the pot holes along the Grand View Point Trail.

The views start from the moment you start this hike. From both the viewpoint and the beginning of the trail around the rim, you can see Monument Basin to your left. It was once known as Standing Rock Basin because of the number of spires in the area. The 305-foot Totem Pole spire is on the left as well. Interpretive signs at the trailhead point out the sights.

As you head southwest, you will follow the rim of the mesa. Look east to see the La Sal Mountains, which may be covered in snow. Though the Colorado and Green Rivers carved this area, neither can be seen from the viewpoints along the trail. But if you have a keen eye, you may spot the remnants of the off-road tracks that bulldozers made while canyon mining for uranium.

Many cairns dot the landscape, and it is virtually impossible to get lost on this trail even in places that aren't well marked. At about 0.5 mile, you can see both sides of the canyon with the Abajo Mountains southeast and the Henry Mountains to the west. When you have westerly views, look for a light colored rock named Cleopatra's Chair. To the north, Candlestick Tower comes into view. A series of steps leads up toward slickrock as you approach the end point. The trail ends when the level ground ends, at a mass of rocks about 15 feet high. You can scramble up for a 360-degree panoramic view of the surrounding area, including Junction Butte and the White Rim. Look for the knobs, spires, and fins across the landscape in the southwest that mark the Maze District of Canyonlands. The Abajo Mountains distinguish the Needles District of Canyonlands.

After taking in the breathtaking views, retrace your steps back across the rim of the canyon to the parking lot. Picnic tables at the trailhead offer a perfect place to enjoy lunch or dinner after a day in the park.

Rank 2

56. Mesa Arch Trail

RATING	Searcher, due to terrain and length
ROUND TRIP DISTANCE	0.5 mile
ROUND-TRIP TIME	30 minutes to 1 hour
ELEVATION CHANGE	100 feet (from 6,100 to 6,180 feet)
MAP	Trails Illustrated Canyonlands
NEAREST LANDMARK	Willow Creek Campground
FEES	$25 a day; National Parks pass; Southeast Utah Parks pass
RESTROOMS	Pit toilets
DOGS	Not allowed
OPERATING HOURS	24 hours

COMMENT: This hike is one of the most popular hikes in the Island in the Sky portion of Canyonlands National Park, especially during sunrise. If you visit at sunrise, bring headlamps and a blanket, and be ready to bump elbows with eager photographers. Pick up a guide at the trailhead describing the local vegetation and other facts about this desert biome trail. The trail is a mix of sand, slickrock, and rock steps. Mesa Arch is a featured landscape desktop background in Windows 7. Hikers can enjoy Mesa Arch year round.

GETTING THERE: From Moab, head north on S. Main St./ UT 191. Turn left onto UT 313 and follow it for almost 15.0 miles. Stay straight onto Island in the Sky Rd., which turns into Grand View Point Rd. a little after 3.0 miles. Continue on Grand View Point Rd. for 3.0 miles to the entrance of Canyonlands National Park. The Mesa Arch Trailhead is a little over 6.0 miles from the Island in the Sky Visitor Center. From the entrance, take the main road past the visitor center and continue to the Mesa Arch Trailhead parking lot.

THE ROUTE: From the parking lot, either head straight up or head left and around to the arch. Straight up is the short climb. Counter-clockwise seems to be the preferred direction for this loop. Because this is such a popular hike, you will most likely be able to follow others on the trail, but the hike has ranger-built cairns and is easy to follow.

The trail climbs from the start on rock steps with pockets of sand in between. At the top of the hill at approximately 0.1 mile, the trail levels off. As you hike along, there are peek-a-boo views of the arch to the left as you begin to descend a hill. Don't

The Sunrise at Mesa Arch is spectacular.

forget to look east for views of the Colorado River. Prickly pear cactus and Mormon tea, pinyon pine, and juniper are some of the vegetation you will see here.

At 0.25 mile, after crossing some sandstone ridges, you will reach the arch. Mesa Arch is a 12-foot high pothole arch spanning 50 feet across the top of a 500-foot cliff. The arch sits at the top of an over 1,200-foot drop into the canyon. The drop off around the ledge is quite steep making it essential to keep little ones close at hand and keep running and scrambling at bay around the arch.

The arch is sometimes referred to as a picture window. Look left and you may be able to see Washing Woman Arch among the pinnacles. Views of Buck Canyon and the peaks of the La Sal Mountains are also visible through, above, and to the side of the arch. In winter and spring, the peaks may be covered in snow. The famous four-by-four 100-mile White Rim Trail can also be seen.

Continue on the loop back to the trailhead. The loop back to the right has views of Aztec Butte and the surrounding area.

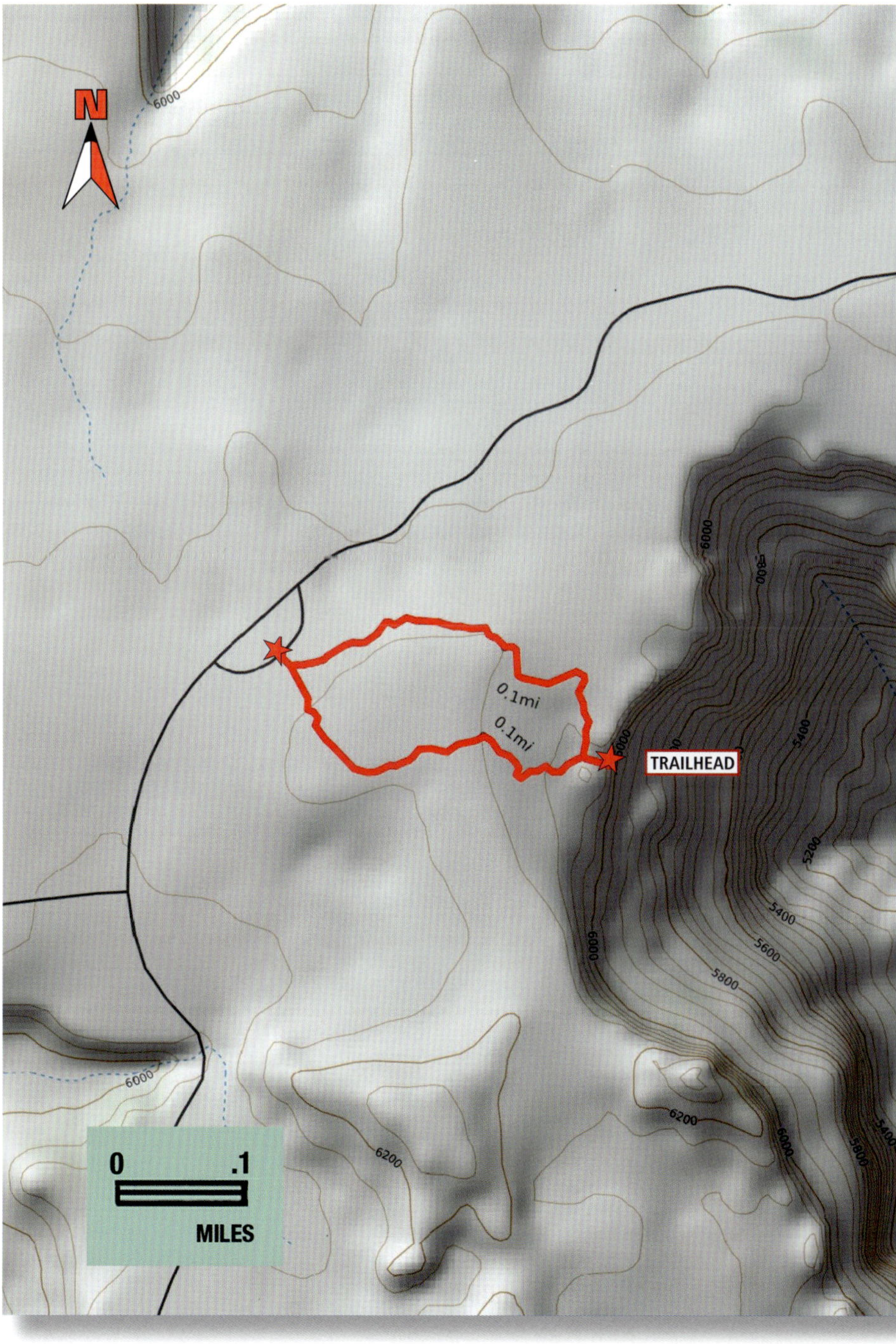

MESA ARCH TRAIL

Rank 2

57. Whale Rock Trail

RATING	Searcher, due to short length but adventurous terrain climbing the whale
ROUND TRIP DISTANCE	1 mile
ROUND-TRIP TIME	0.5–1 hour
ELEVATION CHANGE	77 feet (from 5,715 to 5,793 feet)
MAP	Trails Illustrated Canyonlands
NEAREST LANDMARK	Upheaval Dome
FEES	$25 a day; National Parks pass; Southeast Utah Parks pass
RESTROOMS	None
DOGS	Not allowed
OPERATING HOURS	24 hours

COMMENT: Climbing Whale Rock offers some of the best views of Canyonlands National Park, including Upheaval Dome. While the hike to the whale's tail is not difficult, young hikers may need help and a close eye climbing up the actual whale because of the steepness and drop offs. This trail lacks shade and can be quite windy. Whale Rock and all of Canyonlands is part of the desert biome. While Whale Rock can be enjoyed year round, wet and snowy conditions may make climbing and descending off the rock and the trail more difficult.

GETTING THERE: From Moab, head north on S. Main St./UT 191. Turn left onto UT 313 and follow it for almost 15.0 miles. Stay straight onto Island in the Sky Rd., which turns into Grand View Point Rd. a little after 3.0 miles. Follow Grand View Point Rd. for 3.0 miles to the entrance of Canyonlands National Park. From the Island in the Sky Visitor Center, head south 6.0 miles and turn right onto Upheaval Dome Rd. The parking lot holds approximately 10 vehicles. The Whale Rock Trailhead is about 4.0 miles up the road on the right.

THE ROUTE: From the parking lot, head left (northwest) on the trail. At the start, the trail is a flat mix of sand and gravel. As with all the trails in Canyonlands, take great care in staying on the path to not disturb the cryptobiotic crust. The trail leads through shrubs before it turns to mostly slickrock. From now on, the trail is harder to distinguish. Just follow the cairns to stay on the correct path toward the whale's tale.

The terrain becomes a bit uneven at this point, but is not difficult for youngsters to navigate. They may want some hand holding, but nothing is too challenging. The

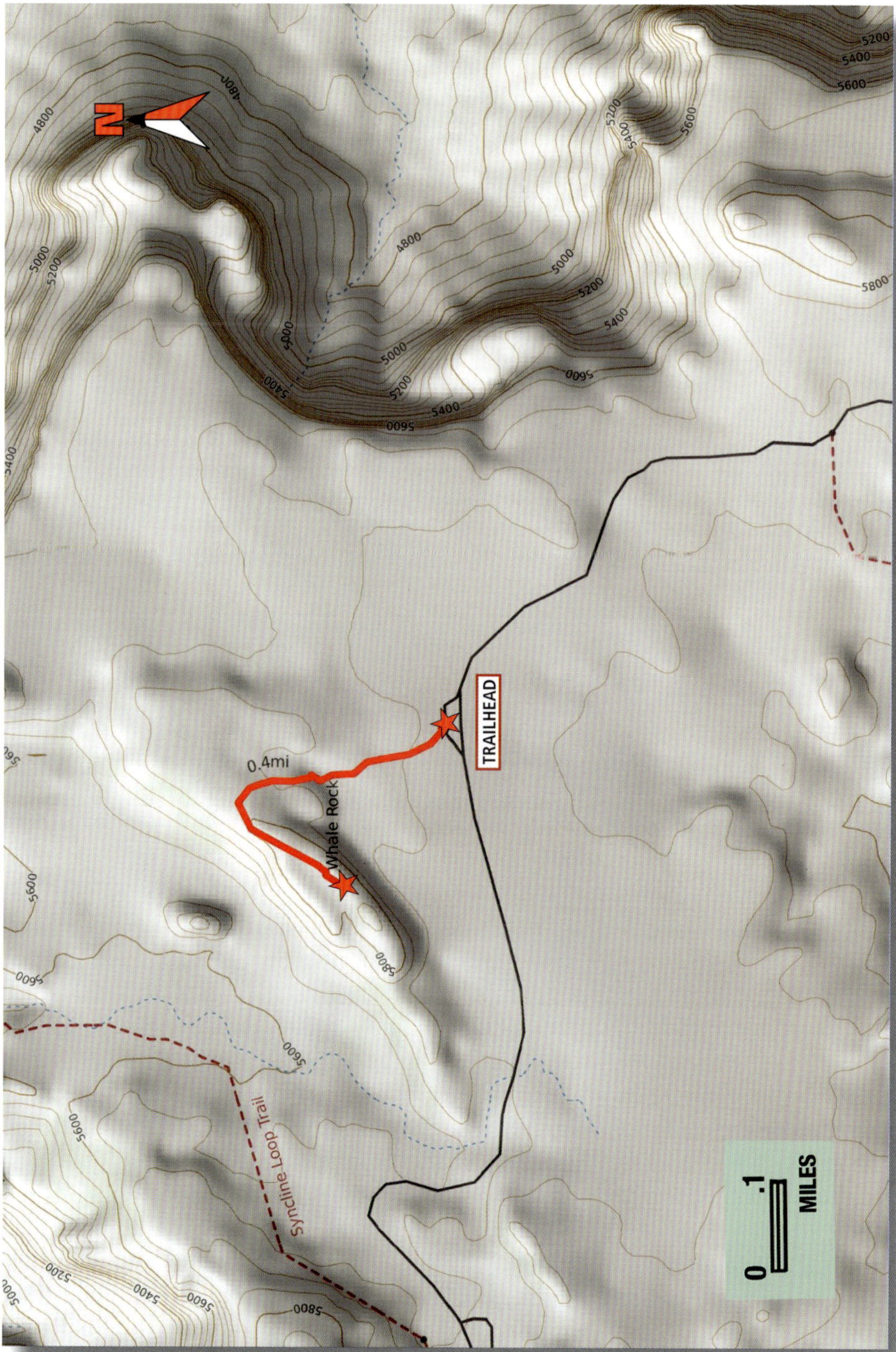

WHALE ROCK TRAIL

It takes some scrambling and butt scooting to get up and down the whale on the Whale Rock Trail.

rock is fairly worn from years of foot traffic, so it may be slick after recent moisture. Without any steep drop offs until you reach the tail section, this is a good trail for introducing children to slickrock and desert hiking.

As you make your way up the whale's body to its tail, cairns continue to dot the landscape. The cairns blend well with the reds of the slickrock, so it may take time to locate the next one. There is a set of uneven rock steps before you get to the whale's tale at about 0.35 mile. Once you arrive at the tail, steep slopes make the hike more challenging for smaller legs. Little ones should be kept close as the drop-offs become longer as you climb higher onto the back of the whale. Potholes dot the back of the whale and may contain water if there was recent rain. Panoramic views greet hikers from the tale to the head.

The red rocks of Canyonlands and Upheaval Dome can be seen in their glory from here. Handrails may or may not be installed to help you navigate the steeper sections up to the top of the whale's head. Butt scooting is encouraged, especially for small hikers. Backtrack to the trailhead after getting your fill of the views.

Arches National Park

Arches National Park was first designated as a national monument in 1929. It was changed into a national park in 1971. It covers 76,679 acres, and has over 2,000 natural stone arches in the park alone. More than a million visitors come to awe at the spires, arches, balanced rocks and fins within the park.

The area around Sandstone Arch is a sand castle building paradise.

Rank 4

58. Delicate Arch Trail

RATING	Wanderer, due to terrain, distance, and elevation change
ROUND TRIP DISTANCE	3.0 miles out and back
ROUND-TRIP TIME	3–4 hours
ELEVATION CHANGE	480 feet (from 4,349 to 4,829 feet)
MAP	Trails Illustrated Arches National Park
NEAREST LANDMARK	Wolfe Ranch
FEES	$25 a day; National Parks pass; Southeast Utah Parks pass
RESTROOMS	Pit toilets
DOGS	Not allowed
OPERATING HOURS	24 hours

COMMENT: One of the most iconic of arches, Delicate Arch is featured on the Utah license plate. The arch has had many names throughout history, including Cowboy's Chaps, Salt Wash Arch, and Old Maid's Bloomers. A writer in 1934 gave it the current name because it was "the most delicately chiseled arch in the entire area." The Olympic torch for the 2002 Winter Olympics also passed through the arch.

The arch faces northeast and is made of Entrada sandstone turned red from iron oxide. It stands approximately 60 feet tall with a 48-foot opening. Like most arches in the area, its true scale can only be fully appreciated from under the arch.

This is also one of the most popular trails in the park, so expect crowds, and plan to stand in line to get your photo under the arch. Potholes along the way may contain water. Look for squirrels, rabbits, and rock wrens. Watch your step as lizards and scorpions enjoy the warm trail. Pinyon pines, Utah Juniper, and other desert vegetation line the trail. There is no shade on this hike. Bring more water than you think you need (fill up at the visitor center) and hike early if visiting in the summer. The trail through the desert biome is very popular at sunset. Spring and fall are the best times to hike this trail. Summer brings intense heat, and winter weather makes the trail very slick.

GETTING THERE: From Denver, take Interstate 70 west about 40 miles to the Georgetown exit (Exit 228). Drive toward town and turn right toward Georgetown at the first four-way stop; look for signs to Guanella Pass. Climb west and then south out of town on Guanella Pass Road/Highway 381 to the pass—10 miles. The pass can be a challenging road in the winter, but it is plowed and generally negotiable in a car with snow tires.

Delicate Arch is the most iconic arch in the park.

On Highway 381, when you break out into the open and see the striking view of the Bierstadt-Evans massif to the east, look for the Guanella Pass trailhead for Bierstadt on the left/east side of the road 10 miles from Georgetown.

THE ROUTE: As you begin, you can see what is left of the John Wesley Wolfe Ranch. The ranch was built in 1888 and abandoned 22 years later. Shortly after the homestead, a small bridge takes you over Salt Wash. Gnats and horseflies are attracted to this area in the warmer months, so wear bug spray and long sleeves.

This trail is wide and open, but be prepared to slow down the pace because of the large number of hikers. Observe trail etiquette and be patient, and use the opportunity for teaching young hikers.

Don't miss the spur trail on your left just past the bridge, which leads to a Ute petroglyph panel featuring a hunt for bighorn sheep and horses. It is about a five minute walk to the panel. The trail climbs slightly for the first mile. The switchbacks make the elevation gain easier as you climb the Morrison Formation. You will pass through another wash before reaching a large slab of slickrock at 0.8 mile. After this area the elevation change is more noticeable. Take your time across the slab; it might be confusing, but there are cairns and a steady stream of other hikers. Also, most of the slickrock is well worn, showing the path. The slab is quite grippy if you have on proper shoes, but if it has recently rained, the slab will be slippery. Steps in

Delicate Arch is used on the license plate for the state of Utah. *Photo: Jamie Recio*

the sandstone help in some of the steeper places. Grab those little hands on this part of the trail!

The views surrounding the trail are quite spectacular. To the north, you may see some hanging gardens where water seeps. The La Sal Mountains often have snow-capped peaks even through late summer.

At 1.2 miles the trail levels off. There is a sand wash with two fins of sandstone surrounding it, followed by alcoves and a bridge on the left at around 1.4 miles. There is another set of stairs that leads to more slickrock, followed by a narrow ledge of approximately 200 feet. You can walk two people across or comfortably with a child backpack if there isn't two-way traffic, but watch the exposure. This area tends to be the most frightening for hikers, especially those afraid of heights. Before you reach Delicate Arch, Frame Arch is on the right. Many photographers use this arch to "frame" Delicate Arch, and you can scramble up the rock to do so.

Keep looking forward as the arch finally comes into view a few steps past Frame Arch, just shy of the 1.5-mile mark. Once you arrive at the arch, be prepared to wait in line if you want that holiday card photo. Thankfully the views help with the waiting. Children enjoy playing in the sandstone amphitheater bowl that surrounds the arch, but it can be quite terrifying for parents to let their children run freely on the steep terrain.

Be sure to look above for white-throated swift nests, which are often seen around the arch in the summer. There are plenty of ledges to rest and take in the view before heading back to the trailhead.

DELICATE ARCH TRAIL

Rank 6

59. Landscape Arch and Double O Arch Trail

RATING	Adventurer, due to distance and terrain, including fins
ROUND TRIP DISTANCE	4.2 miles out and back
ROUND-TRIP TIME	3 hours
ELEVATION CHANGE	650 feet (from 5,200 to 5,850 feet)
MAP	Trails Illustrated Arches National Park
NEAREST LANDMARK	Devil's Garden
FEES	$25 a day; National Parks pass; Southeast Utah Parks pass
RESTROOMS	Pit toilets
DOGS	Not allowed
OPERATING HOURS	24 hours

COMMENT: Landscape Arch was named by Frank Beckwith, the leader of the Arches National Monument Scientific Expedition in the winter of 1933-1934. Landscape Arch is 306 feet long, making it the fifth longest natural rock span in the world. Until the 1990's, you could stand under the arch, but due to rock fall, the National Park Service closed the area. But you can enjoy the arch from a distance behind a fence, and there is a spur sand trail that leads closer to the arch. If you have young children or inexperienced hikers in your group, Landscape Arch is a good place to turnaround for a 1.8 mile round-trip hike. The trail becomes primitive after the arch with sand, fins, and areas of scrambling.

Notice that the soil around the trail is sometimes black in color; this is because the biological soil contains cyanobacteria, a combination of red sand and rock particles. Desert plants, mosses, and fungi grow here. Drought escapers, resistors, and evaders are desert plants that can all be seen on this trail and throughout the park. Escapers such as wildflowers bloom in later spring and early summer. Cacti and yucca are popular resistors, along with Mormon tea. Evaders are not as common, but you may find columbine in the wetter parts of the park. Pinyon pine and juniper provide the small areas of shade on this hike.

The trail to Landscape Arch and Double O Arch passes through the desert biome. While there are bathrooms at the trailhead, there is no access to water. Fill up at the spigot outside of the visitor center.

GETTING THERE: From Moab, drive north on US 191 for 5.0 miles to the park entrance on the right. If traveling from Interstate 70, take the Crescent Junction

The Double O Arch is covered with black desert varnish.

exit at mile marker 181. Drive south on US 191 for 22.0 miles. The park entrance is on the left.

Take the main park road for 18.0 miles to the Devil's Garden Trailhead. The start of the parking lot is on the right; you may see cars lined up along the road waiting to park, as the parking lot serves several trails, a seasonal campground, and a picnic area.

THE ROUTE: Head north from the trailhead through the enclosing walls of Entrada sandstone. Look for a sand area on the left toward the beginning of the hike to enjoy a little playtime. The spur trail for Tunnel Arch and Pine Tree Arch is on the right at 0.3 mile. This is only 0.5 miles round trip. Just before the 1.0-mile mark, you can get a peak of Landscape Arch on the left. Just before Landscape Arch, the trail turns from gravel to deep sand. The sand continues until you reach a rock ramp. The rock ramp is a challenge for little hikers and adults not used to this type of terrain. Take your time to climb the center of the ramp. Follow the cairns to stay on the trail from now on.

Fins make the trail to Double O Arch more challenging.

At 1.3 miles the spur trails for Partition and Navajo Arches are on the left. These add another 0.8 mile to the hike. Previously, Wall Arch was visible on the right, but it collapsed in August 2008. Landscape Arch may also collapse at any time. Climb across several fins, including a mostly flat fin, at around 1.7 miles. The erosion of fins is what created Landscape Arch; you could be making your way across a future arch!

As you cross the fins, you can get a good view of the sky. Search for red-tail hawks and ravens soaring above looking for a kangaroo rat for their next meal. Also look down ahead as a squirrel, chipmunk, or lizard may scurry across your path. Many animals in the park are nocturnal, so mule deer and bighorn sheep are more often seen in the morning or evening. Snakes may be found warming themselves on the rocks. Be wary of strong winds across the fins; check the wind and weather report before heading out on this hike. The trail enters some wash and continues across a few additional fins. As you cross another fin, begin to look for the Double O Arch on the right. Once you can see the arch at a little over two miles, several different social trails lead to the two arches, which are stacked on each other. The top arch spans 71 feet while the bottom arch spans 21 feet. There may be a log or two to help scramble through the hole in the first arch; the other side provides the best view of the arches and the landscape in the distance, including the Book Cliffs.

A brown sign near Double O Arch shows the directions to continue onto the Primitive Trail, the trail to take to the Dark Angel, and the Primitive Trail back to the parking lot. You will notice a different view on your way back to the trailhead. That is another reason this hike is so enjoyable! If you decide to take the spur trail to Pine Tree Arch, you will get the chance to stand under the arch. Retrace your steps to the trailhead.

HIKE EXTENSION: There are many ways to extend the hike from the Devil's Garden Trailhead. You can add the spur trail hike to Navajo Arch and Partition Arch for an additional 0.8 mile on primitive trail. The spur trail near the trailhead leads to Tunnel Arch and Pine Tree Arch for an additional 0.5 mile. If you want to see the Dark Angel, add about another 1.0 mile, depending on the route you take. If you want to complete the full garden including all the spur trails, it is 7.2 miles of mainly primitive trail with scrambling, drop offs, and virtually no shade.

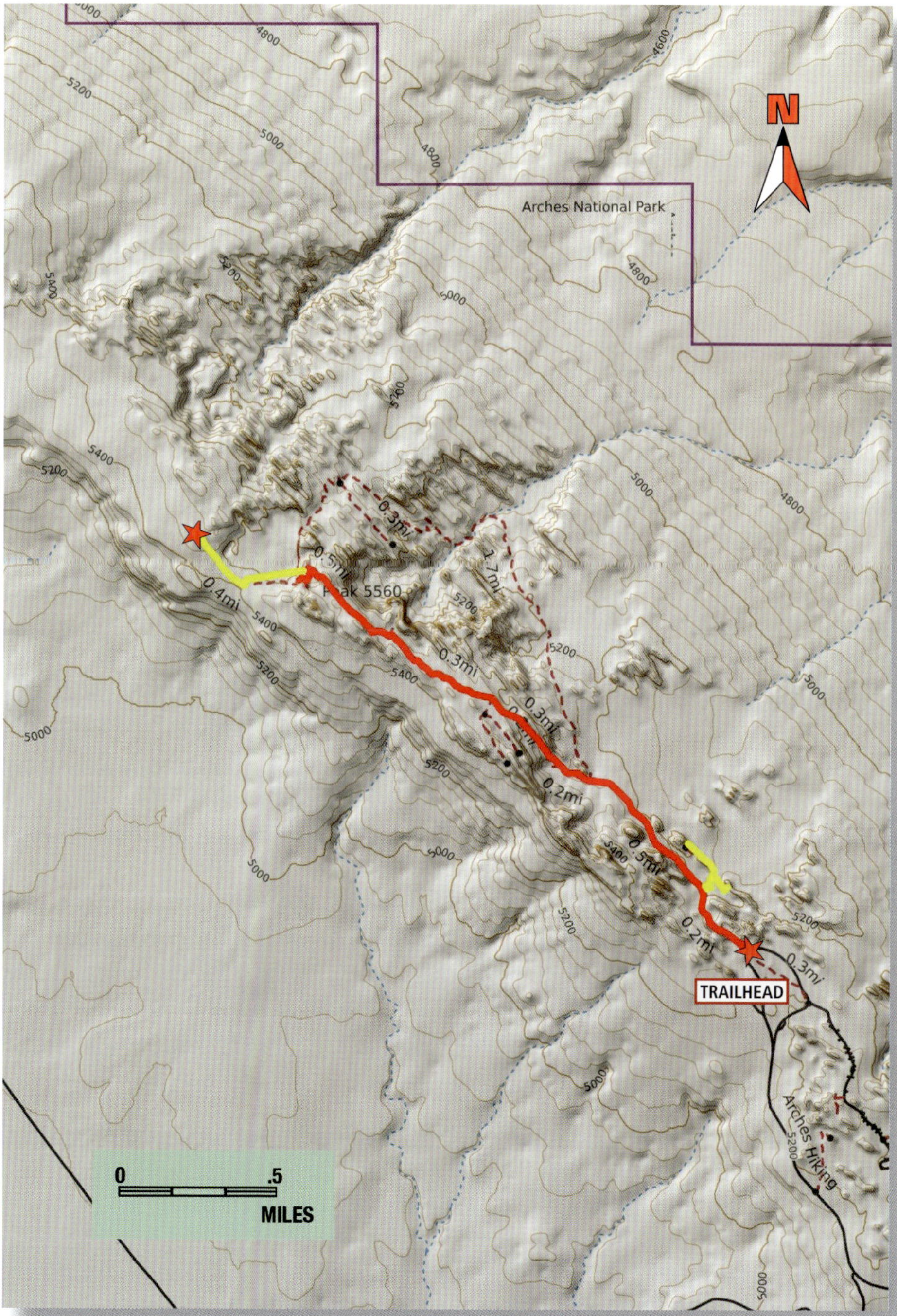

LANDSCAPE ARCH AND DOUBLE O ARCH TRAIL

Rank 2

60. Sand Dune Arch and Broken Arch Loop Trail

RATING	Searcher, due to mostly flat and wide terrain
ROUND TRIP DISTANCE	1.4 miles
ROUND-TRIP TIME	1 hour
ELEVATION CHANGE	177 feet (from 5,137 to 5,278 feet)
MAP	Trails Illustrated Arches National Park
NEAREST LANDMARK	Sand Dune Arch
FEES	$25 a day; National Parks pass; Southeast Utah Parks pass
RESTROOMS	None
DOGS	Not allowed
OPERATING HOURS	24 hours

COMMENT: This is the flattest trail in the park, so it is good for little hikers ready to increase their distance. The short offshoot trail to Sand Dune Arch has the only shade on this hike except for under Broken Arch, so bring water and sun protection. The trail passes through the desert biome. Hikers can enjoy this trail no matter the season.

GETTING THERE: From Moab, drive north on US 191 for 5.0 miles to the park entrance on the right. If traveling from Interstate 70, take the Crescent Junction exit at mile marker 181. Drive south on US 191 for 22 miles. The park entrance is on the left. From the park entrance, follow the main park road for 16.5 miles. The Sand Dune Arch parking lot is on the right and holds about 30 cars with room for an RV or two.

THE ROUTE: This wide trail leaves the trailhead and heads east. At 0.1 mile, you will see an offshoot on the right for the Sand Dune Arch. If you have little ones who tire quickly and you are set on seeing Broken Arch, go to Broken Arch first, as the area around Sand Dune Arch is a climbing playground!

The trail to Sand Dune Arch passes through a mini-slot canyon. Follow the route between the narrow openings of the sandstone walls. It may pose a challenge for little hikers, but they can navigate it with help. The trail turns to deep sand. Many visitors take off their shoes and socks and enjoy the softness and coolness (depending on time of year) of the sand between their toes. At about 0.1 mile, the

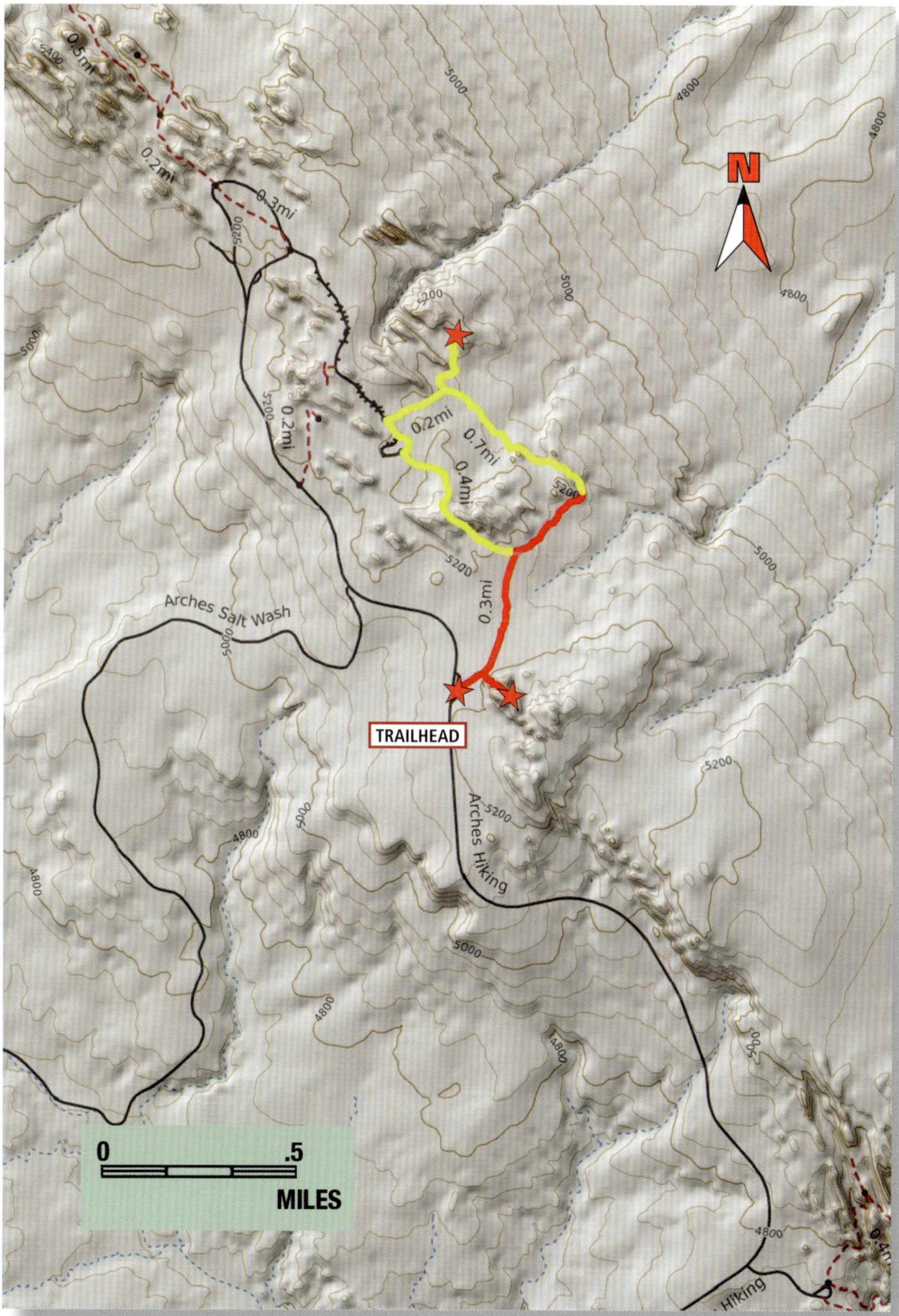

SAND DUNE ARCH AND BROKEN ARCH LOOP TRAIL

Broken Arch stands 43 feet high.

arch is on the right nestled between two sandstone fins. The arch is 30 feet wide and eight feet high.

This is the lone area of shade for most of this hike, so enjoy it. Climbing the arch is not allowed, but there are plenty of places to climb around it. There are many opportunities for fun for kids of all ages here: ledges to climb, a pothole that may be filled with water for splashing, and the sand to run around in. After some sand play, head back to the main trail and follow it northeast toward Broken Arch. The trail is relatively flat toward the arch, making it popular for trail runners. Unobstructed views of the La Sal Mountains can be seen in this area. The vegetation, including juniper and sagebrush, gets thicker as you get closer to the arch. The trail becomes less obvious, so look for cairns and other indicators that you are going the right way. This is where the most elevation change begins, but it is minimal. The trail drops into a wash area that is easy to navigate. Head up and out of the wash, and you have arrived at Broken Arch.

The arch is named for the crack in the middle that seems to divide it in two. It is not in fact broken, but time and erosion will dictate whether it eventually breaks. Broken Arch, at last inside measurement, is 59 feet wide and 43 feet high. With some rock scrambling and jumping, you can stand completely under the arch.

Return to the trailhead the way you came. Stop at Sand Dune Arch if you haven't already done so or if you want more playtime in the sand.

TRAIL EXTENSION: You can continue past Broken Arch to the campground and Tapestry Arch. This adds a little over 0.5 mile to the hike and changes the rating to Seeker for the added distance and rock scrambling.

Dead Horse Point State Park

An International Dark Sky Park, Dead Horse Point State Park was established in 1959. It is named for the natural made horse corral that cowboys used in the 19th century where horses often perished due to exposure. The park sits on the edge of Canyonlands National Park. Dead Horse Point, a mesa 2,000 feet above a gooseneck in the Colorado River, is the most popular destination in the park.

The area of Dead Horse State Park is sometimes called a mini Grand Canyon.

Rank 3

61. East Rim Trail System

RATING	Seeker, due to distance
ROUND TRIP DISTANCE	3.0 miles
ROUND-TRIP TIME	1.5–2 hours
ELEVATION CHANGE	40 feet (from 5,900 to 5,940 feet)
MAP	Trails Illustrated Moab South
NEAREST LANDMARK	Dead Horse Point State Park Visitor Center
FEES	$15 per vehicle; Utah State Parks pass
RESTROOMS	Pit toilets outside of visitor center and at Dead Horse Point
DOGS	Must be leashed
OPERATING HOURS	6 a.m. to 10 p.m.

COMMENT: Dead Horse Point is sometimes referred to as a mini Grand Canyon. In fact, the Grand Canyon scenes in *Driving Miss Daisy* were actually filmed at Dead Horse Point. Park animals are mostly nocturnal, so you might not see much wildlife during the day. But this area is known for birding, so look for scrub jays and birds of prey, including falcons and bald and golden eagles. You might also see wrens, larks, and hummingbirds if you bring some binoculars.

There is no shade on this hike, so plan on an early morning or evening hike if you visit when it's hot. Carry ample water and refill at the overlook. The trail is 2,000 feet above the Colorado River. It tends to not be crowded because most visitors to the park just drive to the various viewpoints. Dead Horse Point is consid ered to be a part of the high desert biome. Perfect picture taking spots can be found all along the trail whether you are looking for a landscape shot or scenic family photo. The trails of Dead Horse Point State Park can be hiked year round. Star gazers will enjoy the night sky views from this trail

GETTING THERE: From Moab, turn left onto Highway 313. Follow Hwy 313 to the top of a mesa. At the top, there is a sign for Dead Horse Point State Park. Turn left (east) to head into the park. Pay the entrance fee and follow the lone road in the park to the visitor center.

THE ROUTE: Beginning from the visitor center, the East Rim Trail is a mix of red sand and slickrock. Look for the brown sign just outside the visitor center noting to go straight to follow the East Rim Trail. The trail follows the east rim to Dead Horse Point, but never gets close to the edge.

The Behind the Rocks area and the La Sal Mountains can be seen from the East Rim Trail.

The trail begins by heading south. It is lined with Utah juniper, sagebrush, and nocturnal plants and wildflowers. Looking over the rim, you can see parts of Arches National Park. At the beginning of the hike, you can also see turquoise-blue solar evaporation ponds for harvesting salt to make potash.

About 0.35 mile up the trail from the visitor center, you will encounter the only hill on this trail. The trail widens at the top and offers expansive views of Dead Horse Point State Park, along with the Behind the Rocks area and the La Sal Mountains. At 0.65 mile, you will see the cutoff trail for the Basin Overlook on the left. Take this spur trail for an additional 0.25 mile each way, or continue on to the Dead Horse Point Overlook.

Close to the 1.0-mile mark, the trail bends around close to the road. Even the car noise doesn't take away from the amazing views. You will reach the east side of "The Neck" at 1.15 miles. The trail narrows here, with just the road separating the East Rim and West Rim Trails. The Neck area holds a lot of superstitions, legends, and myths about ghostly horses and cowboys who were haunted after keeping the best horses and leaving the others to die in the neck.

At 1.25 miles, the trail turns to pavement as you hike the last bit to the lookout area. Follow the pavement for another 0.25 mile until you reach the large parking lot

The East and West Rim Trails meet at the middle at Dead Horse Point.

for Dead Horse Point. Short spurs trails on the left lead to overlooks that are great for picture taking. Many hikers climb higher on the rocks to get a different view. Dead Horse Point is one of the most photographed places in the country, with good reason. The gooseneck of the Colorado River is a sight to be seen. Look down and see if you can make out rafting trips in the horseshoe bend on their way from Moab to Lake Powell. Take a break here and use the restroom, if needed, before you return the 1.5 miles back the way you came to the visitor center.

TRAIL EXTENSION: Take the Basin Overlook Spur to add an additional 0.5 mile to your route. This does not change the rating for this hike, but the spur trail has uneven terrain. Pyramid Butte and Chimney Rock can be seen from this spur trail. Or hike the West Rim Trail back to the visitor center. The West Rim Trail is more primitive and is 2.5 miles one-way, for a total of 4.0 miles.

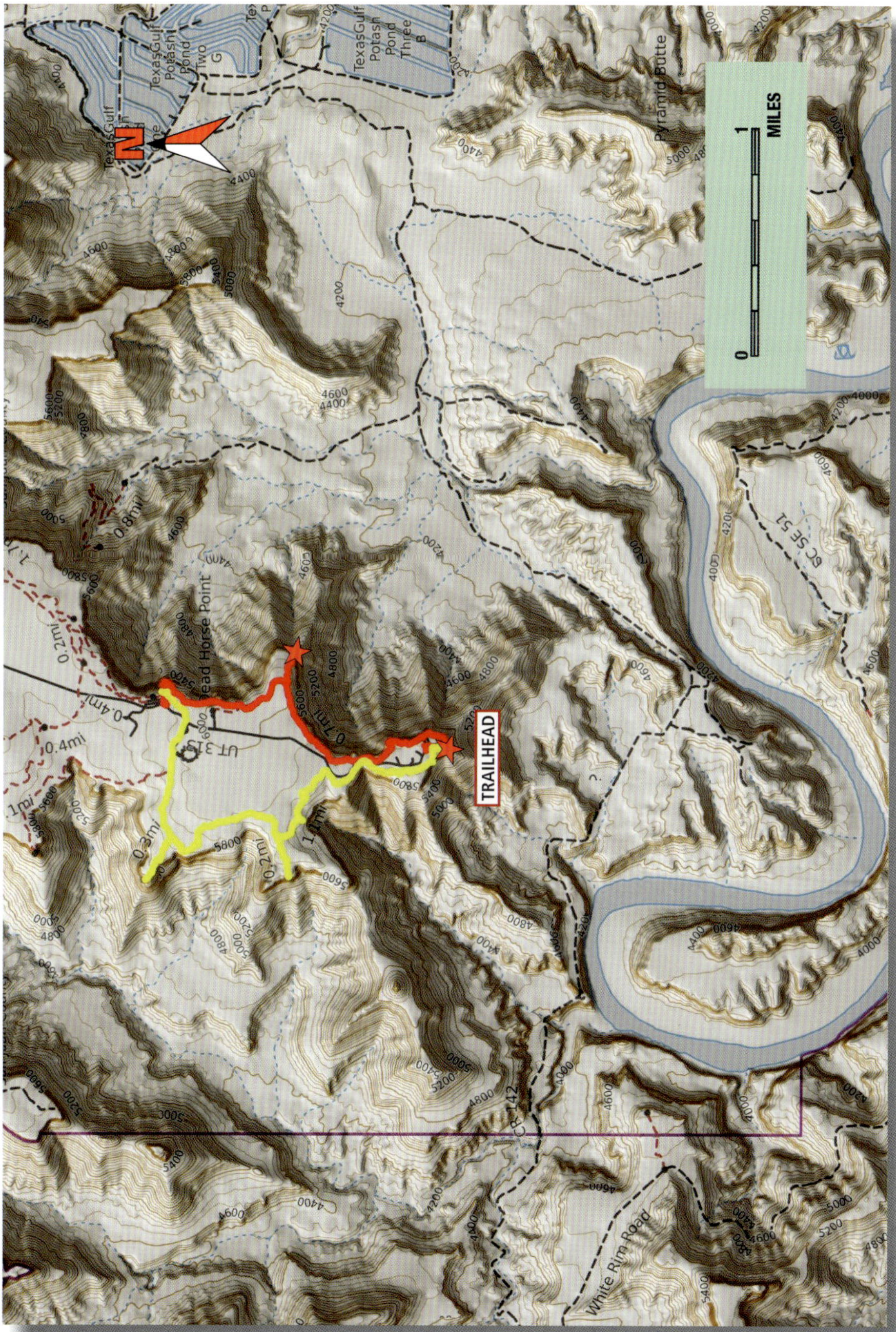

EAST RIM TRAIL SYSTEM

Rank 5

62. West Rim Trail System

RATING	Pathfinder, due to distance and terrain
ROUND TRIP DISTANCE	5.0 miles
ROUND-TRIP TIME	2.5–3 hours
ELEVATION CHANGE	70 feet (from 5,940 to 6,010 feet)
MAP	Trails Illustrated Moab South
NEAREST LANDMARK	Dead Horse Point State Park Visitor Center
FEES	$15 per vehicle; Utah State Parks pass
RESTROOMS	Pit toilets at visitor center and at Dead Horse Point
DOGS	Must be leashed
OPERATING HOURS	6 a.m. to 10 p.m.

COMMENT: This trail is less popular than the East Rim Trail because it goes to a more remote section of the park. The trail is primitive in spots and it takes attention to stay on the trail and follow the cairns at times. Take this trail for a chance to see the sun rise over the Colorado River and the surrounding landscape of this high desert biome.

Because most of the animals are nocturnal, you may not see much wildlife, but look for birds of prey including eagles, and lizards and snakes. There are three official geocaches at Dead Horse Point State Park, Main, East, and West, and it is about 2.0 miles to reach all three points. The trails of Dead Horse Point State Park can be hiked year round.

GETTING THERE: From Moab, turn left onto Highway 313. Follow Hwy 313 to the top of a mesa. At the top, there is a sign for Dead Horse Point State Park. Turn left (east) to head into the park. Pay the entrance fee and follow the lone road in the park to the visitor center.

THE ROUTE: This route, like the East Rim Trail, begins at the visitor center. As you leave the center, look for a brown Bureau of Land Management (BLM) sign and take the trail on the right for the West Rim.

The West Rim Trail starts wide open and level on sandy terrain with views of the state park area. It is easy to follow and relatively obstacle free for the first 1.0 mile. At about 0.33 mile, you will reach the road that leads to the campground and Dead Horse Point. Carefully cross the road to meet up with the trail directly on the other side. The trail runs basically parallel to the road for about a 0.25 mile.

The Big Horn Overlook is the first spur trail on the right about 0.5 mile from the trailhead. This spur trail is 2.5 miles round-trip and takes you to the edge of the rim with sheer drop offs. At just shy of 1.0 mile, there is a sign on the right for the Rim Overlook. This is a short spur trail of 0.5 mile round-trip that takes you to the edge of the rim for views of Shafer Canyon. The spur trail for Shafer Canyon is 0.5 mile long and is also on the right marked with a brown BLM sign around 1.7 miles. Once you pass the spur trail for Shafer Canyon, the trail changes from sand to a mix of sand and uneven slickrock. This is where following the trail gets more difficult, so look for those cairns to guide you on the safest route.

The Meander Overlook spur trail is another 0.5 mile down the trail on the right. If you aren't afraid of heights and trust the balance of your little hikers, this overlook is well worth getting off the beaten path for. The views of the Colorado River are incredible, and you can see several layers of rock that make up the rim, including the Cutler Formation and Kayenta sandstone. It is a short 0.2 mile round-trip.

There are views of the Colorado River along the West Rim Trail.

Just shy of the 2.0-mile mark, the trail heads to the south, close to the road, and it narrows. This is "The Neck" from the west side. Here only the road separates the West Rim and the East Rim Trails. The Neck area holds a lot of superstitions, legends, and myths about ghostly horses and cowboys who were haunted after keeping the best horses and leaving the others to die in the neck. After passing through The Neck the trail opens up again. Continuing south, the trail follows the rim at a distance with some climbs over slickrock. It curves to the southeast as you follow the cairns the last half mile toward Dead Horse Point.

HIKE ALTERNATIVE: Alternatively, take the East Rim Trail back to the visitor center for a total of 4.0 miles.

The makings of small hoodoos can be found around the park.

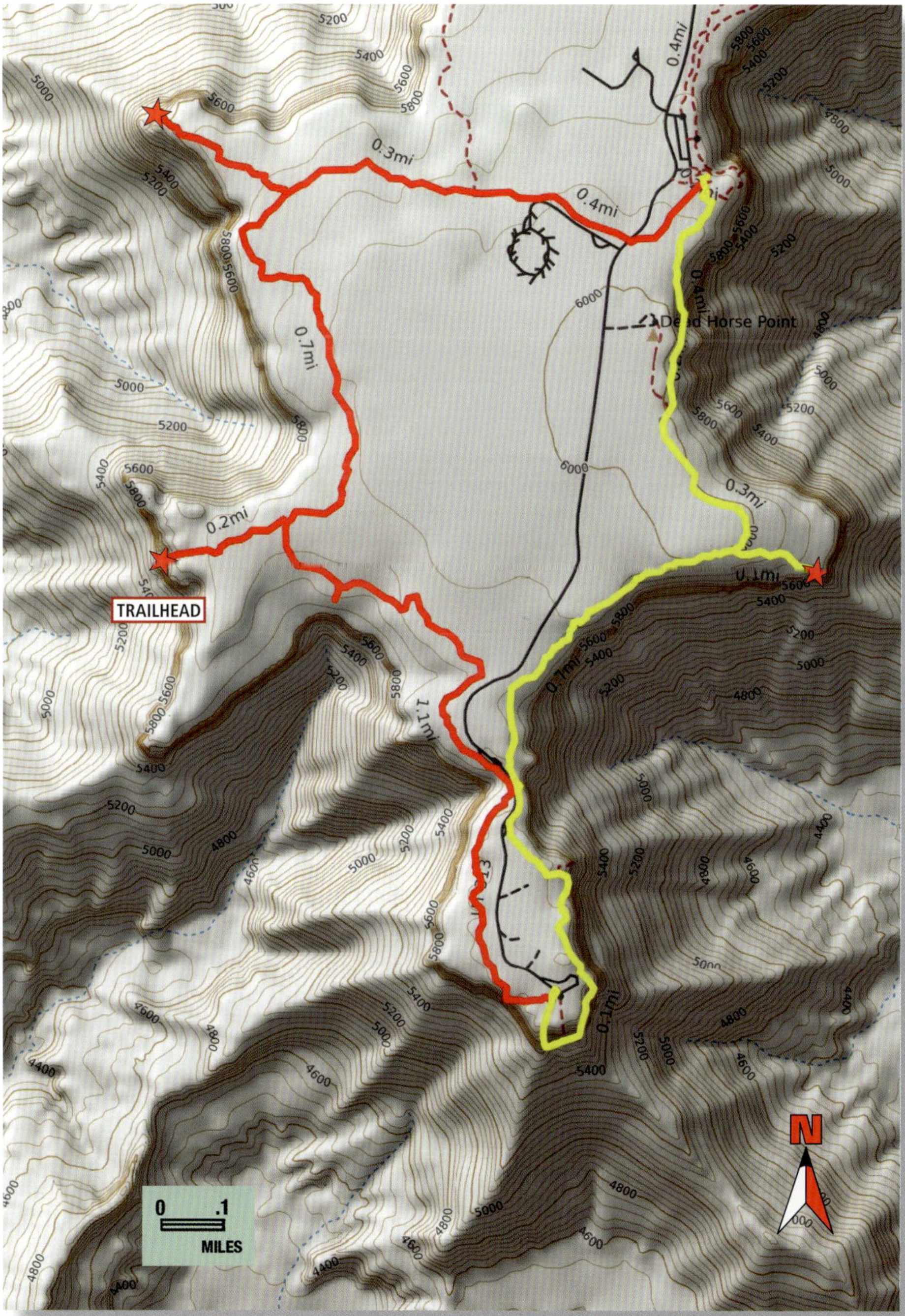

WEST RIM TRAIL SYSTEM

The Rim of Dead Horse Point State Park.

On the Way Home

DEAD HORSE POINT STATE PARK VISITOR CENTER

The museum located in the Dead Horse Point State Park Visitor Center is worth a visit. Learn about cryptobiotic soil, the different layers of rock, local geology, and much more. The history of the park area and the adaptation of local animals and vegetation can also be explored. In the summer evenings, rangers lead interpretive programs in the amphitheater. It also features a small kids play area with interactive tools. You can also pick up materials to participate in the park's Jr. Ranger program at the museum. A special rotating exhibit in the gallery may also be open.

You can also learn about geocaching in the park. A ranger can also tell and show you why Dead Horse Point State Park is an International Dark Sky Park.

Dead Horse Point State Park Visitor Center

P.O. Box 609
Moab, UT 84532
(435) 259-2614
https://stateparks.utah.gov/parks/dead-horse
Admission: $15 per vehicle; Utah Parks pass
Hours: Monday through Sunday 9 a.m. to 5 p.m.; closed on Thanksgiving, Christmas, and New Year's Day

Cedar Mesa Area

Located in southeast Utah within San Juan County, Cedar Mesa is covered by sandstone cliffs and large canyons. Both Bears Ears National Monument and Natural Bridges National Monument fall within the area. Ruins, cliff dwellings and pictographs are common along the canyon walls evidence of Puebloans that once lived there. The area is growing in popularity for outdoor enthusiasts including rock climbers, hikers, mountain bikers and paddlers.

Cliff dwellings found in Bear Ears National Monument.

Rank 5

63. Kane Gulch to Turkey Pen Ruins and Stimper Arch Trail

RATING	Pathfinder, due to distance and terrain
ROUND TRIP DISTANCE	9.5 miles out and back
ROUND-TRIP TIME	4.5 hours
ELEVATION CHANGE	600 feet (from 5,875 to 6,450 feet)
MAP	Trails Illustrated Grand Gulch Cedar Mesa Plateau
NEAREST LANDMARK	Bears Ears
FEES	$2 day use fee payable at Kane Gulch Ranger Office
RESTROOMS	Pit toilets
DOGS	Not allowed
OPERATING HOURS	24 hours

COMMENT: Located at the junction of Kane Gulch and Grand Gulch, Junction Ruins is said to be the most visited ruins in the Cedar Mesa area. Turkey Pen Ruins is just shy of 4.5 miles down the wash of Grand Gulch. Not far from Turkey Pen Ruins is Stimper Arch, with an opening of six feet and a span of 20 feet. Remember to enjoy the artifacts and ruins from a distance, and obey the fencing and keep out signs. The trail is mostly exposed making spring and fall ideal times for hiking. The Cedar Mesa area is a high desert biome. The trail can be hiked year round.

GETTING THERE: From Highway 95, turn south onto UT 261 for 4.0 miles. The Kane Gulch Ranger Station is on the left. There are over 20 parking spots at the Kane Gulch Ranger Station.

THE ROUTE: The trail through Kane Gulch begins across the main road on the other side of the Kane Gulch Ranger Station. Cross the road carefully to begin the hike into Cedar Mesa and the Bears Ears National Monument area. Cairns guide you for the beginning part of the hike as you walk across slickrock and through the wash. Be sure to follow the cairns as you pass through the livestock gate at 0.4 mile. If the gate is open, keep it open. If it is closed, close it behind you. Social-looking trails, especially on the right, are created by animals, so make sure to not take any of those.

The trail soon turns south as you pass through a tunnel of grass. It closes you in as you hike closer to the canyon. At 1.0 mile, the trail enters the canyon. Make note of the aspen trees, which typically grow in higher elevations, making this grove at lower elevation extra special.

Stimper Arch spans 20 feet.

As you enter the canyon, you will pass through a fun small slot. The desert varnished sandstone begins to hug you. Green moss brings vibrant color to the walls. The trail meanders up and down and through wash that may or may not contain water. Old growth trees arch over you, and birds will likely chirp as you inhale the scent of pine.

Continue to follow the cairns, as there is very few trail signs. Water may pool in the low areas of the sandstone. The sandstone looks like waves in places from water erosion. The high route is usually the best route if you are trying to avoid water. The trail passes by a rock fall area as you leave the slickrock for a red sand path. The sand isn't deep, which helps keep the terrain on this longer hike easier. Not long after, the trail turns to slickrock again.

At 2.0 miles, there is a sign denoting the area as part of a wilderness study. Be sure to stop and take in the beauty of the landscape in. There are many places for photos. Granaries and dwellings are visible on the east side of the canyon high above. There are several more potential water crossings as the trail follows west through the wash toward the junction of Kane Gulch and Grand Gulch. Just before the junction, two hoodoos signal that you are close.

At 3.5 miles, Kane and Grand Gulch meet. Look right at the trail junction and you may be able to see Junction Ruins off in the distance between the cottonwood trees. There are many social trails to the ruins. This large three-level Anasazi cliff dwelling served as dwellings and places of worship. Two levels of the ruins are cur-

The Kane Gulch Ranger Station should be your first stop before heading towards the ruins.

rently accessible. It takes a fair bit of scrambling to access the second level. An overhang of sandstone protects the kivas and habitation rooms. Stories of the past are told through pictographs, while pieces of broken pottery and old cornhusks dot the landscape. When you finish exploring Junction Ruins, head back to the junction of Kane and Grand Gulches. Continue west into Grand Gulch.

At 4.3 miles, look for social trails on the right (north) again. These trails lead away from the wash and toward the sandstone walls. After cresting a large hill of sand, you will see the Turkey Pen Ruins. The ruins were believed to be built by the Anasazi between 1000 and 1250 AD. Protected by an alcove of sandstone, areas of the ruins are roped off for protection for both the ruins and visitors. The second level is no longer accessible. Don't miss the roped off roofless structure. This "pen" made of sticks covered in mud with a south facing opening is where these ruins got their name. No proof ever has been found that the structure was used for housing turkeys, but the name remains. Take time to appreciate the silence at both ruins and to understand the importance of protecting these lands.

Stimper Arch is 0.25 mile farther than Turkey Pen Ruins. Shy of the trail's 5.0-mile mark, it sits above the sandstone walls to the east. The arch almost looks like an eye and is popular with photographers.

Retrace your steps across the red sand, slickrock, and sandstone. Remember the entire hike back is uphill. The elevation changes gradually over several miles, but little ones may need more breaks for water and snacks on the way back. Close or keep open the livestock gate according to how you found it. Take one last final look into Kane Gulch before you cross the street back to the parking lot and ranger station.

KANE GULCH TO TURKEY PEN RUINS AND STIMPER ARCH TRAIL

Natural Bridges National Monument was established as a national monument by President Theodore Roosevelt in 1906.

Natural Bridges National Monument

The first national monument designated in Utah, the bridges were first brought to the world's eye in a 1904 issue of *National Geographic* Magazine. Although established as a national monument by President Theodore Roosevelt in 1906, it wasn't until roads were built in the 1950s to support the mining of uranium that the national monument saw visitors. Although the bridges are the main feature, the park is known for stargazing as well being designated as the first International Dark Sky Park by the International Dark Sky Association in 2007.

The trail to Sipapu Bridge overlooks the north part of Natural Bridges National Monument.

Rank 2

64. Owachomo Bridge Trail

RATING	Searcher, due to uneven terrain and elevation change
ROUND TRIP DISTANCE	0.5 mile
ROUND-TRIP TIME	30 minutes
ELEVATION CHANGE	175 feet (from 5,944 to 6,119 feet)
MAP	Trails Illustrated Grand Gulch Cedar Mesa Plateau
NEAREST LANDMARK	Owachomo Bridge Overlook
FEES	$15 a day; National Parks pass; Southeast Utah Parks pass
RESTROOMS	None
DOGS	Not allowed
OPERATING HOURS	24 hours

COMMENT: Meaning "rock mound" in Hopi, the trail is named after a mound of rock visible on the top of the southeast end of the bridge. The bridge is also referred to as "Little Bridge," "Edwin," or lastly "Congressman," which is the name given to the bridge by miner Cass Hite. Surveyor William Douglas named it Owachomo Bridge in 1908. The trail is a mix of slickrock, steps, and soil. Owachomo Bridge is a part of the high desert biome. Remember that this area is covered in cryptobiotic soil, so stay on the trail. The bridges can be enjoyed year round and are especially impressive at night under the stars.

GETTING THERE: Head south from Blanding on US 191 to UT 95. Take UT 95 for 35 miles to UT 275. The entrance to Natural Bridges National Monument is at the end of UT 275.

From the visitor center, follow the nine-mile main park road that runs one-way. You will pass the Sipapu Bridge viewpoint and trailhead on the right as well as the Horsecollar Ruin Overlook and the Kachina Bridge Trailhead and overlook. Continue on the paved one-away road for approximately 5.0 miles to the Owachomo Bridge Trailhead. The paved parking lot is on the right and holds fewer than 20 cars.

THE ROUTE: From the parking lot, head south on pavement toward the Owachomo Bridge viewpoint. Before you reach the viewpoint, there is a wooden sign on the right designating the trail down to the bridge. Take sometime at the viewpoint before or after your short hike to the bridge to catch another view of the bridge and the famous Bears Ears buttes to the east.

Owachomo Bridge is 106 feet tall and spans 180 feet.

The trail heads south/southwest and descends into Armstrong Canyon rather quickly. Permian-era Cedar Mesa Formation sandstone slabs, wooden stairs, and rock stairs take you down to the bridge area. While there is some vegetation on the trail from pinyon pine to Mormon tea, there is very little if any shade on this trail.

It's easy to stay on this trail with the signage and the worn path. Be on the lookout for lizards basking in the sun and bunnies scampering across the sandstone and in the vegetation. Bears, mountain lions, mule deer, and wild turkey also frequent the monument area. Blue pinyon jays may be seen, most likely feeding on the pinyon pine seeds that are a staple of their diet.

Compared to the two other bridge hikes in Natural Bridges National Monument, this is the easiest hike and the most photographed bridge. This means the trail may be crowded, especially around and under the bridge. Depending on the time of year, a large pool of water may exist near the bridge. Known as Zeke's bathtub (named for the first park custodian, Zeke Johnson), wading in the water is against park regulations. Recent rain or occasional snowmelt may create a waterfall to the left of the bridge.

As you enjoy the view from underneath, observe the height of the Owachomo Bridge at 106 feet tall and the span of 180 feet. The bridge is 9 feet thick and 27 feet wide. The Tuwa Creek ran under the bridge thousands of years ago, giving this

Follow the wooden trail sign to Owachomo Bridge.

natural feature its bridge designation. This area is a good place to stop and enjoy lunch or a snack.

You can see remnants of Zeke's Trail, which is on the National Register of Historic Places, if you look across the canyon below the bridge. Return to the trailhead the way you came, stopping at the viewpoint at the top if you haven't already.

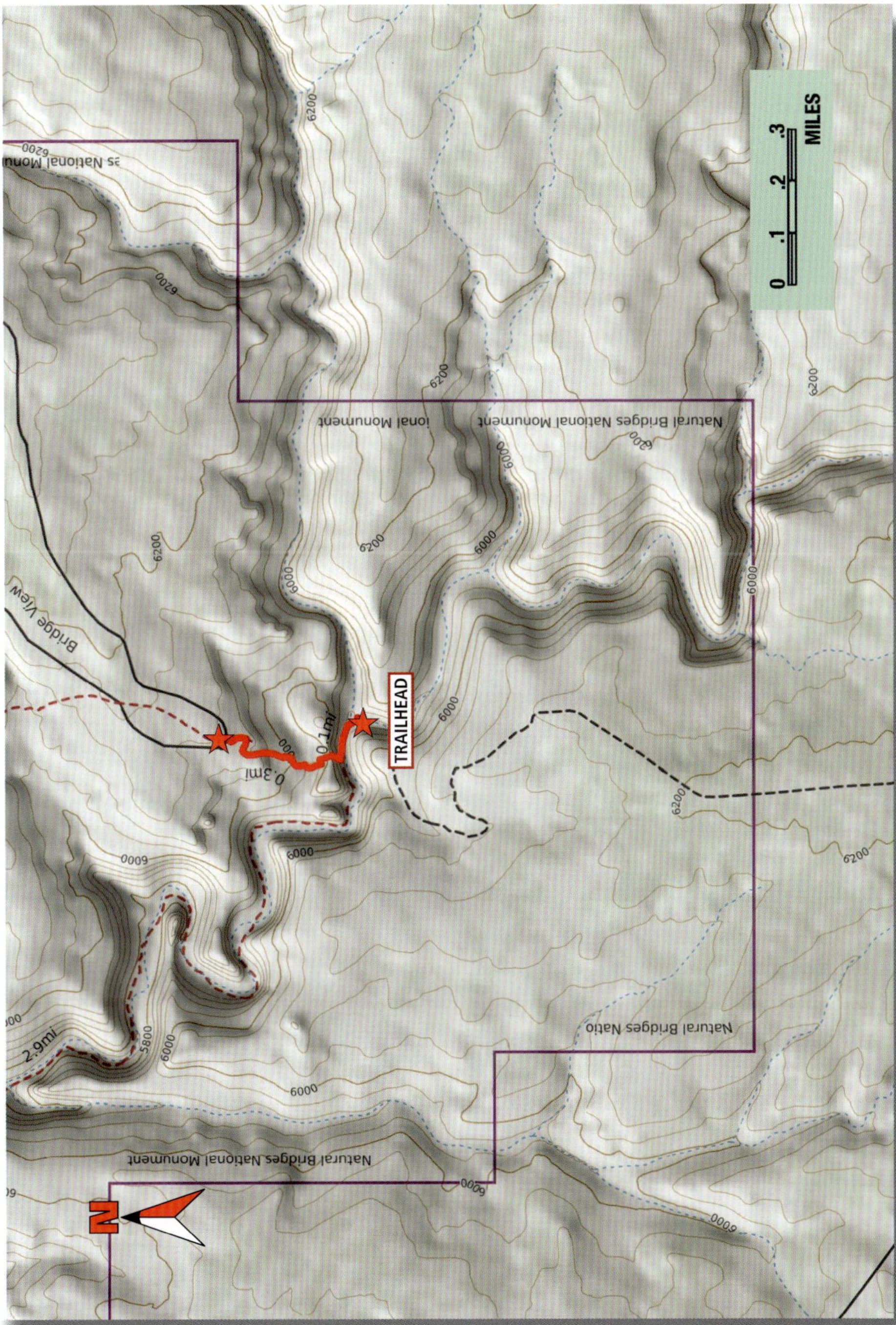

OWACHOMO BRIDGE TRAIL

Rank 4

65. Sipapu Bridge Trail

RATING	Wanderer, due to elevation change, steps, and ladders
ROUND TRIP DISTANCE	1.4 miles
ROUND-TRIP TIME	1.5–2 hours
ELEVATION CHANGE	436 feet (from 5,768 to 6,204 feet)
MAP	Trails Illustrated Grand Gulch Cedar Mesa Plateau
NEAREST LANDMARK	Sipapu Bridge Overlook
FEES	$15 a day; National Parks pass; Southeast Utah Parks pass
RESTROOMS	None
DOGS	Not allowed
OPERATING HOURS	24 hours

COMMENT: The Sipapu Bridge is the second largest natural bridge in the United States and is the largest bridge in the United States that one can pass under. Sipapu is a Hopi word for the symbolic portal from which the first human ancestors emerged. While the bridge has had several names, including President and Augusta, William Douglas, who mapped the monument boundaries, gave its permanent name in 1908.

There are several ladders, stairs made of both steel and rock, and railings along this trail. There is very little shade except at the bottom, so hiking in early morning or later in the day is recommended. While Armstrong Creek may be running underneath the bridge, fill your bottle up at the visitor center. Natural Bridges National Monument is part of the high desert biome.

Look for signs of life in the ephemeral pools, also known as potholes. Keep an eye out for birds of prey soaring above the canyon walls and lizards darting back and forth across the rock. The soil surrounding the trail is biological soil crust and may be black in color.

GETTING THERE: Head south from Blanding on US 191 to UT 95. Take UT 95 for 35 miles to UT 275. The entrance to Natural Bridges National Monument is at the end of UT 275. From the visitor center, follow the main park road that runs one-way. You will pass the overlook for the Sipapu Bridge on the right. Continue for a short distance to the Sipapu Bridge Trailhead. The paved parking lot is on the right with approximately 15 parking spots.

Sipapu Bridge is the second largest bridge in the United States.

THE ROUTE: From the parking lot, you will begin to descend slickrock. Steps within the rock help with footing as the trail leads down into White Canyon. The trail switches back and forth. As you descend into the canyon, a large overhang denotes that you are close to the set of steel steps that make it possible to cross over the otherwise impossible to navigate cliff areas. Take a few more steps, and you will reach the first of three ladders leading down the cliffside. The wooden ladder is bolted into the wall of sandstone. The trail continues to slowly descend as the walls of White Canyon surround you.

At almost 0.4 mile, there are ruins on the right under an overhang. This was once an Anasazi Granary. You may view the ruins, but do not disturb them. There are additional ruins on the cliffs throughout the hike if your keen eye can spot them. A wooden sign denotes the direction of the trail. Head right to continue on the trail down to the canyon floor and for an overhead view of Sipapu Bridge. If you head straight, you will end up at the viewpoint. The viewpoint, at about 6,000 feet, offers a view of the expansive Sipapu Bridge without the major elevation changes. At the viewpoint, overhangs may provide a bit of shade to stop and get some water.

The viewpoint is a good place to turn around if you have had too much adventure for the day. The trail gets considerably more difficult after this point due to elevation changes that occur as you switch back and forth on the trail between red sand, dirt, and man-made steps. The most vegetation on the trail grows along these switchbacks, including Mormon tea, Indian paintbrush, buffaloberry, and juniper trees. Cottonwoods show their best golden color in the fall.

The trail turns back to slickrock less than 0.25 mile from the viewpoint. A railing on the left helps you down the steep and slippery slickrock. This area is known to be icy in winter, and rain and algae grow across the rock in the spring, so this can be the toughest part of the hike to navigate. Shortly after the railing, there are two other ladders making the slickrock areas easier to negotiate. After another set of stairs, you will finally be on the canyon floor among the much desired shade of Gambel oaks.

Armstrong Creek has a seasonal flow. The run level depends on the time of year and recent weather. Look up at the expansiveness of the bridge, with its height of 220 feet and span of 286 feet. Farther down is a sandbar that offers a tree-free view of Sipapu Bridge. This area offers a view of the canyon from another angle.

Remember what goes down, must come up. Enjoy some time in the shade and take a break on the sandy wash before the climb back. There is no shame in taking as many breaks as you need as you climb the switchbacks, ladders, and stairs up and out of the canyon. The trail divide at the viewpoint spot is also a good place to rest the legs and lungs. Follow your footsteps back to the trailhead.

TRAIL EXTENSION: You can loop between Owachomo Bridge and Kachina Bridge or take the full loop trail that passes all three bridges. From Owachomo Bridge to Kachina Bridge it is 5.4 miles with an elevation change of 400 feet. Add 1.5 to 2 hours minimum to complete this hike. If you continue on to Sipapu Bridge, the full loop is 8.6 miles and 500 feet of elevation change. Expect this hike to take 4 to 6 hours. The trails to Kachina Bridge and Sipapu Bridge are advanced trails requiring the use of ladders and have steep drop offs. The trail between the bridges is primitive and you may have to cross water as well.

The ruins of an Anasazi Granary can be seen on the Sipapu Bridge Trail.

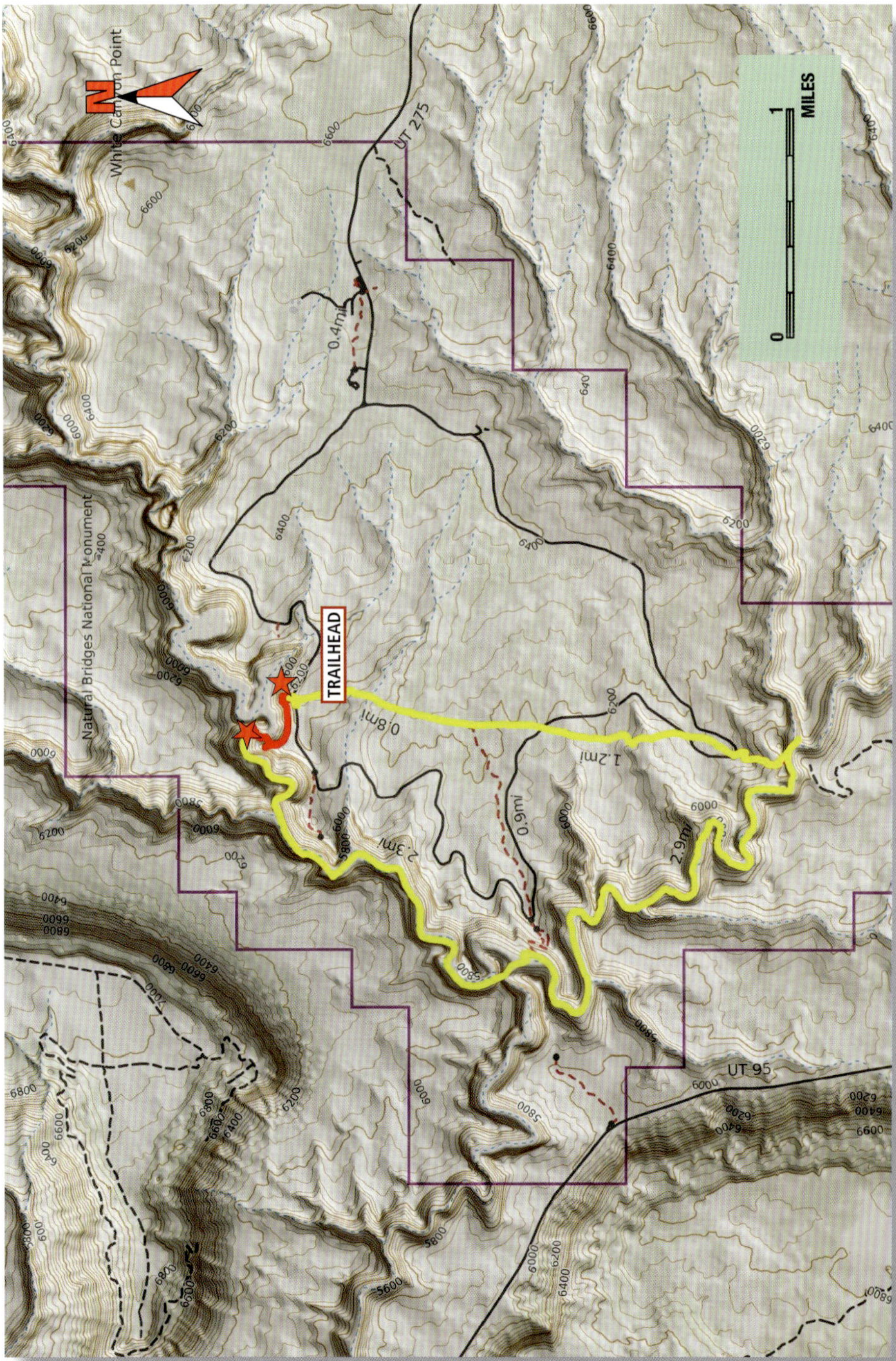

SIPAPU BRIDGE TRAIL

CHECKLIST

ROUTE	RANK	PAGE	DATE	NOTE
☐ Limber Pine Trail	Rank 2	34		
☐ Birdsong Trail	Rank 3	40		
☐ Quail Loop Trail	Rank 1	44		
☐ Wheeler Creek Trail	Rank 5	47		
☐ Adams Canyon Trail	Rank 5	52		
☐ Fairy Forest Trail	Rank 1	58		
☐ Mirror Lake Shoreline Trail	Rank 3	61		
☐ Wild Rose Trail	Rank 3	66		
☐ Buffalo Point Trail	Rank 3	70		
☐ Dooley Knob Spur Trail	Rank 4	73		
☐ Ladyfinger Trail	Rank 3	75		
☐ Albion Meadows Trail	Rank 4	82		
☐ Cecret Lake Trail	Rank 2	86		
☐ Donut Falls Trail	Rank 2	92		
☐ Hidden Falls Trail	Rank 1	96		
☐ Lake Solitude Trail	Rank 4	100		
☐ Silver Lake Trail	Rank 1	104		
☐ Bonneville Shoreline Trail to the Wadsworth Suspension Bridge	Rank 2	108		
☐ Lower Bells Reservoir Trail from the Boulders Trailhead	Rank 3	111		
☐ Rocky Mouth Falls Trail	Rank 3	115		
☐ Cascade Springs Interpretive Trail	Rank 3	120		
☐ Stewart Falls/Stewart Cascade Trail	Rank 4	124		

CHECKLIST

ROUTE	RANK	PAGE	DATE	NOTE
☐ Timpanogos Cave Trail	Rank 5	129		
☐ Battle Creek Falls Trail	Rank 3	134		
☐ Buffalo Peak to Squaw Valley Trail	Rank 3	140		
☐ Fifth Water Hot Springs Trail/ Diamond Fork/Hot Springs Trail	Rank 3	146		
☐ Cottontail Loop (Dutch Hollow Trail System)	Rank 1	152		
☐ Mid Mountain Trail	Rank 4	156		
☐ PC Hill Trail	Rank 4	159		
☐ Round Valley Trails	Rank 4	162		
☐ Black Dragon Canyon Trail	Rank 3	168		
☐ Curtis Bench Trail	Rank 2	174		
☐ Entrada Canyon Trail	Rank 3	178		
☐ Valley of the Goblins Trail	Rank 2	182		
☐ Lower Emerald Pools Trail	Rank 2	188		
☐ Riverside Walk Trail	Rank 2	192		
☐ Mossy Cave Trail	Rank 1	198		
☐ Queen's Garden to Navajo Loop Trail	Rank 4	201		
☐ The Rim Trail	Rank 1	205		
☐ Grand Parade Trail	Rank 2	210		
☐ Panorama Point Trail	Rank 3	213		
☐ Shakespeare Arch/Sentinel Arch Trail	Rank 1, Rank 3	217		
☐ Devil's Garden Trail	Rank 2	222		
☐ Lower Calf Creek Falls Trail	Rank 6	226		

CHECKLIST

ROUTE	RANK	PAGE	DATE	NOTE
☐ Sunset Point Trail	Rank 1	232		
☐ Cohab Canyon Trail	Rank 4	236		
☐ Hickman Bridge Trail	Rank 3	240		
☐ Red Fleet Dinosaur Track Site	Rank 3	246		
☐ Fossil Discovery Trail	Rank 3	252		
☐ Pioneer Park Trail	Rank 1, Rank 3	258		
☐ Petrified Dunes Trail	Rank 3	264		
☐ Red Sands Trail/Three Ponds Trail	Rank 4	267		
☐ Corona Arch Trail	Rank 4	272		
☐ Grandstaff Canyon to Morning Glory Bridge Trail	Rank 4	276		
☐ Grand View Point Trail	Rank 2	282		
☐ Mesa Arch Trail	Rank 2	285		
☐ Whale Rock Trail	Rank 2	288		
☐ Delicate Arch Trail	Rank 4	292		
☐ Landscape Arch and Double O Arch Trail	Rank 6	296		
☐ Sand Dune Arch and Broken Arch Loop Trail	Rank 2	300		
☐ East Rim Trail System	Rank 3	304		
☐ West Rim Trail System	Rank 5	308		
☐ Kane Gulch to Turkey Pen Ruins and Stimper Arch Trail	Rank 5	314		
☐ Owachomo Bridge Trail	Rank 2	320		
☐ Sipapu Bridge Trail	Rank 4	324		

ABOUT THE AUTHOR

Courtney Johnson really discovered her love for the outdoors at age 9 after a hiking trip to view Halley's Comet with her father and Girl Scout troop in 1986. Hiking, mountain biking, and stand up paddling are just some of the activities Johnson enjoys with her husband AJ and little ripper Emma. If not exploring her home state of Colorado, you can find her most often enjoying the Utah mountains, especially the Uintas. She lives in Erie, Colorado where she is a freelance writer, photographer, and substitute teacher. *The Best Utah Children's Hikes* is Johnson's first book.

Johnson and her family at Double O Arch.

Illustration by Jesse Crock